THE HUMAN ADVENTURE

READINGS IN WORLD HISTORY

VOLUME TWO

Selected and Edited by
SYDNEY EISEN
MAURICE FILLER

General Editor: LEWIS PAUL TODD

HARCOURT, BRACE & WORLD, INC.

New York   Chicago   San Francisco   Atlanta   Dallas

ABOUT THE EDITORS

SYDNEY EISEN is Associate Professor of History and Humanities at York University in Toronto, Ontario. He formerly taught at Williams College and at The City College of New York, where he was also acting Assistant Dean of the College of Liberal Arts. Professor Eisen received his B.A. from the University of Toronto and his Ph.D. from The Johns Hopkins University. In 1953 he was the recipient of a Canadian Social Science Research Council Fellowship for study in England. He has taught history to high school students on the advanced placement level and has given courses and conducted seminars for secondary school teachers. Professor Eisen is a member of the CEEB Advanced Placement Committee in European History.

MAURICE FILLER is the Coordinator of the History Department at the Mt. Greylock Regional High School in Williamstown, Massachusetts. He received his Master's Degree from Boston University and has done additional graduate work in history at the University of Michigan and Columbia University. In the summer of 1960 he received a John Hay Fellowship for further study in the humanities. For the past fifteen years he has taught social studies courses at all levels from grade seven through grade twelve. He is a member of a number of professional organizations, among them the National Council for the Social Studies and the American Historical Association.

THE GENERAL EDITOR

LEWIS PAUL TODD is the editor of *Social Education*, the official journal of the National Council for the Social Studies. He has had many years of experience as a teacher in schools and colleges and has made many contributions to the professional literature of the social studies.

EDITORIAL CONSULTANTS

Consultation and advice on these volumes were given by Dr. Anatole G. Mazour and Dr. John M. Peoples. Dr. Mazour is Professor of History at Stanford University, and Dr. Peoples is a teacher of history at the Alameda High School, Alameda, California. They are co-authors of *Men and Nations: A World History*.

Printed in the United States of America

PREFACE

This collection of primary and secondary sources provides supplementary material for courses in world history. It is our hope that these readings will make the study of history a more exciting and meaningful experience, an experience that will help recapture the spirit of the past as well as reveal the complex nature of human development.

What is to be omitted and what is to be included in a collection of this nature often becomes a matter of individual preference. In our selection we have tried to choose documents that are both significant and interesting as well as to maintain a balance of political, social, and intellectual history. For the most part, documents that are summarized in every textbook have been omitted, though a few, such as Magna Carta and the Declaration of Independence, have been included so that the reader may get some sense of the original. We have sought to keep the collection small and manageable and yet provide a body of readings for each of the basic divisions of world history.

The collection is divided into two volumes, the first covering the period from the dawn of history to 1815, and the second from 1815 to the present. There are ten basic parts, of which Parts One through Six are included in Volume One and Parts Seven through Ten in Volume Two. The general order of the selections is chronological, but rather than adhere rigidly to chronology, we have grouped together within each of the appropriate sections those readings that pertain to the same topic.

The divisions used in Western history are not suitable for the civilizations of India, China, and Japan. The selections drawn from the histories of these areas before about the middle of the nineteenth century first appear at the end of Volume One as Part Six. For those who wish to use only the second volume and who meet the Asian civilizations for the first time in the Age of Imperialism in the nineteenth century, we have reprinted all the material on India, China, and Japan in Volume Two, Part Eight, together with material on Africa.

All documents, or groups of documents, are preceded by brief introductions that provide the historical setting against which the sources are to be read. In order to allow the reader the maximum freedom of interpretation, we have generally refrained from using the introductions to analyze the documents. Where necessary, footnotes and textual explanations have been added to make the meanings of the documents clear. We have followed accepted American spelling, capitalization, and punctuation. In a very few instances we have altered the word order to make a statement more comprehensible.

In preparing this book we have beset our friends and colleagues with numerous queries of fact and opinion; we are very grateful to them for their patience and advice. We appreciate the generous cooperation we received from the staff of the Stetson Library of Williams College, where much of the work was done over several summers. We are grateful to Emanuel S. Chill, Dante A. Puzzo, Conrad Schirokauer, and George Schwab, all in the Department of History of The City College, and to John W. Baldwin of the Department of History, The Johns Hopkins University, who read portions of the introductions and made valuable suggestions. We are indebted to the members of the Department of History at Mt. Greylock Regional High School, especially Lawrence Vadnais and John Good, and to Mrs. Doris Eisen and Mrs. Myril Filler, for reading the book and making perceptive comments. We also wish to acknowledge our obvious debt to those scholars who have previously made translations and compilations of sources for the study of history.

SYDNEY EISEN
MAURICE FILLER

CONTENTS

PART EIGHT The Non-European
Civilizations and
European Imperialism

PART TEN   Hope and Distress
in the Nuclear Age

PART SEVEN

Industrialization and the Supremacy of Europe

A Plea for Laissez-faire

Enlightened thinkers of the eighteenth century frowned upon mercantilist regulations which resulted in senseless government interference in business, inefficient production, and constant warfare among nations. For the sake of peace and prosperity they urged that government interference be eliminated and that the laws of supply and demand be allowed to guide economic behavior.

The most popular and influential book on this subject was written by Adam Smith, a Scottish philosopher. The Wealth of Nations (1776) offers a compelling argument for government to leave things alone — except in the areas of defense, preservation of property, and upholding contracts. The theory of laissez-faire was very influential in the nineteenth century, especially among businessmen. It was partly responsible for the lowering of tariffs and for a reluctance to interfere with deplorable social conditions. Smith did not intend his theories to become a justification for the inhumane treatment of workers. He was certain that in the long run his ideas would benefit all humanity.

Every individual is continually exerting himself to find out the most advantageous employment for whatever capital he can command. It is his own advantage, indeed, and not that of the society which he has in view. But the study of his own advantage naturally, or rather necessarily, leads him to prefer that employment which is most advantageous to the society.

First, every individual endeavors to employ his capital as near home as he can and consequently as much as he can in the support of domestic industry, provided always that he can thereby obtain the ordinary, or not a great deal less than the ordinary profits of stock. . . .

Secondly, every individual who employs his capital in the support of domestic industry necessarily endeavors so to direct that industry, that its produce may be of the greatest possible value. . . .

Source: Adam Smith, *An Inquiry into the Nature and Causes of the Wealth of Nations*, London: J. Maynard, 1811, Vol. II, pp. 239–43.

2

In proportion as the value of this produce is great or small, so will likewise be the profits of the employer. But it is only for the sake of profit that any man employs a capital in the support of industry; and he will always, therefore, endeavor to employ it in the support of that industry of which the produce is likely to be of the greatest value. . . .

As every individual therefore endeavors as much as he can both to employ his capital in the support of domestic industry and so to direct that industry that its produce may be of the greatest value, every individual necessarily labors to render the annual revenue of the society as great as he can. He generally, indeed, neither intends to promote the public interest, nor knows how much he is promoting it. By preferring the support of domestic to that of foreign industry, he intends only his own security; and by directing that industry in such a manner as its produce may be of the greatest value, he intends only his own gain; and he is in this, as in many other cases, led by an invisible hand to promote an end which was no part of his intention. Nor is it always the worse for the society that it was no part of it. By pursuing his own interest, he frequently promotes that of the society more effectually than when he really intends to promote it. I have never known much good done by those who affected to trade for the public good. . . .

What is the species of domestic industry which his capital can employ and of which the produce is likely to be of the greatest value, every individual, it is evident, can in his local situation judge much better than any statesman or lawgiver can do for him. The statesman who should attempt to direct private people in what manner they ought to employ their capitals would not only load himself with a most unnecessary attention, but assume an authority which could safely be trusted not only to no single person, but to no council or senate whatever, and which would nowhere be so dangerous as in the hands of a man who had folly and presumption enough to fancy himself fit to exercise it.

Child Labor in the Factories

Higher wages and the opportunity for a better life first attracted labor from the farms to the factories in eighteenth-century England. As time went on, the life of the laborer deteriorated. There were more people than jobs, depressions threw thousands

3

out of work, and employers discovered that women and children could operate machines efficiently and at a much lower cost than men.

The conditions in the factories became the scandal of the nation. Cries for reform were raised by statesmen, novelists, and even manufacturers. In spite of the obvious horrors which existed in many factories and towns, there was stubborn resistance to government interference from those who believed that such problems were unavoidable.

The following evidence was gathered by a parliamentary committee investigating the working conditions of children in the textile mills. The resulting report shocked the nation and led to the enactment of factory legislation in 1833.

[Elizabeth Bently is questioned, June 4, 1832]
What age are you? — Twenty-three. . . .

What time did you begin work at the factory? — When I was six years old. . . .

What kind of mill is it? — Flax mill.

What was your business in that mill? — I was a little doffer.*

What were your hours of labor in that mill? — From five in the morning till nine at night, when they were thronged [very busy].

For how long a time together have you worked that excessive length of time? — For about half a year.

What were your usual hours of labor when you were not so thronged? — From six in the morning till seven at night.

What time was allowed for your meals? — Forty minutes at noon.

Had you any time to get your breakfast or drinking? — No, we got it as we could.

And when your work was bad, you had hardly any time to eat . . . at all? — No; we were obliged to leave [our food] or take it home, and when we did not take it, the overlooker took it and gave it to his pigs. . . .

* **doffer:** a worker who removes full spindles from a cotton-combing machine.

Source: House of Commons, *Reports from Committees — Labor of Children in Factories*, Vol. XV, Session 6 December 1831–16 August 1832: Report from the Committee on the "Bill to Regulate the Labor of Children in Mills and Factories of the United Kingdom." Minutes of evidence taken before the Committee on the Factories Bill, pp. 195–98.

Were the children [beaten] . . . ? — Yes.

With what? — A strap; I have seen the overlooker go to the top end of the room, . . . and sometimes he has got a chain and chained them, and strapped them all down the room. . . .

What was the reason for that? — He was angry.

Had the children committed any fault? — They were too slow.

Were the children excessively fatigued at that time? — Yes, it was in the afternoon.

Were the girls so struck as to leave marks upon their skin? — Yes, they have had black marks many times, and their parents dare not come to him about it. They were afraid of losing their work.

If the parents were to complain of this excessive ill-usage, the probable consequence would be the loss of the situation of the child? — Yes. . . .

You dragged the baskets? — Yes; down the rooms to where they worked.

And as you had been weakened by excessive labor, you could not stand that labor? — No.

It has had the effect of pulling your shoulders out? — Yes, it was a great basket that stood higher than this table a good deal. . . .

Did you perceive that many other girls were made ill by that long labor? — Yes, a good many of them. . . .

Were you heated with your employment . . . ? — No, it was not so very hot as in the summertime; in the wintertime they were obliged to have the windows open, it made no matter what the weather was, and sometimes we got very severe colds in frost and snow. . . .

Could you eat your food in that factory? — No, indeed I had not much to eat, and the little I had I could not eat it, my appetite was so poor. . . .

Did you live far from the mill? — Yes, two miles.

Had you a clock? — No, we had not.

Supposing you had not been in time enough in the morning at these mills, what would have been the consequence? — We should have been quartered.

What do you mean by that? — If we were a quarter of an hour too late, they would take off half an hour; we only got a penny an hour, and they would take a halfpenny more.

The fine was much more considerable than the loss of time? — Yes. . . .

5

Were you generally there in time? — Yes, my mother has been up at four o'clock in the morning, and at two o'clock in the morning. . . .

Was it a matter of anxiety and difficulty for you to [get up] to be early enough for those hours of labor? — Yes.

You are considerably deformed in your person in consequence of this labor? — Yes, I am.

At what time did it come on? — I was about thirteen years old when it began coming, and it has got worse since.

The Liverpool–Manchester Railway

Like so many beneficial inventions, the railroad did not win immediate public approval. The speed was terrifying, the noise was irritating, the dark smoke polluted the air, and the ugliness of the tracks and the cars disfigured the pleasant green countryside. Those individuals who had recently invested their money in canals and turnpikes were especially not congenial toward locomotives.

The first passenger line, between Stockton and Darlington, was opened in 1825, and the second, between Liverpool and Manchester, in 1830. During the next ten years only a few hundred miles of track were added. Then the idea took hold. England was gripped by a railway-building mania as it had been by a canal-building mania in the latter part of the eighteenth century. By 1848 five thousand miles of track had been put down, and the railway was spreading through other lands.

From the actress Fanny Kemble we have a description of the Liverpool–Manchester line in 1830.

She [the engine] . . . consisted of a boiler, a stove, a small platform, a bench, and . . . a barrel containing enough water to prevent her being thirsty for fifteen miles — the whole machine not bigger

Source: Frances Anne Kemble, *Record of a Girlhood*, London: R. Bentley & Son, 1878, Vol. II, pp. 160–64.

than a common fire engine. She goes upon two wheels which are her feet and are moved by bright steel legs called pistons; these are propelled by steam. . . . The reins, bit, and bridle of this wonderful beast is a small steel handle which applies or withdraws the steam from its legs or pistons, so that a child might manage it. The coals, which are its oats, were under the bench, and there was a small glass tube affixed to the boiler with water in it, which indicates by its fullness or emptiness when the creature wants water, which is immediately conveyed to it from its reservoirs. There is a chimney to the stove, but as they burn coke there is none of the dreadful black smoke which accompanies the progress of a steam vessel. This snorting little animal, which I felt rather inclined to pat, was then harnessed to our carriage, and Mr. Stephenson * having taken me on the bench of the engine with him, we started at about ten miles an hour. The steam horse being ill adapted for going up and down hill, the road was kept at a certain level, and appeared sometimes to sink below the surface of the earth and sometimes to rise above it. Almost at starting it was cut through the solid rock, which formed a wall on either side of it about sixty feet high. You can't imagine how strange it seemed to be journeying on thus, without any visible cause of progress other than the magical machine, with its flying white breath and rhythmical, unvarying pace between these rocky walls, . . . and when I reflected that these great masses of stone had been cut [apart] to allow our passage thus far below the surface of the earth, I felt as if no fairy tale was ever half so wonderful as what I saw. Bridges were thrown from side to side across the top of these cliffs, and the people looking down upon us from them seemed like pygmies standing in the sky. . . .

We had now come fifteen miles and stopped where the road traversed a wide and deep valley. Stephenson made me alight and led me down to the bottom of this ravine over which, in order to keep his road level, he has thrown a magnificent viaduct of nine arches, the middle one of which is seventy feet high, through which we saw the whole of this beautiful little valley. It was lovely and wonderful beyond all words. . . . He explained to me the whole construction of the steam engine and said he could soon make a famous engineer of me, which, considering the wonderful things he has achieved, I dare not say is impossible. His way of explaining himself is peculiar but very striking, and I understood without difficulty all that he said to me. We then rejoined the rest of the party, and the engine having received its supply of water,

* **George Stephenson:** railway pioneer and inventor.

7

the carriage was placed behind it, for it cannot turn, and was set off at its utmost speed, thirty-five miles an hour, swifter than a bird flies. . . . You cannot conceive what that sensation of cutting the air was; the motion is as smooth as possible, too. I could either have read or written; and as it was, I stood up and with my bonnet off "drank the air before me." The wind, which was strong, or perhaps the force of our own thrusting against it, absolutely weighed my eyelids down. . . . When I closed my eyes this sensation of flying was quite delightful and strange beyond description; yet strange as it was, I had a perfect sense of security and not the slightest fear. At one time, to exhibit the power of the engine, having met another steam carriage which was unsupplied with water, Mr. Stephenson caused it to be fastened in front of ours; moreover, a wagon laden with timber was also chained to us, and thus propelling the idle steam engine and dragging the loaded wagon which was beside it and our own carriage full of people behind, this brave little she-dragon of ours flew on. Farther on she met three carts, which being fastened in front of her she pushed on before her without the slightest delay or difficulty; when I add that this pretty little creature can run with equal facility either backwards or forwards, I believe I have given you an account of all her capacities.

Marx Predicts the Workers' Revolution

The Communist Manifesto (1848) was a call to revolution. It also claimed to offer a key to the understanding of all human history. According to the views of Karl Marx and Friedrich Engels, the history of human development is the story of class struggle, and the nature of all institutions and ideas — political, economic, social, and religious — is always determined by the exploiting class, made up of those who controlled the means of production. With the coming of the Industrial Revolution, the means of production were taken over by the industrialists. The Manifesto predicted that they would grow richer and become fewer in number while the masses would sink into degrading poverty. Then the workers would rise in revolution, dispossess the exploiters, and after a transition period of dictatorship establish a classless society in which each person would give according to his ability and each receive according to his needs.

Marx and Engels were relatively unknown when they wrote the Manifesto and for the time being their ideas were barely noticed. Both were German, the former a journalist and a student of law and philosophy, the latter a well-to-do manufacturer whose family owned a factory in Manchester, England. Conditions in the 1840's led them to believe that the predicted revolution was near at hand. This revolution did not materialize, and over the years the position of labor steadily improved in a number of European countries.

A specter is haunting Europe — the specter of Communism. All the powers of old Europe have entered into a holy alliance to [destroy] this specter: Pope and Czar, Metternich, . . . French radicals, and German police spies.

Communism is already acknowledged by all European powers to be itself a power.

It is high time that Communists should openly, in the face of the whole world, publish their views, their aims, their tendencies, and meet this nursery tale of the specter of Communism with a manifesto of the Party itself. . . .

The history of all hitherto existing society is the history of class struggles.

Freeman and slave, patrician and plebeian, lord and serf, guild master and journeyman, in a word, oppressor and oppressed, stood in constant opposition to one another, carried on an uninterrupted, now hidden, now open fight; a fight that each time ended either in a revolutionary reconstitution of society at large, or in the common ruin of the contending classes. . . .

The modern bourgeois [middle-class] society that has sprouted from the ruins of feudal society has not done away with class antagonisms. It has but established new classes, new conditions of oppression, new forms of struggle in place of the old ones.

Our epoch, the epoch of the bourgeoisie [the middle class], pos-

Source: Karl Marx and Friedrich Engels, *Manifesto of the Communist Party*, Moscow: Co-operative Publishing Society of Foreign Workers in the U.S.S.R., 1935, pp. 15–63.

sesses, however, this distinctive feature: it has simplified the class antagonisms. Society as a whole is more and more splitting up into two great hostile camps, into two great classes directly facing each other — bourgeoisie and proletariat.*. . .

The feudal system of industry, in which industrial production was monopolized by closed guilds, now no longer sufficed for the growing wants of the new markets. The manufacturing system [in the preindustrial period] took its place. The guild masters were pushed aside by the manufacturing middle class. . . .

Meantime the markets kept ever growing, the demand ever rising. Even manufacture † no longer sufficed. Thereupon, steam and machinery revolutionized industrial production. The place of manufacture was taken by the giant, modern industry; the place of the industrial middle class, by industrial millionaires, [the modern bourgeoisie who became] the leaders of whole industrial armies. . . .

We see, therefore, how the modern bourgeoisie is itself the product of a long course of development, of a series of revolutions in the modes of production and of exchange. Each step in the development of the bourgeoisie was accompanied by a corresponding political advance of that class. . . . The bourgeoisie has at last, since the establishment of modern industry and of the world market, conquered for itself in the modern representative state exclusive political sway. The executive of the modern state is but a committee for managing the common affairs of the whole bourgeoisie.

The bourgeoisie . . . has played a most revolutionary role in history. . . .

In proportion as the bourgeoisie, i.e., capital, is developed, in the same proportion is the proletariat, the working class, developed — a class of laborers who live only so long as they find work, and who find work only so long as their labor increases capital. These laborers, who must sell themselves piecemeal, are a commodity, like every other article of commerce and are consequently exposed to all the vicissitudes of competition, to all the fluctuations of the market.

Owing to the extensive use of machinery and to division of labor, the work of the proletarians has lost all individual character, and consequently all charm for the workman. He becomes an appendage of the

---

* **proletariat:** the class of industrial laborers who make a living working for other men.

† **manufacture:** that is, handwork.

machine, and it is only the most simple, most monotonous, and most easily acquired knack that is required of him. Hence the cost of production of a workman is restricted almost entirely to the means of subsistence that he requires for his maintenance. . . .

With the development of industry, the proletariat not only increases in number, it becomes concentrated in greater masses, its strength grows, and it feels that strength more. The various interests and conditions of life within the ranks of the proletariat are more and more equalized, in proportion as machinery obliterates all distinctions of labor and nearly everywhere reduces wages to the same low level. The growing competition among the bourgeoisie and the resulting commercial crises make the wages of the workers ever more fluctuating. The unceasing improvement of machinery, ever more rapidly developing, makes their livelihood more and more precarious. . . . Thereupon the workers begin to form combinations . . . against the bougeoisie; they club together in order to keep up the rate of wages; they found permanent associations in order to make provision beforehand for these occasional revolts. Here and there the contest breaks out in riots. . . .

The modern laborer, . . . instead of rising with the progress of industry, sinks deeper and deeper below the conditions of existence of his own class. He becomes a pauper, and pauperism develops more rapidly than population and wealth. And here it becomes evident that the bourgeoisie is unfit any longer to be the ruling class in society and to impose its conditions of existence upon society as an overriding law. . . . Society can no longer live under this bourgeoisie; in other words, its existence is no longer compatible with society. . . .

What the bourgeoisie therefore produces, above all, are its own gravediggers. Its fall and the victory of the proletariat are equally inevitable.

In what relation do the Communists stand to the proletarians as a whole? . . .

The Communists . . . are on the one hand — practically — the most advanced and resolute section of the working-class parties of every country, that section which pushes forward all others; on the other hand — theoretically — they have over the great mass of the proletariat the advantage of clearly understanding the line of march, the conditions, and the ultimate general results of the proletarian movement.

The immediate aim of the Communists is the same as that of all the other proletarian parties: formation of the proletariat into a class, overthrow of bourgeois supremacy, conquest of political power by the proletariat. . . .

The distinguishing feature of Communism is not the abolition of property generally, but the abolition of bourgeois property. Modern bourgeois private property is the final and most complete expression of the system of producing and appropriating products that is based on class antagonisms, on the exploitation of the many by the few.

In this sense, the theory of the Communists may be summed up in the single phrase: abolition of private property. . . .

Communism deprives no man of the power to appropriate the products of society; all that it does is to deprive him of the power to subjugate the labor of others by means of such appropriation. . . .

We have seen . . . that the first step in the revolution by the working class is to raise the proletariat to the position of ruling class. . . .

The proletariat will use its political supremacy to wrest by degrees all capital from the bourgeoisie; to centralize all instruments of production in the hands of the state, i.e., of the proletariat organized as the ruling class; and to increase the total of productive forces as rapidly as possible. . . .

The Communists disdain to conceal their views and aims. They openly declare that their ends can be attained only by the forcible overthrow of all existing social conditions. Let the ruling classes tremble at a Communist revolution. The proletarians have nothing to lose but their chains. They have a world to win.

Workingmen of all countries, unite!

The Paris Workers in Revolt—June 1848

What are the fundamental causes of revolution? asked the French aristocrat Alexis de Tocqueville. Governments are overthrown, he decided, when corruption, indifference, and selfishness render the rulers "incapable and unworthy of governing." Such was the state of the government of King Louis Philippe, he warned; the nation was in the hands of a small, wealthy, corrupt group, deaf and indifferent to the cries for extending liberty, broadening the franchise, and relieving the misery of the working class.

Shortly after this warning, in February 1848, a Paris revolution overthrew the French monarchy and established a moderately conservative republic. Continued discontent among the workers and some provocation from the new government resulted in a bloody battle in June in which the workers were totally defeated. This event, known as "The June Days," left a legacy of distrust and hatred between workers and the middle class in France.

Tocqueville was a member of the Chamber of Deputies (the lower house of the French legislature) when the revolution broke out in February 1848.

I come at last to the insurrection of June, the most extensive and the most singular that has occurred in our history and perhaps in any other: the most extensive, because during four days more than a hundred thousand men were engaged in it; the most singular, because the insurgents fought without a war cry, without leaders, without flags, and yet with a marvelous harmony and an amount of military experience that astonished the oldest officers.

What distinguished it also, among all the events of this kind which have succeeded one another in France for sixty years, is that it did not aim at changing the form of government, but at altering the order of society. It was not, strictly speaking, a political struggle in the sense which until then we had given to the word, but a combat of class against class. . . . We behold in it nothing more than a blind and rude but powerful effort on the part of the workmen to escape from the necessities of their condition. . . . It was this mixture of greed and false theory which first gave birth to the insurrection and then made it so formidable. These poor people had been told that the wealth of the rich was in some way the produce of a theft practiced upon themselves. . . .

It must also be observed that this formidable insurrection was not the enterprise of a certain number of conspirators, but the revolt of one whole section of the population against another. Women took part in

Source: Alexis de Tocqueville, *The Recollections of Alexis de Tocqueville*, translated by Alexander T. de Mattos, London: H. Henry & Co., Ltd., 1896, pp. 187–88, 199–200, 212, 230–31.

13

it as well as men. While the latter fought, the former prepared and carried ammunition; and when at last the time had come to surrender, the women were the last to yield. These women went to battle with, as it were, a housewifely ardor: they looked to victory for the comfort of their husbands and the education of their children. . . .

Nevertheless, we succeeded in triumphing over this so formidable insurrection; nay more, it was just that which rendered it so terrible which saved us. . . . Had the revolt borne a less radical character and a less ferocious aspect, it is probable that the greater part of the middle class would have stayed at home; France would not have come to our aid; the National Assembly itself would perhaps have yielded. . . . But the insurrection was of such a nature that any commerce with it became at once impossible, and from the first it left us no alternative but to defeat it or to be destroyed ourselves.

Thousands of men were hastening to our aid from every part of France and entering the city by all the roads not commanded by the insurgents. Thanks to the railroads, some had already come from fifty leagues' distance, although the fighting had only begun the night before. On the next and the subsequent days, they came from distances of a hundred and two hundred leagues. These men belonged indiscriminately to every class of society; among them were many peasants, many shopkeepers, many landlords and nobles, all mingled together in the same ranks. They were armed in an irregular and insufficient manner, but they rushed into Paris with unequaled ardor: a spectacle as strange and unprecedented in our revolutionary annals as that offered by the insurrection itself. It was evident from that moment that we should end by gaining the day [winning], for the insurgents received no reinforcements, whereas we had all France for reserves.

Such were the days of June, necessary and disastrous days. They did not extinguish revolutionary ardor in France. . . . They delivered the nation from the tyranny of the Paris workmen and restored it to possession of itself.

Personally I . . . was indifferent to the Republic; but I adored Liberty, and I conceived great apprehensions for it immediately after these days. I at once looked upon the June fighting as a necessary crisis, after which, however, the temper of the nation would undergo a certain change. The love of independence was to be followed by a dread of, and perhaps a distaste for, free institutions; after such an abuse of liberty a return of this sort [the regime of Louis Napoleon] was inevitable.

The Revolution of 1848 in Berlin

There is a saying that when France sneezes Europe catches cold. Less than a month after the beginning of the February Revolution in Paris, in spite of all Metternich's quarantines, revolution broke out in the Austrian Empire, Germany, and Italy. During a brief moment of liberal triumph, nationalities proclaimed their independence, and monarchs made pious promises of granting constitutions; nevertheless, within a few months, the revolutions were crushed and the conservative forces were again firmly in power. Dissension among the liberals, mutual hatred among the aspiring nationalities, and the loyalty and efficiency of the armies had all helped to turn the tide.

When revolution broke out in Berlin, the King of Prussia, Frederick William IV, believing that his subjects had been aroused by foreigners, offered a number of concessions. Then some shots were fired, and the people began to erect barricades. Frederick William avoided greater bloodshed by giving in to popular demands. But by the middle of 1849, the King was again in control.

[An eyewitness reports:]

At eleven A.M. I found the city perfectly quiet and cheerful enough. . . . In the Castle Square about two thousand citizens were assembled in groups, all well dressed and very respectable people. . . . They told each other of the urgent representations which the deputation from the Rhine had made; they said they had been informed of a partial change in the Ministry, etc. I found the people in an excited mood but not at all hostile. On the contrary, the groups gave loud cheers for the King time after time. Quite in the background, at the corners of the streets leading into the Square, I saw workingmen and common people standing. . . . All the shops in the Square were open, and ladies had occupied the windows. . . . Inside the Castle the troops from Potsdam were bivouacked; they were smoking and walking about the courtyard,

Source: J. C. Legge, *Rhyme and Revolution in Germany*, London: Constable & Company, Ltd., 1918, pp. 284–86. Reprinted by permission of the publishers.

mingling with the citizens. Meanwhile the Castle Square was more thronged than ever, and the people began to discuss the suggestion put forward that it was absolutely necessary that the soldiers [brought] from outside should leave Berlin, and that the troops in barracks round about Berlin should withdraw as well. It was then quite plain that great bitterness against the troops prevailed — a fairly instinctive bitterness not affected by politics, . . . and one that gave cause to fear the worst. Further, about one P.M. the crowd pressed unmistakably toward the porch leading to the King's apartments. . . . About half past one the King appeared on the balcony and attempted to speak. A gentleman with him . . . said with a loud voice something to this effect:

It is the King's will that the Press shall be free;

It is the King's will that the Diet be summoned at once;

It is the King's will that there shall be a constitution on the most liberal basis to include all German countries;

It is the King's will that there shall be a German national flag;

It is the King's will that all customs barriers shall be done away with in Germany. . . .

The enthusiasm that prevailed in the Square was so violent that it might almost have been taken to be the result of intoxication. People of the most highly educated classes jumped up on to vehicles in order to spread the good news. The King came out on the balcony again and was greeted with enthusiastic signs of rejoicing; he waved his handkerchief. . . . About this time I left the Square and went to the Königstrasse to have my midday meal there. I saw people embracing each other and crying for joy; women at the windows waved their handkerchiefs; materials for bonfires in the evening were carried through the streets, and the citizens who met me shouted, "We want to go to the Castle Square too, we want to cheer our beloved King too." It was two P.M.; I was seated at a table in the Crown Prince restaurant half way along the Königstrasse; collections for the poor were made as a token of rejoicing; people from the city came in to celebrate the joyful day at the table d'hôte; congratulations went round on the fact that the great day of freedom and new birth had dawned for Prussia too, and had dawned gloriously, without the shedding of blood.

[Then came the catastrophe. Two shots were fired by the soldiers on the crowd at the Long Bridge. The King always stoutly maintained that the guns went off by accident. . . .

Accident or not, the result was disastrous. The following is the vivid account of an eyewitness:]

At one moment everybody was rejoicing and shouting "Hurrah!" and a few minutes later all was changed to yells of rage and cries for revenge. In one hour the appearance of the city was entirely different. . . . "To the church towers!" was the cry, "To the alarm bells!" and the church doors were broken open by force, for no one would wait till the sexton arrived with the keys. . . . As if by magic, barricades arose. At every street corner people gathered, young and old, of high and low degree, to build barricades. Stalls, carriages, omnibuses, cabs, heavy transport wagons, postal and brewery carts, and scaffolding poles were collected by thousands of hands in all parts of the city. Even women and children took part; the unity which prevailed in building was marvelous. All were equal: two men would be seen dragging a beam, one a workman with a torn shirt and the other a well-dressed gentleman. The chief materials of the barricades nearly everywhere were torn-up pavements, stone flags, beams, and the many boards and planks lying across the gutters, or carriages, carts, etc., which were upset. Beds, sacks of flour, and furniture were brought out of the houses; everyone gave willingly what he had; gates, doors, fences, palings, hooks, bars, etc. Everything was done in perfect order, and everywhere with the same remarkable speed and contempt of death. People cooperated throughout.

The Chartists Present a Petition to the House of Commons

The English Poor Law of 1834 imposed degrading hardships upon the workers by making poverty the equivalent of crime. Paupers could not collect relief without going into wretched workhouses. Idleness was to be discouraged by making these workhouses less palatable than holding the worst job. The workers felt that only by getting the vote could they improve their state.

In 1836 a group of intelligent workingmen drew up the People's Charter demanding political rights for the workers. It remained a force in British politics for over ten years. Petitions were signed, rallies were held, and at times revolution was in the air.

The Chartists, though numerous, were not united. The government rejected their appeal and was determined to resist force. Because of the resolute calm of the government, there was little violence. None of the Chartists' demands were met at the time, but within little more than fifty years, all, except annual elections for the House of Commons, had been made into law.

The following account deals with the presentation of the Chartist Petition to the House of Commons in 1842.

The Petition itself . . . recited the usual theory of democracy; it described the various well-known anomalies [irregularities] of representation, complained of bribery "which exists to an extent best known by your honorable House"; it described the grievous burdens of debt and taxes and the rigors of the Poor Law; it spoke feelingly of the great inequality of riches between those who produce and those "whose comparative usefulness ought to be questioned," such as the Queen, the Prince Consort, . . . and the Archbishop of Canterbury. . . . Then came the praises of the Charter and the final demand "that your honorable House . . . do immediately, without alteration, . . . pass into law the document entitled the People's Charter." It was indeed a tremendous and comprehensive document.

[The Petition] had 3,317,702 signatures, said the *Northern Star*. It was to be delivered at the House of Commons on May 2. At very early hours of that morning detachments of Chartists assembled in various parts of London and marched to the rendezvous in Lincoln's Inn Fields. At noon the Petition arrived, mounted on a huge wooden frame, on the front of which were painted the figures "3,317,702.". . . At the back appeared the same figures and "Liberty." On the sides were set forth the "six points" of the Charter. The Petition was just over six miles long. The great . . . frame was mounted on poles for the thirty bearers. The journey to the House began. MacDouall and Ruffy Ridley, a London Chartist worthy, headed a procession on horseback. Then

Source: Mark Hovell, *The Chartist Movement*, edited and compiled by T. F. Tout, Manchester, England: Manchester University Press, 1918, pp. 254–57. Reprinted by permission of the publishers.

came the Petition. . . . Delegates from various towns and Chartist rank and file brought up the rear of what, if the *Northern Star* is to be credited, was an uncommonly long column. It took a devious route, and the head reached the House when the rear was at Oxford Circus, a length of nearly two miles. When the Petition reached the Houses of Parliament, the huge framework was found much too large to enter, and it had to be broken up. The Petition was carried in in lumps and bundles and strewed all over the floor of the House. It looked as if it had been snowing paper. Nevertheless the Petition made a very impressive show.

Next day, May 3, Duncombe brought forward his motion that the petitioners should be heard at the bar of the House. . . . He described, in language borrowed largely from Chartist sources, the great distress in the manufacturing districts, distress which was due partly at least to the fact that the interests of the industrious classes were not represented in Parliament. Leader, Bowring, and Fielden supported the motion. Sir James Graham opposed. Then arose Macaulay. . . . Macaulay's chief objection was to universal suffrage. "I believe that universal suffrage would be fatal to all purposes for which government exists and for which aristocracies and all other things exist, and that it is utterly incompatible with the very existence of civilization. I conceive that civilization rests upon the security of property. . . ."

Not less extraordinary was the outburst of Roebuck, who spoke . . . in favor of the Petition. Government, said he, was constituted to counteract the natural desire of every man to live upon the labor of others. Therefore, to exclude a majority of citizens from the control of public affairs was in effect to allow the minority to oppress the majority. Roebuck denied that the petitioners were hostile to property, which was as essential to their welfare as it was to its owners'. . . .

Let us hear Lord John Russell. Lord John had as great a respect for the petition as abhorrence of its demands. Even to discuss such demands would bring into question the ancient . . . institutions of the country. It would drive capital out of the country by throwing doubts upon the rights of property. . . . Property, intelligence, and knowledge were the qualifications for a constituency. Citizens, moreover, had no natural and inherent right to the franchise [right to vote], for the franchise was granted by the laws and institutions of the country in so far as the grant was considered conducive to better government. . . .

[The motion to hear the Petition was defeated by a very large majority.]

The Objects and Methods of the Fabian Society

Some Socialists abhorred violent revolution; this was especially true of the Fabian Society of England, founded in 1883. The Fabians took their name and motto from the Roman general Fabius, who refused to meet Hannibal in pitched battle. Fabius helped defeat Hannibal by slowly and patiently wearing him down. In this way the British Fabians sought to cope with the problems of capitalist society in their day. According to their outlook, every piece of social legislation was a step in the right direction.

The society was composed of middle-class intellectuals. Among the original members was George Bernard Shaw, whose biting humor was heard from many platforms. The Fabians believed that reform could be achieved by peaceful evolutionary means. They rejected class struggle, and they entertained no notions about family and religion that were disturbing to society. Perfectly respectable themselves, they helped make Socialism respectable in England. Many members of the present Labor Party in England are Fabians.

The object of the Fabian Society is to persuade the English people to make their political constitution thoroughly democratic and so to socialize their industries as to make the livelihood of the people entirely independent of private capitalism.

The Fabian Society endeavors to pursue its Socialist and democratic objects with complete singleness of aim. . . .

It brings all the pressure and persuasion in its power to bear on existing forces, caring nothing by what name any party calls itself or what principles, Socialist or other, it professes, but having regard solely to the tendency of its actions, supporting those which make for Socialism and democracy, and opposing those which are reactionary.

It does not propose that the practical steps toward social democracy should be carried out by itself, or by any other specially organized society or party.

Source: *Fabian Tract* No. 70, London: The Fabian Society, 1896, pp. 3–8.

It does not ask the English people to join the Fabian Society.

The Fabian Society does not claim to be the people of England, or even the Socialist Party, and therefore does not seek direct political representation by putting forward Fabian candidates at elections. But it loses no opportunity of influencing elections and inducing constituencies to select Socialists as their candidates. No person, however, can obtain the support of the Fabian Society, or escape its opposition, by merely repeating a few shibboleths [pet phrases] and calling himself a Socialist or Social Democrat. . . .

The Fabian Society, far from holding aloof from other bodies, urges its members to lose no opportunity of joining them and permeating them with the Fabian ideas as far as possible. Almost all organizations and movements contain elements making for Socialism, no matter how remote the sympathies and intentions of their founders may be from those of the Socialists. . . .

The Fabian Society is perfectly constitutional in its attitude, and its methods are those usual in political life in England.

The Fabian Society accepts the conditions imposed on it by human nature and by the national character and political circumstances of the English people. It sympathizes with the ordinary citizen's desire for gradual, peaceful changes, as against revolution, conflict with the army and police, and martyrdom. . . . The Fabian Society . . . begs those Socialists who are looking forward to a sensational historical crisis to join some other society.

Democracy, as understood by the Fabian Society, means simply the control of the administration by freely elected representatives of the people. The Fabian Society energetically repudiates all conceptions of democracy as a system by which the technical work of government administration and the appointment of public officials shall be carried on by referendum or any other form of direct popular decision. Such arrangements may be practical in a village community, but not in the complicated industrial civilizations which are ripening for social democracy. . . .

Democracy, as understood by the Fabian Society, makes no political distinction between men and women.

The Fabian Society, having learned from experience that Socialists cannot have their own way in everything any more than other people, recognizes that in a democratic community compromise is a necessary condition of political progress.

Socialism, as understood by the Fabian Society, means the organization and conduct of the necessary industries of the country and the appropriation of all forms of economic rent of land and capital by the nation as a whole, through the most suitable public authorities, parochial, municipal, provincial, or central.

The Fabian Society does not suggest that the state should monopolize industry as against private enterprise or individual initiative further than may be necessary to make the livelihood of the people and their access to the sources of production completely independent of both. The freedom of individuals to test the social value of new inventions, to initiate improved methods of production, to anticipate and lead public enterprise in catering for new social wants, to practice all arts, crafts, and professions independently . . . is . . . as highly valued by the Fabian Society as freedom of speech, freedom of the press, or any other article in the charter of popular liberties.

The Fabian Society strenuously maintains its freedom of thought and speech with regard to the errors of socialist authors, economists, leaders, and parties, no less than to those of its opponents. For instance, it insists on the necessity of maintaining as critical an attitude toward Marx and Lassalle,* some of whose views must by this time be discarded as erroneous or obsolete, as these eminent socialists themselves maintained toward their predecessors. . . .

The Fabian Society desires to offer to all projectors and founders of Utopian communities in South America, Africa, and other remote localities its apologies for its impatience of such adventures. . . .

The Fabian Society does not put socialism forward as a panacea for the ills of human society, but only for those produced by defective organization of industry and by a radically bad distribution of wealth.

* Ferdinand Lassalle (1825–1864): a German Socialist.

Improvement in the Condition of the British Working Class

The failure of Chartism in England discouraged labor from political action for some time. Instead, the skilled workers concentrated on organizing unions for purposes of mutual benefit and collective bargaining. The stubborn resistance and opposition of manufacturers did not succeed in smashing the unions. In the meantime the political maturity of these workers impressed itself on the rulers of the nation. In the middle of the 1860's both the Liberal Party and the Conservative Party competed to give the right to vote to the more prosperous workers. It was the Conservatives at this time, under the shrewd guidance of Benjamin Disraeli, who extended the franchise to a million workers in 1867. Rising economic productivity, prosperity, and the new legislation all tended to improve the lot of the workingman. The unskilled laborers were less fortunate. At the end of the nineteenth century millions of them still lived on the edge of starvation.

The author of the following selection, G. D. H. Cole, was a British scholar who wrote numerous volumes on the history of labor.

Within the limits of the factory system, there is no doubt that on the whole working-class conditions were getting better. The factory code was being stiffened up, both by legislation and by better inspection and administration; and the methods of the Factory Acts were being gradually applied to fresh industries, including the mines. The hours of labor, still very long, were being slowly reduced, especially at first for children and women. Factories were becoming rather less vile and insanitary; and very slowly sanitary and housing conditions in the towns were being improved. It is, however, a notable fact that overcrowding remained nearly as bad as ever. . . . Nevertheless, the death rate in England and Wales had been reduced from 22.7 per thousand in 1851–55 to 16 per thousand in 1901–05, and the birth rate from 34 to 28. The infant mortality rate, on the other hand, had actually risen, from 14.6 percent in 1850 to 15.4 percent in 1900.

There had been a great decrease in crime, due in part to the diminished ferocity of the criminal law; and the number of paupers had fallen from over a million in 1850 to under 800,000 in 1900, despite the increase in population. An almost universal system of public elementary education had been built up. In 1851 the state spent only £150,000

Source: G. D. H. Cole, *A Short History of the British Working-Class Movement*, London: Macmillan and Co., Ltd., 1927, Vol. II, pp. 188–90, 194–96. Reprinted by permission of the publishers.

on this service. In 1901 it was already spending nearly eleven millions, in addition to the sums expended out of local rates. The services of local government in the sphere of public health were practically created during the second half of the century. The conception that it was the state's business to take at least some precautions to safeguard the health of its citizens found expression in a remodeled system of local government to which large powers were entrusted.

These changes undoubtedly made life more tolerable for the ordinary man and gave him something to hope for in a world that to the generations before had seemed to offer no hope at all. . . .

Of course, it was not for the workers alone that better times came with the settling down of industrialism in the second half of the century. A huge new middle class came into being; the professions, the managerial grades in industry, the middlemen of every sort increased enormously in numbers. Employers and financiers made fortunes undreamed of by the greatest magnates of the Industrial Revolution. In 1851 the professional classes were 2.2 percent of the total population and the commercial classes 4.3 percent. By 1881 the corresponding figures were 6.2 and 7.8. . . . There can be no doubt that, up to 1880 at least, profits were rising considerably faster than wages.

Wages, however, were rising, both in money and in purchasing power. In the absence of reliable statistics, it is not easy to present any comprehensive view of the change in the wages of the whole industrial population, and it is necessary to fall back on estimates which are admittedly based on somewhat inadequate data. . . . There were setbacks; but between 1850 and 1900 the average real wage, measured in purchasing power, rose at least by 70, and perhaps by as much as 80 percent.

General elementary education, of course, had made a huge difference to manners, habits, and social outlook. The rise in wages had made possible ways of living which were beyond the reach of the workers during the bad times of the Industrial Revolution. The improvement in sanitary conditions had profoundly altered, save for the unfortunate slum dwellers, the conditions of urban life. The sort of appeals which had roused the workers in the thirties and forties would have made no impression on their successors in the latter part of the century. Though there were still, even in 1900, many thousands of hopelessly exploited "bottom dogs," such as Charles Booth's famous survey had brought to common knowledge ten years before, these were not typical of the organized or organizable working class. In the great industries the workers had ceased to be a ragged and starving mob, easily roused . . . by some one of the many "Messiahs" who sprang up in the early years of the century. They had acquired a status. . . .

No longer were mass uprisings, huge sudden revolts bred of despair and spreading like wildfire none knew how, likely or even possible. Strikes had become, for the most part, orderly movements, prepared for in advance and conducted by organized bodies and under duly constituted leadership. . . . Socialist propaganda had become far less an appeal to emotions and instincts and far more an appeal to reason. . . .

In certain respects the wide differences of education hampered the working-class propagandists. In the early part of the century, the workers were left to provide their own newspapers because it was not worth anyone else's while to provide for them. . . .

The coming of popular education altered the whole position. It became worthwhile commercially to provide reading matter for the poor as well as the rich. The result was seen in a flood of cheap novels, cheap magazines, cheap newspapers. The commercial classes vied with the working-class propagandists in catering for the workers' reading. . . .

During the Victorian era, it is beyond doubt that working-class standards were very greatly improved.

The Dedication of Young Italy

The passion for Italian unity, freedom, and independence that had been kindled by the French Revolution and the promises of Napoleon was kept alive after 1815 in societies of conspirators. Complicated rituals, secret passwords, and poor leadership generally characterized these groups. Their attempts at revolution ended in disaster and resulted in many executions. In 1831 Giuseppe ("Joseph" in English) Mazzini, who had already been involved in underground activities, founded a new type of secret society — Young Italy.

Mazzini had the qualities of a prophet, and Young Italy was a society with a high ethical ideal. The achievement of the unity of Italy became something of a religious mission. Devotion to duty and disciplined self-sacrifice were cultivated as a preparation for achieving national unity. Although this society suffered serious setbacks, Mazzini's ideas spread everywhere. An ardent republican, he was ultimately disappointed by the unification of Italy under a monarch.

The oath of Young Italy is indicative of the inspiring quality of Mazzini's character and the romantic nature of the whole movement.

Each member will, upon his initiation into the association of Young Italy, pronounce the following form of oath, in the presence of the initiator:

In the name of God and of Italy —

In the name of all the martyrs of the holy Italian cause who have fallen beneath foreign and domestic tyranny —

By the duties which bind me to the land wherein God has placed me and to the brothers whom God has given me —

By the love, innate in all men, I bear to the country that gave my mother birth and will be the home of my children —

By the hatred, innate in all men, I bear to evil, injustice, usurpation, and arbitrary rule —

By the blush that rises to my brow when I stand before the citizens of other lands, to know that I have no rights of citizenship, no country, and no national flag —

By the aspiration that thrills my soul toward that liberty for which it was created and is impotent to exert; toward the good it was created to strive after and is impotent to achieve in the silence and isolation of slavery —

By the memory of our former greatness and sense of our present degradation —

By the tears of Italian mothers for their sons dead on the scaffold, in prison, or in exile —

By the sufferings of the millions —

I, ———, believing in the mission entrusted by God to Italy and the duty of every Italian to strive to attempt its fulfillment —

Convinced that where God has ordained that a nation shall be, he has given the requisite power to create it; that the people are the depositories of that power, and that in its right direction for the people and by the people lies the secret of victory —

Source: Joseph Mazzini, *The Life and Writings of Joseph Mazzini*, London: Smith, Elder & Co., 1891, Vol. I, pp. 110–12.

Convinced that virtue consists in action and sacrifice, and strength in union and constancy of purpose —

I give my name to Young Italy, an association of men holding the same faith, and swear to dedicate myself wholly and forever to endeavor with them to constitute Italy one free, independent, republican nation.

Cavour and the Emperor Napoleon III Plan a War

It would have been a miracle if weak and disunited Italy had been able to free itself from Austrian domination. Count Camillo di Cavour, however, was not one to wait for miracles. A liberal and a patriot, his plan for Italian unification was hardheaded and practical. As the Prime Minister of the King of Piedmont-Sardinia, he strengthened his state and prepared it to become the nucleus of a unified Italy. He joined France and England in the Crimean War in order to display the valor of Italian troops and to win support for the cause of Italian unity in Europe.

In the French Emperor Louis Napoleon, Cavour found the military ally he needed against Austria. Napoleon III believed that he was following in the footsteps of his illustrious uncle in giving support to Italian independence. As a practical man himself, he was also interested in territorial compensation for his participation.

At a secret meeting at Plombières in July 1858, Cavour and the Emperor planned the war with Austria. Cavour gave the following report of the meeting to his sovereign, King Victor Emmanuel II.

My position became embarrassing, for I no longer had anything definite to propose. The Emperor came to my aid and together we ran through all the states of Italy, to seek there this cause of war so difficult to find. After having traveled the whole peninsula without success, we arrived almost without suspecting it at Massa and Carrara,* and there discovered what we had been seeking so eagerly. After we had given the Emperor a precise description, . . . we agreed that an address of the inhabitants to your Majesty would be provoked to ask your protection and even to demand the annexation of these duchies to Sardinia. Your Majesty would not accept this offer, but, taking the part of these oppressed peoples, would address to the Duke of Modena a haughty and threatening note. The Duke, confident of the support of Austria, would reply to it impertinently. Thereupon your Majesty would occupy Massa and war would begin.

As it would be the Duke of Modena who would be the cause of it, the Emperor thinks that it would be popular not only in France but equally in England and in the rest of Europe, since the prince is, wrongly or rightly, considered as the scapegoat of despotism.†. . .

We passed to the great question: what would be the aim of the war? The Emperor admitted easily that the Austrians must be chased completely out of Italy. . . . But then, how is Italy to be organized? After long discussion, we agreed in general on the following bases, while recognizing that they might be modified by the events of the war. The valley of the Po, Romagna, and the Legations ‡ would constitute the kingdom of Upper Italy, over which the House of Savoy would reign. For the Pope would be kept Rome and its environs. The rest of the Papal States would form, with Tuscany, the kingdom of Central Italy. The frontiers of the kingdom of Naples would not be touched. The four Italian states would form a confederation like the Germanic Con-

* **Massa and Carrara:** discontented areas under the jurisdiction of the Duke of Modena.

† Although Austria was later provoked into an attack on Piedmont in April 1859, it did not happen according to this plan.

‡ **Legations:** the Legations were Ravenna, Ferrara, and Bologna, provinces of the Papal States.

Source: Thomas C. Mendenhall, Basil O. Henning, and Archibald S. Foord, *The Quest for a Principle of Authority in Europe, 1715–Present*, New York: Holt, Rinehart & Winston, Inc., 1948, pp. 188–89. Reprinted by permission of the publishers.

federation, with the Pope given the presidency to console him for the loss of the best part of his states.

This arrangement appears to me completely acceptable, for your Majesty, by being sovereign by right of the richest and strongest part of Italy, would be sovereign in fact of the whole peninsula.

After having regulated the future fate of Italy, the Emperor asked me what France would get and if your Majesty would cede Savoy and the county of Nice. I replied that your Majesty, professing the principle of nationality, understood that it followed that Savoy should be reunited to France; that consequently you were ready to sacrifice it, although it would cost you much to renounce a country which had been the cradle of your family and a people which had given so many proofs of affection and devotion to your ancestors; that, as for Nice, the question was different, since the Niceans held by origin, language, and customs more to Piedmont than to France, and that consequently their accession to the Empire would be contrary to that very principle for which we were going to fight. Thereupon the Emperor caressed his moustache several times and contented himself with adding that these were for him completely secondary questions with which there would be time to occupy ourselves later. . . .

The Emperor has not made the marriage of the Princess Clotilde [daughter of King Victor Emmanuel] with his cousin a condition . . . of the alliance; but he clearly showed that he counts much on it. If the marriage does not take place, . . . what will happen? . . . The alliance will be made. But the Emperor will bring to it a spirit entirely different from that which he would bring if, as the price of the crown of Italy which he offers your Majesty, you would give him the hand of your daughter for his nearest relative. . . . What is certain is that the success of the war, the glorious consequences which should result from it for your Majesty and your people, depend in great part on the goodwill of the Emperor, on his friendship for your Majesty. . . . I do not hesitate to declare, with the deepest conviction, that to accept the alliance and to refuse the marriage would be immense political error, which could draw down on your Majesty and our country great misfortunes.

Bismarck's Formula for Success

Otto von Bismarck had nothing but contempt for the liberal democratic revolutionaries of 1848 who had attempted and utterly failed to establish a unified Germany. A hardheaded Prussian, he relied on unscrupulous diplomacy and brute force to achieve this end. In 1862, after a long career as a diplomat, he was appointed chief minister of Prussia. King William I was at the time deeply involved in a conflict with his legislature, which had refused to grant appropriations to reform and strengthen the army. The King was so dejected that he even considered abdication. It was then suggested to him that he call on Bismarck. Bismarck boldly collected the taxes and carried out the military reforms in the face of violent parliamentary protest. After Bismarck's great victory over Austria in 1866, the Prussian legislature, overcome with national pride, voted to forgive him for his highhanded actions and legalize his unconstitutional behavior.

Bismarck's behavior in the early days of his appointment is reconstructed from contemporary accounts.

"Bismarck plays his comedy thoroughly, trying to intimidate the King and all the parties. It amuses him to take everyone in. He is trying to induce the King to give way about the period of military service. To the members of the Upper House he paints in such dark colors the reaction he proposed to install that, so he fancies, they are positively alarmed. . . . He sometimes takes a very strong line as regards the members of the Lower House; at other times he behaves in a way designed to encourage them to come to terms. . . . This much is certain, that he has so far made a great impression by the brilliancy of his genius. . . ."

For the time being he practices the utmost politeness, even when he is sorely tried. He had hardly been minister a week before he took advantage of a sitting of one of the . . . committees to make some personal admissions. In the course of the debate he opened his cigar

Source: Emil Ludwig, *Bismarck: The Story of a Fighter*, translated by Eden and Cedar Paul, Boston: Little, Brown and Co., 1927, pp. 206–07. Reprinted by permission of Frank J. Horch Associates.

case and showed his opponents a small olive branch, saying: "I recently picked this at Avignon, intending to offer it to the people's party in token of peace. I see, however, that the time for such an action has not yet arrived.". . . A moment afterward, the virtuoso changes his tone and declares that the accusations leveled at him by the press (which asserts that he designs to make war in order to distract attention from the confusions at home) are false, and goes on to say:

"It is true that we can hardly escape complications in Germany, though we do not seek them. Germany does not look to Prussia's liberalism but to her power. The South German States would like to indulge in liberalism, and therefore no one will assign Prussia's role to them! Prussia must collect her forces and hold them in reserve for a favorable moment, which has already come and gone several times. Since the treaties of Vienna, our frontiers have been ill-designed for a healthy body politic. The great questions of the time will be decided not by speeches and resolutions of majorities (that was the mistake of 1848 and 1849), but by iron and blood.". . .

No shorthand writer took [these sentences] down, but when they ran like wildfire all over Germany, when press and people had changed the rhythm of the phrase to "blood and iron" and had expressed real or feigned alarm, the speaker did not repudiate the words.

Prussia's Reluctance to Wound Defeated Austria

Europe watched bewildered as the Prussian army crushed the Austrians in a matter of seven weeks in 1866. Bismarck had been planning this war for several years. The Prussian army had been trained to precision, equipped with rapid-firing rifles, and made more mobile by the building of railways. Austria's prospective allies had been neutralized in one way or another by Bismarck's shrewd diplomacy and vague promises.

Bismarck did not wish to destroy Austria. On the contrary, he wanted Austria as an ally. His aim was to break Austria's power in the German states to clear the way for German unification under Prussia. Against the wishes of the Prussian ruler

*and some of the generals, Bismarck stubbornly resisted inflicting
further humiliation on Austria and offered a generous peace.*

*Bismarck discusses his attitude toward defeated Austria in
his memoirs.*

It was my object, in view of our subsequent relations with
Austria, as far as possible to avoid cause for mortifying reminiscences,
if it could be managed without prejudice to our German policy. A triumphant entry of the Prussian army into the hostile capital [Vienna]
would naturally have been a gratifying recollection for our soldiers, but
it was not necessary to our policy. It would have left behind it . . . a
wound to the pride of Austria which, without being a pressing necessity
for us, would have unnecessarily increased the difficulty of our future
mutual relations. It was already quite clear to me that we should have
to defend the conquests of the campaign in further wars. . . . That a
war with France would follow a war with Austria lay in the logic of history. . . . We could not foresee how far the later wars would make
for the maintenance of what had already been won; but in any case it
would be of great importance whether or not . . . the wounds we had
inflicted upon them [the Austrians] and their self-respect were incurable.
Moved by this consideration, I had a political motive for avoiding,
rather than bringing about, a triumphal entry into Vienna in the Napo-
leonic style. In positions such as ours was then, it is a political maxim
after a victory not to inquire how much you can squeeze out of your
opponent, but only to consider what is politically necessary. The ill-
feeling which my attitude earned for me in military circles . . . was the
result of a military departmental policy to which I could not concede a
decisive influence on the policy of the state and its future. . . .

We had to avoid wounding Austria too severely; we had to avoid
leaving behind in her any unnecessary bitterness of feeling or desire for
revenge; we ought rather to reserve the possibility of becoming friends
again with our adversary of the moment, and in any case to regard the
Austrian state as a piece on the European chessboard and the renewal of
friendly relations with her as a move open to us. If Austria were se-

Source: Otto von Bismarck, *Bismarck; the Man and the Statesman*, translated
under the supervision of A. J. Butler, New York: Harper & Brothers, 1899, Vol. II,
pp. 42–43, 50.

verely injured, she would become the ally of France and of every other opponent of ours; she would even sacrifice her anti-Russian interests for the sake of revenge on Prussia.

Bismarck Edits
a Telegram from His Monarch

Bismarck tricked the French into declaring war on Germany in July 1870. The war had long been part of his strategy, for it was his means of frightening the independent states in southern Germany into joining his Prussian-dominated North German Confederation. Bismarck's opportunity came when France and Prussia were at odds over the succession to the throne of Spain. Bismarck proceeded to edit a perfectly innocent telegram from his King in such a way that when it was published it infuriated both the French and the Prussians. Napoleon III took the bait and Paris cried "To Berlin!" Within a few short months the French were completely crushed and the South German States were in the arms of Prussia. In January 1871, in the magnificent Hall of Mirrors at the palace of Versailles, the King of Prussia, William I, read a proclamation which announced the creation of the German Empire.

In his memoirs, Bismarck relates the story of the telegram sent from Ems, the resort where the King was staying.

All considerations, conscious and unconscious, strengthened my opinion that war could be avoided only at the cost of the honor of Prussia and of the national confidence in it. Under this conviction I made use of the royal authorization communicated to me . . . to publish the contents of the telegram; and in the presence of my two guests [Generals Moltke and Roon] I reduced the telegram by striking out words, but without adding or altering. . . .

Source: Otto von Bismarck, *Bismarck; the Man and the Statesman*, translated under the supervision of A. J. Butler, New York: Harper & Brothers, 1899, Vol. II, pp. 100–02.

The difference in the effect of the abbreviated text of the Ems telegram as compared with that produced by the original was not the result of stronger words but of the form, which made this announcement appear decisive. . . .

After I had read out the concentrated edition to my two guests, Moltke remarked: "Now it has a different ring; it sounded before like a parley; now it is like a flourish in answer to a challenge." I went on to explain: "If in execution of his Majesty's order I at once communicate this text, which contains no alteration in, or addition to, the telegram, not only to the newspapers, but also by telegraph to all our embassies, it will be known in Paris before midnight, and not only on account of its contents, but also on account of the manner of its distribution, it will have the effect of a red flag upon the Gallic bull.

"Fight we must if we do not want to act the part of the vanquished without a battle. Success, however, essentially depends upon the impression which the origination of the war makes upon us and others; it is important that we should be the party attacked and this Gallic . . . touchiness will [play into our hands] if we announce in the face of Europe . . . that we fearlessly meet the public threats of France."

This explanation brought about in the two generals . . . a more joyous mood, the liveliness of which surprised me. They had suddenly recovered their pleasure in eating and drinking and spoke in a more cheerful vein. Roon said: "Our God of old lives still, and will not let us perish in disgrace." Moltke so far relinquished his passive equanimity that, glancing up joyously toward the ceiling and abandoning his usual punctiliousness [carefulness] of speech, he smote his hand upon his breast and said, "If I may but live to lead our armies in such a war, then the devil may come directly afterward and fetch away [my] old carcass."

The Degradation
of Captain Dreyfus

The Dreyfus Case almost destroyed the Third French Republic. The Republic had already been shaken by threats from Royalists and would-be Napoleons when, in 1894, Captain Alfred Dreyfus, the only Jew on the French General Staff, was accused of giving military secrets to the Germans. The denials of Dreyfus were of no avail and his excellent record as a soldier did not help him; he was tried by a military court, convicted, stripped of his rank, and sent to Devil's Island. Within a few years, on the basis of accumulated evidence, it became clear that the real culprit was an unscrupulous and indebted aristocrat, Major Esterhazy, and that Dreyfus had been framed by forged documents.

By this time all France had taken sides. Many important reputations were involved, including that of the French Army. Esterhazy was brought to trial and acquitted. Dreyfus was granted another trial in 1899 and again found guilty. The world was aghast at this scandalous miscarriage of justice in democratic France. The President of France "pardoned" Dreyfus, but not until 1906 was the unfortunate army officer completely exonerated and restored to his position.

One of the dramatic incidents in the affair is given below as recounted in a work on Dreyfus by Nicholas Halasz.

Colonel Maurel read the verdict. It was unanimous. Dreyfus was found guilty of treason and condemned to dishonorable discharge from the Army, deportation from France, and exile for life in a fortified place.

It was late in the day when Dreyfus himself was informed. He was led out of his cell and brought under guard to the deserted courtroom. The guard presented arms. A candelabrum had been lighted. The clerk of the court read out the sentence by its light.

Dreyfus stood at attention. He listened stiffly, made a smart about-face, and returned to his cell. But when he was alone, he decided to kill himself. He ran against the wall head first to shatter his skull. . . . The prison director came running. He persuaded Dreyfus that suicide would only confirm his guilt in the eyes of the world and leave an ineradicable stain on his family. . . .

It was in character that the day Dreyfus dreaded above all others in the grim years that lay ahead was the day on which he would be publicly drummed out of the army. On January 4 [1895] he wrote Lucie

Source: Nicholas Halasz, *Captain Dreyfus: The Story of a Mass Hysteria*, New York: Simon and Schuster, Inc., 1955, pp. 54–56. Copyright 1955 by Nicholas Halasz. Reprinted by permission of the publishers.

[Mme Dreyfus]: "Tomorrow I am going to suffer the supreme ordeal for your sake and for the sake of our children." And on that morrow, January 5, great crowds began pressing toward the Champ de Mars, where the punishment would be carried out on the parade grounds of the École Militaire [the French military academy].

The crowd was a mob. It was in a lynching mood. . . . But a heavy military cordon kept them at bay. A double line of guards had been thrown around the outside of the iron railing which fenced in the quadrangle where the proceedings — formal as an execution — were to take place. They confined the mob to looking on over their shoulders.

Each regiment of the Paris garrison had sent a unit to represent it. A trumpet sounded, commands were barked, and a small door was thrown open. From it stepped a giant sergeant of the Republican Guard. He led four soldiers with drawn swords in whose midst walked Captain Dreyfus. They marched up to General Darras, who sat waiting for them on horseback.

The vast crowd hemming in the quadrangle densely on all four sides was so silent that the heels of the little group of men could be heard thudding. They ground to a halt before General Darras. The general drew his sword. In a voice that sounded tiny in that huge, silent space he cried: "Alfred Dreyfus, you are unworthy of carrying arms. We herewith degrade you in the name of the people of France."

Dreyfus stirred. He had been standing at attention. Now he lifted up his head. "Soldiers!" he shouted. "An innocent is dishonored. Long live France!" His voice, too, sounded tiny in that huge silent space, but it carried to the crowd outside. A great rumbling roar came from them. . . .

The giant sergeant rushed at Dreyfus. He tore the epaulets from the captain's shoulders and then tore the red stripes, marking him as a General Staff officer, from the captain's trousers. Finally he took the captain's sword and broke it in two. He threw the pieces on the ground. With the epaulets and the red stripes, it made a little pile of refuse.

Dreyfus was then marched past the soldiers ranked column after column in lines of parade dress. He walked with the unbending precision of a staff officer on inspection. The effect was ghastly. His uniform seemed suddenly naked. At regular intervals, he threw up his arms and with a face that was nearly maniacal in its effort to conceal its suffering cried: "I am innocent. Long live France!"

The Village Community in Russia

The village community was the whole world of the Russian peasant. (In fact "mir," which is the Russian word for village community, is also the word for "peace" and for "world".) Before the emancipation of the serfs, the mir was responsible for the collective farming of the village and the collective payment of taxes. Under the scrutiny of the local noble, it elected an elder to direct its affairs.

With the emancipation of the serfs in 1861, the mir retained its authority. The lands received by the serfs were held collectively by the mir. It was still responsible for the collection of taxes and retained the right to restrict travel. Whereas in Western Europe the system of holding land in common began to disappear at the end of the Middle Ages, in Russia the communal village continued to dominate agricultural life. To all but the most enterprising peasants the system was quite satisfactory, for it offered security and protection.

Sir Donald Mackenzie Wallace spent many years in Russia in the late nineteenth century, observing and recording the life of the people.

A Russian village is something very different from a village in our sense of the term. . . . The villagers are bound together by ties quite unknown to the English rural population. A family living in an English village has little reason to take an interest in the affairs of its neighbors. . . . So long as the Jones family does not commit any culpable breach of public order, such as putting obstructions on the highway or habitually setting their house on fire, their neighbor Brown takes probably no interest in their affairs and has no ground for interfering with their perfect liberty of action. Among the families composing a Russian village, such a state of isolation is impossible. The heads of households must often meet together and consult in the village assembly, and

Source: Sir Donald Mackenzie Wallace, *Russia*, New York: Henry Holt & Co., 1905, pp. 110–17.

their daily occupation must be influenced by the communal decrees. They cannot begin to mow the hay or plow the fallow field until the village assembly has passed a resolution on the subject. If a peasant becomes a drunkard or takes some equally efficient means to become insolvent, every family in the village has a right to complain, not merely in the interests of public morality but from selfish motives, because all the families are collectively responsible for his taxes. For the same reason no peasant can permanently leave the village without the consent of the commune, and this consent will not be granted until the applicant gives satisfactory security for the fulfillment of his actual and future liabilities. If a peasant wishes to go away for a short time in order to work elsewhere, he must obtain a written permission, which serves him as a passport during his absence; and he may be recalled at any moment by a communal decree. In reality he is rarely recalled so long as he sends home regularly the full amount of his taxes — including the dues which he has to pay for the temporary passport — but sometimes the commune uses the power of recall for purposes of extortion. If it becomes known, for instance, that an absent member is receiving a good salary or otherwise making money, he may one day receive a formal order to return at once to his native village, but he is probably informed at the same time, unofficially, that his presence will be dispensed with if he will send to the commune a certain specified sum. The money thus sent is generally used by the commune for convivial purposes. . . .

All male peasants in every part of the Empire are inscribed in census lists, which form the basis of the direct taxation. These lists are revised at irregular intervals, and all males alive at the time of the "revision," from the newborn babe to the centenarian, are duly inscribed. Each commune has a list of this kind and pays to the government an annual sum proportionate to the number of names which the list contains, or in popular language, according to the number of "revision souls." During the intervals between the revisions the financial authorities take no notice of the births and deaths. A commune which has a hundred male members at the time of the revision may have in a few years considerably more or considerably less than that number, but it has to pay taxes for a hundred members all the same until a new revision is made for the whole Empire.

Now in Russia, so far at least as the rural population is concerned, the payment of taxes is inseparably connected with the possession of land. Every peasant who pays taxes is supposed to have a share of the land belonging to the commune. If the communal revision lists contain a hundred names, the communal land ought to be divided into a hundred shares and each "revision soul" should enjoy his share in return for the taxes which he pays. . . .

At the present day the constitution of all the village communes is of the English type — a body of unwritten traditional conceptions which have grown up and modified themselves under the influence of ever-changing practical necessity. . . .

The absence of all formal procedure at the assemblies illustrates admirably the essentially practical character of the institution. The meetings are held in the open air, because in the village there is no building — except the church, which can be used only for religious purposes — large enough to contain all the members; and they almost always take place on Sundays or holidays, when the peasants have plenty of leisure. Any open space may serve as a forum. The discussions are occasionally very animated, but there is rarely any attempt at speech-making. If any young member should show an inclination to indulge in oratory, he is sure to be unceremoniously interrupted by some of the older members, who have never any sympathy with fine talking. The assemblage has the appearance of a crowd of people who have accidentally come together and are discussing in little groups subjects of local interest. Gradually some one group, containing two or three peasants who have more moral influence than their fellows, attracts the others, and the discussion becomes general. . . .

Theoretically speaking, the village parliament has a speaker in the person of the village elder. . . . The elder comes prominently forward only when it is necessary to take the sense of the meeting. On such occasions he may stand back a little from the crowd and say, "Well, . . . have you decided so?" and the crowd will probably shout, "*Ládno! ládno!*" that is to say, "Agreed! agreed!"

Communal measures are generally carried in this way by acclamation; but it sometimes happens that there is such a diversity of opinion that it is difficult to tell which of the two parties has a majority. In this case the elder requests the one party to stand to the right and the other to the left. The two groups are then counted and the minority submits, for no one ever dreams of opposing openly the will of the mir.

Enlightening the Russian People

The autocracy of the czars tended to make extremists and terrorists out of Russian reformers. Without an outlet for action in the practical world of politics, reformers gathered in secret revolutionary organizations and dreamed of utopias. Some pinned their revolutionary hopes on the relatively small number of industrial workers; others on the masses of peasants living in village communities.

In the early 1870's, intelligent and enthusiastic young men and women flocked by the thousands to the peasant villages and to the factories to educate and enlighten the people. The peasants were both talkative and suspicious, and the police had no difficulty rounding up the reformers. This movement was a failure, but its spirit continued to live on.

Sergei M. Kravchinski, who wrote under the pseudonym Stepnyak, was one of the first to answer the call "to the people." Here he describes the mood of the 1870's.

The men and women who had come back from abroad inflamed the public mind with the recital of the great struggle already undertaken by the proletariat of the West . . . and prepared to go "among the people". . . in order to put their ideas in practice. And both turned anxiously to those, who were few then, who had come back from the work of propagandism, to ask them what were these powerful and mysterious beings — the people — whom their fathers taught them to fear and whom, without knowing, they already loved with all the impetuosity of their youthful hearts. And those appealed to, who just before had the same mistrust of the peasants, . . . said, overflowing with exultation, that the terrible people were good, simple, trusting as children; that they not only did not mistrust, but welcomed them with open arms and hearts; that they listened to their words with the deepest sympathy, and that old and young after a long day of toil pressed attentively around them in some dark and smoky hovel in which, by the uncertain light of a chip of resinous wood in place of a candle, they spoke of Socialism, or read one of the few propagandist books which they had

Source: Stepnyak, *Underground Russia*, 2nd ed., New York: Charles Scribner's Sons, 1883, pp. 21–26.

brought. . . . And after having depicted all the terrible sufferings of these unhappy people, seen with their own eyes, heard with their own ears, they told of little signs and tokens, exaggerated perhaps by their imaginations, which showed . . . that there were indications and rumors denoting that their patience was coming to an end, and that some great storm was felt to be approaching.

All these numerous and powerful influences, acting upon the impressionable minds, so prone to enthusiasm, of the Russian youth, produced that vast movement of 1873–74 which inaugurated the new Russian revolutionary era.

Nothing similar had been seen before nor since. It was a revelation rather than a propaganda. At first the book or the individual could be traced out that had impelled such or such a person to join the movement; but after some time this became impossible. It was a powerful cry which arose no one knew where and summoned the ardent to the great work of the redemption of the country and of humanity. And the ardent, hearing this cry, arose, overflowing with sorrow and indignation for their past life, and abandoning home, wealth, honors, family, threw themselves into the movement with a joy, an enthusiasm, a faith, such as are experienced only once in a life and when lost are never found again.

I will not speak of the many, many young men and young women of the most aristocratic families who labored for fifteen hours a day in the factories, in the workshops, in the fields. Youth is always generous and ready for sacrifice. The characteristic fact was that the contagion spread even to people in years who had already a future clearly marked out and a position gained by the sweat of their brows: judges, doctors, officers, officials; and these were not among the least ardent.

Yet it was not a political movement. It rather resembled a religious movement and had all the contagious and absorbing character of one. People not only sought to attain a distinct practical object but also to satisfy an inward sentiment of duty, an aspiration toward their own moral perfection. . . .

But this noble movement, in contact with harsh reality, was shattered like a precious Sèvres * vase, struck by a heavy and dirty stone.

A revolution always requires a powerful organization which can only be formed by a propaganda, either Socialist or purely revolutionary. As this could not be openly carried on, it was necessary to have recourse

* **Sèvres ware:** a costly porcelain manufactured at Sèvres, France.

to a secret propaganda; and that was absolutely impossible in our villages.

Everyone who settles there, whether as artisan, or as communal teacher, or clerk, is immediately under the eyes of all. He is observed and his every movement is watched as though he were a bird in a glass cage. Then too, the peasant is absolutely incapable of keeping secret the propaganda in his midst. How can you expect him not to speak to his neighbor whom he has known for so many years of a fact so extraordinary as the reading of a book, especially when it concerns a matter which appears to him so just, good, and natural as that which the Socialist tells him about? Thus, whenever a propagandist visits any of his friends, the news immediately spreads throughout the village. . . .

It is quite evident that with these customs the government would have no difficulty in hearing of the agitation which was being carried on among the peasants. Arrest followed arrest, thick and fast. . . . The total number of arrests was never known. . . .

But legion after legion boldly descended into the lists, when owing to the number of the fallen, the battle seemed to be slackening. The movement lasted for two years with various degrees of intensity. But the fact had at last to be recognized that it was like running one's head against a wall.

The Assassins of Alexander II Explain Their Deed

After several miscalculations and failures, The Will of the People, a terrorist organization, finally succeeded in 1881 in assassinating Czar Alexander II. Alexander's reforms, extensive though they were, had not satisfied even the moderates. The terrorists, disdaining any compromise with the autocracy, lived only to destroy it. Alexander III, after the assassination of his father, received a letter of explanation from the revolutionary executive committee of The Will of the People. The new Czar turned his back on reform and was determined to crush even the mildest criticism of the existing order.

The following selection is taken from the letter that was sent to Alexander III.

Your Majesty: The Executive Committee thoroughly understands the mental prostration you must now be experiencing. It does not, however, consider that it should from a feeling of delicacy defer the following declaration. There is something higher even than legitimate human feeling; it is the duty toward our country, a duty to which every citizen should sacrifice himself, his own feelings, and even those of others. . . .

Your Majesty will admit that the government of the late Emperor cannot be accused of "want of energy." The innocent and the guilty were hanged alike; the prisons, like the remotest provinces, were filled with the condemned. The so-called "leaders" were taken and hanged by the dozen.

They died tranquilly and with the calmness of martyrs, but this did not stop the movement; on the contrary, the movement increased and continually gained in strength. A revolutionary movement, your Majesty, does not depend on individuals. It is a process of the social organism, and against it the gibbets * erected for the most energetic representatives of that process are as powerless to save the existing order of things as the punishment of the cross, inflicted upon the Nazarene, was powerless to save the decaying ancient world from the triumph of reforming Christianity.

The government may continue to arrest and hang as long as it likes and may succeed in oppressing single revolutionary bodies. We will even admit that it may succeed in destroying the essential organization of the revolution. But this will not change the state of things. Revolutionists will be created by events, by the general discontent of the whole of the people. . . .

An entire nation cannot be suppressed; and still less can the discontent of a nation be suppressed by rigorous measures. These instead, will increase its bitterness, its energy, and its forces. . . . Thus, with the progress of time, the revolutionary organizations cannot but increase in number and in efficiency. . . .

A terrible explosion, a sanguinary revolution, a spasmodic convul-

* **gibbets:** a kind of gallows.

Source: Stepnyak, *Underground Russia*, 2nd ed., New York: Charles Scribner's Sons, 1883, pp. 313–19.

sion throughout all Russia, will complete the destruction of the old order of things. . . .

But why the sad necessity for this sanguinary [bloody] struggle?

For this reason, your Majesty; that a just government, in the true sense of the word, does not exist among us. A government should, in conformity with the essential principle of its existence, be the expression of the aspirations of the people, should carry out only the will of the people. With us, however — pardon us for saying so — the government . . . deserves the name of a "band of usurpers.". . .

Only the bloodsucking officials, whose knavish exactions remain unpunished, enjoy the protection of the government and the laws.

How frightful, on the other hand, is the fate of an upright man who labors for the common welfare! Your Majesty, you yourself well know that it is not the Socialists alone who are persecuted and transported. . . .

This is why the government in Russia has no moral influence over the people; this is why Russia produces so many revolutionists; this is why even an event like the killing of the czar excites sympathy among a great part of this very people. . . .

There are only two outlets from such a situation: either a revolution, which will neither be averted nor prevented by condemnations to death, or the spontaneous surrender of supreme authority to the people to assist in the work of government.

In the interests of the country and to avoid a useless waste of talent and energy and those terrible disasters by which the Revolution is always accompanied, the Executive Committee addresses itself to your Majesty and counsels you to select the latter course. . . .

We hope that personal resentment will not suppress in you either the sentiment of duty or the desire of hearing the truth.

We also might feel resentment. You have lost your father: we have lost not only our fathers, but our brothers, wives, sons, and best friends. Nevertheless, we are ready to forget all personal rancor if the welfare of Russia demands it, and we expect as much from you.

We impose upon you no conditions of any kind. Do not take offense at our proposals. The conditions which are necessary in order that the revolutionary movement should give place to a pacific development have not been created by us but by events. We simply record them. These conditions, according to our view, should be based upon two principal stipulations.

44

First, a general amnesty for all political offenders, since they have committed no crime but have simply done their duty as citizens.

Second, the convocation of the representatives of the whole of the people for the examination of the best forms of social and political life, according to the wants and desires of the people. . . .

And now, your Majesty, decide. The choice rests with you. We, on our side, can only express the hope that your judgment and your conscience will suggest to you the only decision which can accord with the welfare of Russia, with your own dignity, and with your duties toward the country.

THE EXECUTIVE COMMITTEE

Darwin Searches for the Origin of Species

Although Charles Darwin's Origin of Species (1859) did not present the idea of evolution for the first time, it did offer an explanation of how evolution worked. Over a period of thirty years, Darwin had gathered an overwhelming body of evidence to support the theory. Darwin's ideas of variation of offspring, struggle for existence, adaptation, natural selection, and survival of the fittest, although accepted at once by a small group of men, caused a general furor among his contemporaries.

Darwin had spent five years on the H.M.S. Beagle collecting, observing, and classifying biological specimens found in the South Atlantic and Pacific. Years of continued study and research produced no more than a temporary written outline of his work. The Origin of Species finally emerged as a book because Darwin realized that he would be anticipated by another author if he delayed in publishing his findings.

In his short Autobiography, Darwin discusses his search for a solution to the problem of species.

45

After my return to England it appeared to me that by following the example of Lyell in geology and by collecting all facts which bore in any way on the variation of animals and plants under domestication and nature, some light might perhaps be thrown on the whole subject. My first notebook was opened in July 1837. I worked on true Baconian principles, and without any theory collected facts on a wholesale scale, more especially with respect to domesticated productions, by printed enquiries, by conversation with skillful breeders and gardeners, and by extensive reading. When I see the list of books of all kinds which I read and abstracted, including whole series of journals and transactions, I am surprised at my industry. I soon perceived that selection was the keystone of man's success in making useful races of animals and plants. But how selection could be applied to organisms living in a state of nature remained for some time a mystery to me.

In October 1838, that is, fifteen months after I had begun my systematic enquiry, I happened to read for amusement Malthus on *Population*, and being well prepared to appreciate the struggle for existence which everywhere goes on from long-continued observation of the habits of animals and plants, it at once struck me that under these circumstances favorable variations would tend to be preserved and unfavorable ones to be destroyed. The result of this would be the formation of new species. Here, then, I had at last got a theory by which to work; but I was so anxious to avoid prejudice that I determined not for some time to write even the briefest sketch of it. In June 1842 I first allowed myself the satisfaction of writing a very brief abstract of my theory in pencil in 35 pages; and this was enlarged during the summer of 1844 into one of 230 pages, which I had fairly copied out and still possess.

But at that time I overlooked one problem of great importance; and it is astonishing to me . . . how I could have overlooked it and its solution. This problem is the tendency in organic beings descended from the same stock to diverge in character as they become modified. That they have diverged greatly is obvious from the manner in which species of all kinds can be classed under genera, genera under families, families under suborders, and so forth; and I can remember the very spot in the road, while in my carriage, when to my joy the solution oc-

Source: Charles Darwin, *The Autobiography of Charles Darwin*, edited by Nora Barlow, London: William Collins Sons & Co., Ltd., 1958, pp. 119–21. Reprinted by permission of A. D. Peters, London.

curred to me. . . . The solution, as I believe, is that the modified off-spring of all dominant and increasing forms tend to become adapted to many and highly diversified places in the economy of nature.

Pasteur Discovers a Cure for Rabies

The busy life of Louis Pasteur was dedicated to solving scientific riddles and throwing light on mysteries. By the use of the microscope he was able to prove that there was no such thing as "spontaneous generation." He learned that certain strains of bacteria were the cause of disease, and he discovered a way of destroying them by the process that bears his name — "pasteurization." He came to the conclusion that the many deaths each year from rabies were caused by bacteria. After conducting extensive experiments, he developed a serum in 1885 which he first used successfully on dogs who had themselves been bitten by rabid dogs.

The story of the first human being to be inoculated against rabies is told by one of Pasteur's biographers.

On Monday, July 6, Pasteur saw a little Alsatian boy, Joseph Meister, enter his laboratory accompanied by his mother. He was only nine years old and had been bitten two days before by a mad dog. . . .

Pasteur's emotion was great at the sight of the fourteen wounds of the little boy, who suffered so much that he could hardly walk. What should he do for this child? Could he risk the preventive treatment which had been constantly successful on his dogs? Pasteur was divided between his hopes and his scruples, painful in their acuteness. Before deciding on a course of action, he made arrangements for the comfort of this poor woman and her child, alone in Paris, and gave them an appointment for five o'clock. He did not wish to attempt anything with-

Source: René Vallery-Radot, *The Life of Pasteur*, translated by R. L. Devonshire, New York: McClure Phillips & Co., 1906, pp. 414–17, 422.

47

out having seen Vulpian and talked it over with him. Since the Rabies Commission had been constituted, Pasteur had formed a growing esteem of the great judgment of Vulpian, who in his lectures on the . . . nervous system had already mentioned the profit to human clinics to be drawn from experimenting on animals. . . .

Vulpian expressed the opinion that Pasteur's experiments on dogs were sufficiently conclusive to authorize him to foresee the same success in human pathology. Why not try this treatment? . . . Was there any other . . . treatment against hydrophobia? . . .

This was also the opinion of Dr. Grancher, whom Pasteur consulted. M. Grancher worked at the laboratory. . . .

Vulpian and M. Grancher examined little Meister in the evening, and seeing the number of bites, some of which, on one hand especially, were very deep, they decided on performing the first inoculation immediately; the substance chosen was fourteen days old and had quite lost its virulence: it was to be followed by further inoculations gradually increasing in strength.

It was a very slight operation, a mere injection into the side of a few drops of a liquid. . . . The child, who cried very much before the operation, soon dried his tears when he found the slight prick was all that he had to undergo.

Pasteur had had a bedroom comfortably arranged for the mother and child. . . .

"All is going well," Pasteur wrote to his son-in-law on July 11, "the child sleeps well, has a good appetite, and the inoculated matter is absorbed into the system from one day to another without leaving a trace. It is true that I have not yet come to the test inoculations, which will take place on Tuesday, Wednesday, and Thursday. If the lad keeps well during the three following weeks, I think the experiment will be safe to succeed. . . ."

But, as the inoculations were becoming more virulent, Pasteur became a prey to anxiety: "My dear children," wrote Mme Pasteur, "your father has had another bad night; he is dreading the last inoculations on the child. And yet there can be no drawing back now! The boy continues in perfect health."

Renewed hopes were expressed in the following letter from Pasteur:

"My dear René, I think great things are coming to pass. Joseph Meister has just left the laboratory. The three last inoculations have left some pink marks under the skin, gradually widening and not at all tender. There is some action, which is becoming more intense as we approach the final inoculation, which will take place on Thursday, July 16. The lad is very well this morning and has slept well, though slightly restless; he has a good appetite and no feverishness. He had a slight hysterical attack yesterday."

The letter ended with an affectionate invitation. "Perhaps one of the great medical facts of the century is going to take place; you would regret not having seen it!"

Pasteur was going through a succession of hopes, fears, anguish, and an ardent yearning to snatch little Meister from death; he could no longer work. At nights, feverish visions came to him of this child whom he had seen playing in the garden, suffocating in the mad struggles of hydrophobia, like the dying child he had seen at the Trousseau Hospital in 1880. Vainly his experimental genius assured him that the virus of that most terrible of diseases was about to be vanquished, that humanity was about to be delivered from this dread horror. . . .

The treatment lasted ten days; Meister was inoculated twelve times. . . .

Cured from his wounds, delighted with all he saw, gaily running about as if he had been on his own Alsatian farm, little Meister, whose blue eyes now showed neither fear nor shyness, merrily received the last inoculation; in the evening, after claiming a kiss from "dear Monsieur Pasteur," as he called him, he went to bed and slept peacefully. Pasteur spent a terrible night of insomnia; in those slow dark hours of night when all vision is distorted, Pasteur, losing sight of the accumulation of experiments which guaranteed his success, imagined that the little boy would die.

The treatment being now completed, Pasteur left little Meister to the care of Dr. Grancher (the lad was not to return to Alsace until July 27) and consented to take a few days' rest. . . .

He wrote from Arbois to his son August 3, 1885: "Very good news last night of the bitten lad. I am looking forward with great hopes to the time when I can draw a conclusion. It will be thirty-one days tomorrow since he was bitten.". . .

On October 26, Pasteur, in a statement at the Academy of Sciences, described the treatment followed for Meister. Three months and three days had passed, and the child remained perfectly well.

The Flight at Kitty Hawk

Only three newspapers bothered to report the event which in-augurated a revolution in transportation and communication. Orville and Wilbur Wright were two young mechanics from Ohio who had selected Kitty Hawk, North Carolina, as a spot favorable for their experiments in flight. First they built a glider, then added to it a tail and rudder, and finally equipped it with an engine. Their airplane looked like two boards strung to-gether with wire. On December 17, 1903, Orville Wright be-came the first man to fly a motor-driven airplane that was heav-ier than air. He managed to stay up about twelve seconds. The Wrights continued to improve their machine, but it was some time before the significance of their accomplishment was rec-ognized.

The story of the flight is told by Orville Wright.

During the night of December 16, 1903, a strong cold wind blew from the north. When we arose on the morning of the seventeenth, the puddles of water which had been standing about camp since the recent rains were covered with ice. . . . We thought that by facing the flyer into a strong wind, there ought to be no trouble in launching it from the level ground about camp. We realized the difficulties of flying in so high a wind, but estimated that the added dangers in flight would be partly compensated for by the slower speed in landing. . . . Measurements made just before starting the first flight showed veloci-ties of 11 to 12 meters per second, or 24 to 27 miles per hour. . . .

With all the knowledge and skill acquired in thousands of flights in the last ten years, I would hardly think today of making my first flight on a strange machine in twenty-seven-mile wind, even if I knew that the machine had already been flown and was safe. After these years of experience, I look with amazement upon our audacity in at-tempting flights with a new and untried machine under such circum-stances. Yet faith in our calculations and the design of this first machine, based upon our tables of air pressures secured by months of careful lab-

Source: Orville Wright, "How We Made the First Flight," in *Flying*, Vol. II, December, 1913, pp. 35–36.

oratory work, and confidence in our system of control developed by three years of actual experience in balancing gliders in the air had convinced us that the machine was capable of lifting and maintaining itself in the air, and that with a little practice, it would be safely flown.

Wilbur having used his turn * in the unsuccessful attempt on the fourteenth, the right to the first trial now belonged to me. After running the motor a few minutes to heat it up, I released the wire that held the machine to the track, and the machine started forward into the wind. Wilbur ran at the side of the machine, holding the wing to balance it on the track. . . . Wilbur was able to stay with it till it lifted from the track after a forty-foot run. . . .

The course of the flight up and down was exceedingly erratic, partly due to the irregularity of the air and partly to lack of experience in handling this machine. . . . A sudden dart when a little over 100 feet from the end of the track, or a little over 120 feet from the point at which it rose into the air, ended the flight. . . . This flight lasted only 12 seconds, but it was nevertheless the first in the history of the world in which a machine carrying a man had raised itself by its own power into the air in full flight, had sailed forward without reduction of speed, and had finally landed at a point as high as that from which it started.

* The brothers took turns in attempting the flight.

PART EIGHT

The Non-European
Civilizations and
European Imperialism

A Hindu View
of the Four Classes

It is a basic premise of Hinduism that men are not born the same. They differ in character, in station, and in obligations. In accordance with the doctrine of rebirth, the behavior of an individual in the previous life determines the station into which he will be born in the next. In each case, he must fulfill the tasks which are appropriate to his particular position.

Originally there were four basic classes (these were not castes) in Hindu society, as well as a large number of untouchables. Within each class there developed in time many castes. The castes did not grow out of the classes but were based on ancient divisions of tribe, profession, or religion. The untouchables, who do menial work such as disposing of corpses, have their own castes. Altogether there are now about three thousand castes in India.

The Code of Manu, the most famous of the Hindu books of sacred law, was written sometime during the first and second centuries B.C. *It outlines the duties of the four classes as seen from the traditional Hindu viewpoint.*

For the sake of the preservation of this entire creation, Purusha, the exceedingly resplendent one, assigned separate duties to the classes which had sprung from his mouth, arms, thighs, and feet.

Teaching, studying, performing sacrificial rites, so too making others perform sacrificial rites, and giving away and receiving gifts — these he assigned to the brahmans.

Protection of the people, giving away of wealth, performance of sacrificial rites, study, and nonattachment to sensual pleasures — these are, in short, the duties of a kshatriya.

Source: Wm. Theodore de Bary *et al.*, editors, *Oriental Civilizations: Sources of Indian Tradition*, New York: Columbia University Press, 1958, p. 225. Reprinted by permission of the publishers.

Tending of cattle, giving away of wealth, performance of sacrificial rites, study, trade and commerce, . . . and agriculture — these are the occupations of a vaishya.

The Lord has prescribed only one occupation . . . for a shudra; namely, service without malice of . . . these other three classes.

The Meaning and Practice of Yoga

In the Hindu religion yoga is the training and practice which enable an individual to achieve unity with God. Because men differ by temperament, they will practice yoga in different ways — some by the use of the mind, some by emotion and love, some by work and activity, and some by rigid mental control. The yogi, by means of long and rigorous training, tries to come in contact with the divine spirit. To succeed in this quest he must first make himself oblivious of any outside influence, including that of his body. Only when this has been achieved will the yogi be in a state of pure contemplation.

In the Bhagavad Gita (Song of the Lord), one of the most popular of Hindu sacred texts, Lord Krishna, an incarnation of the god Vishnu, the Preserver, discusses the discipline of a yogi. Lord Krishna is addressing Arjuna, a member of the warrior class who is reluctant to go into battle because he is repelled by bloodshed. Lord Krishna informs him that he must do his duty, and in the course of the discussion outlines the meaning and practice of yoga.

Work alone art thou entitled to, and not to its fruit. So never work for rewards, nor yet desist from work. Work with an even mind, O Arjuna. . . . Be of even mind in success and in failure. Evenness of

Source: *The Bhagavad Gita*, translated by D. S. Sarma, published by the *Madras Law Journal*, India, 1945, as found in *The Religion of the Hindus*, edited by Kenneth W. Morgan, New York: The Ronald Press Company, 1953, pp. 378–80, 386–88. Reprinted by permission of D. S. Sarma, the *Madras Law Journal*, and The Ronald Press Company.

mind is called yoga. Far inferior indeed is mere action, O Arjuna, to equanimity of mind. So take refuge in equanimity; miserable are they who work for results.

When a man puts away all the desires of his mind, O Arjuna, and when his spirit finds comfort in itself — then is he called a man of steadfast wisdom. He who is not perturbed in mind by adversity and has no eagerness amidst prosperity, he from whom desire, fear, and anger have fallen away — he is called a sage of firm understanding. . . .

The man who gives up all desires and goes about free from any longing . . . — he attains to peace. This is a divine state, O Arjuna. He who has reached it is deluded no longer, and he who is established in it even at the hour of death — he attains to the bliss of God.

Sages look upon all alike, whether it be a learned and lowly Brahman or a cow or an elephant or even a dog or an outcaste. . . . His soul being unattached to external objects, he finds the happiness that is in himself; he is in union with God, and he enjoys undying bliss.

For the pleasures that arise from attachments are only sources of pain. They have a beginning and an end, O Arjuna, and no wise man delights in them. He who is able to resist the force of desire and anger even here before he quits his body — he is a yogi, he is a blessed man. The yogi who is happy within becomes divine, and attains to the beatitude of God.

Those whose sins are destroyed and whose doubts are removed, whose minds are disciplined and who rejoice in the good of all beings — such holy men attain to the beatitude of God. Those who are free from desire and anger, and who have subdued their minds and realized themselves — around such austere men lies the beatitude of God.

Shutting out all external objects, fixing the gaze of his eyes between his brows, and equalizing the inward and the outward breath moving in his nostrils, the sage who has controlled his senses, mind, understanding, and who puts away desire, fear, and anger, and who is ever bent on liberation — he is indeed ever liberated. And having known me who am the Recipient of all sacrifices and austerities, the Lord of all the worlds and the Friend of all creatures, he attains peace. . . .

He who has conquered himself is the friend of himself; but he who has not conquered himself is hostile to himself as a foe. The spirit of a man who has conquered himself and attained to serenity is steadfast in cold and heat, in pleasure and pain, and in honor and dishonor. He is said to be a steadfast yogi whose mind derives satisfaction from knowledge and experience, who having conquered his senses, never vacillates, and to whom a clod, a stone, and a piece of gold are the same. He who has equal regard for friends, companions, and foes, for those who are indifferent, for those who are impartial, for those who are hateful, for those who are righteous and those who are sinful — he stands supreme.

A yogi should always try to concentrate his mind in absolute solitude, having retired to a secret place, and subdued his mind and body and got rid of his desires and possessions. Having in a clean place firmly fixed his seat neither too high nor too low, and having spread over it the sacred grass, and then a deerskin, and then a cloth, he should practice yoga for his own purification, restraining his thoughts and senses, and bringing his mind to a point. Sitting firm he should hold his body, head, and neck erect and still, and gaze steadfastly on the point of his nose, without looking around. Serene and fearless, steadfast in the vow of celibacy, and subdued in mind, he should sit in yoga, thinking on me and intent on me alone.

Keeping himself ever steadfast in this manner, the yogi of subdued mind attains to the peace which abides in me and which leads to bliss. Yoga is not for him who eats too much, nor for him who eats too little. It is not for him, O Arjuna, who is given to too much sleep, nor for him who keeps vigil too long. But for the man who is temperate in his food and recreation, who is restrained in all his actions, and who is regulated in his sleep and vigil, yoga puts an end to all sorrow. When the disciplined mind of a man is established in the Spirit alone, free from the desire of any object, then he is said to possess concentration. "As a lamp in a place sheltered from the wind does not flicker" — that is the figure employed of a yogi who, with a subdued mind, practices concentration of the Spirit.

Renouncing entirely all the desires born of the imagination and restraining with his mind all his senses on every side, a man should gain tranquillity little by little, and with a steadfast purpose concentrate his mind on the Spirit, and think of nothing else. Whatsoever makes the wavering and fickle mind wander away — it should be withdrawn from that and brought back to the control of the Spirit. . . . Supreme happiness comes to the yogi whose mind is at rest, whose passions are composed, and who is pure and has become one with God.

The Four Noble Truths of Buddhism

Buddhism, the religion of many millions throughout the world, traces its origin to a handsome, wealthy young prince of a northern Indian tribe who left his family and home to live apart from the world and search for truth. Touched by human misery and suffering, Siddhartha Gautama (c. 560– c. 480 B.C.) longed to find a way to release men from pain. After rejecting extreme seclusion and self-deprivation as a possible solution, enlightenment came to him one day while he was contemplating under a tree. Thereafter he was called Buddha — the Enlightened One — or more exactly, "the One who is awake."

Buddha believed that it was his mission to enlighten the world. For about fifty years he preached his message throughout India, gaining followers and disciples wherever he went. His teachings were a reaction to Hinduism. They provided a means whereby every individual, without ritual, without a priesthood, and without supernatural aid, could attain the blissful state of Nirvana in which desire is totally extinguished and perfect peace attained.

"The Four Noble Truths" was the first sermon preached by Buddha after his enlightenment. Before an audience of five, he set forth the causes of evil and suffering, as well as the means to cope with them.

What are these Four Noble Truths? They are the Noble Truth of Suffering, the Noble Truth of the Origin of Suffering, the Noble Truth of the Extinction of Suffering, and the Noble Truth of the Path that leads to the Extinction of Suffering. . . .

What now is the Noble Truth of Suffering?

Birth is suffering; decay is suffering; death is suffering; sorrow, lamentation, pain, grief, and despair are suffering; not to get what one desires is suffering. . . .

And what is decay? The decay of beings . . . getting aged, frail,

Source: Dwight Goddard, editor, A Buddhist Bible, New York: E. P. Dutton & Co., Inc., 1938, pp. 22–24, 29–33. Reprinted by permission of the publishers.

gray and wrinkled; the failing of their vital force, the wearing out of the senses — this is called decay.

And what is death? The parting and vanishing of beings; . . . their destruction, disappearance, death, the completion of their life period, . . . the discarding of the body — this is called death.

And what is sorrow? The sorrow arising through this or that loss or misfortune which one encounters, the worrying oneself, the state of being alarmed, inward sorrow, inward woe — this is called sorrow.

And what is lamentation? Whatsoever, through this or that loss or misfortune which befalls one, is wail and lament, wailing and lamenting . . . — this is called lamentation.

And what is pain? The bodily pain and unpleasantness, the painful and unpleasant feeling produced by bodily contact — this is called pain.

And what is grief? Mental pain and unpleasantness. . . .

And what is despair? Distress and despair arising through this or that loss or misfortune . . . — this is called despair. . . .

What now is the Noble Truth of the Origin of Suffering? It is that craving which gives rise to fresh rebirth and, bound up with pleasure, . . . now here, now there, finds ever fresh delight. . . .

But where does this craving arise and take root? Wherever in the world there is the delightful and pleasurable, there this craving arises and takes root. Eye, ear, nose, tongue, body, and mind are delightful and pleasurable, there this craving arises and takes root.

Forms, sounds, smells, tastes, . . . and ideas are delightful and pleasurable: there this craving arises and takes root.

If namely, when perceiving a visible form, a sound, odor, taste, bodily contact, or an idea in the mind, the object is pleasant, one is attracted, and if unpleasant, one is repelled.

Thus, whatever kind of feeling one experiences — pleasant, unpleasant, or indifferent — one approves of and cherishes the feeling and clings to it; . . . but lust for feelings means clinging to existence, . . . and on clinging to existence depends the . . . process of becoming; . . . on the process of becoming depends [future] birth; . . . and dependent on birth are decay and death, sorrow, lamentation, pain, grief, and despair. Thus arises this whole mass of suffering.

This is called the Noble Truth of the Origin of Suffering. . . .

What now is called the Noble Truth of the Extinction of Suffering? It is the complete fading away and extinction of this craving, its forsaking and giving up, the liberation and detachment from it.

But where may this craving vanish, where may it be extinguished? Wherever in the world there are delightful and pleasurable things, there this craving may vanish, there it may be extinguished.

Be it in the past, present, or future: whosoever of the monks or priests regard the delightful and pleasurable things in the world as impermanent, . . . as a disease and sorrow, it is he who overcomes the craving.

For, through the total fading away and extinction of craving, . . . decay and death, sorrow, lamentation, suffering, grief, and despair are extinguished. Thus comes about the extinction of this whole mass of suffering. . . .

To give oneself up to indulgence — . . . the base, common, vulgar, unholy, unprofitable; and also to give oneself up to self-mortification — the painful, unholy, unprofitable: both these two extremes the Perfect One [Buddha] has avoided and found out the Middle Path which makes one both to see and to know, which leads to peace, to discernment, to enlightenment, to Nibbana [Nirvana].

It is the Noble Eightfold Path, the way that leads to the extinction of suffering, namely:

1. Right Understanding
2. Right Mindedness
3. Right Speech
4. Right Action
5. Right Living
6. Right Effort
7. Right Attentiveness
8. Right Concentration

This is the Middle Path which the Perfect One has found out, which makes one both to see and to know, which leads to peace, to discernment, to enlightenment, to Nibbana.

Free from pain and torture is this path, free from groaning and suffering: it is the perfect path.

An Indian Moslem's Impressions of England

Among the European states that fought one another for control of India, the British emerged supreme in the middle of the eighteenth century. The Indians reacted in various ways to the Europeans. Some admired their efficiency; others despised them for their materialism; most were indifferent.

At the end of the eighteenth century Abu Taleb Khan, a Moslem civil servant, was invited by a Scottish friend to go to Europe. For about three years he traveled extensively and recorded his observations. English society flocked to meet him, and on the whole, he seems to have had a wonderful time.

The first and greatest defect I observed in the English is their want of faith in religion and their great inclination to philosophy [atheism]. The effects of these principles, or rather want of principle, is very conspicuous in the lower orders of people, who are totally devoid of honesty. They are, indeed, cautious how they transgress against the laws, from fear of punishment; but whenever an opportunity offers of [stealing] anything without the risk of detection, they never pass it by. They are also ever on the watch to appropriate to themselves the property of the rich who, on this account, are obliged constantly to keep their doors shut and never to permit an unknown person to enter them. . . .

The second defect most conspicuous in the English character is pride, or insolence. Puffed up with their power and good fortune for the last fifty years, they are not [afraid] of adversity, and take no pains to avert it. Thus, when the people of London some time ago assembled in mobs on account of the great increase of taxes and high price of provisions, and were nearly in a state of insurrection — although the magistrates, by their vigilance in watching them, and by causing parties of soldiers to patrol the streets day and night to disperse all persons whom they saw assembling together, succeeded in quieting the disturbance —

Source: Wm. Theodore de Bary *et al.*, editors, *Oriental Civilizations: Sources of Indian Tradition*, New York: Columbia University Press, 1958, pp. 563–64. Reprinted by permission of the publishers.

yet no pains were afterward taken to eradicate the evil. Some of the men in power said it had been merely a plan of the [workers] to obtain higher wages (an attempt frequently made by the English tradesmen); others were of the opinion that no remedy could be applied; therefore no further notice was taken of the affair. All this, I say, betrays a blind confidence which, instead of meeting the danger and endeavoring to prevent it, waits till the misfortune arrives and then attempts to remedy it. Such was the case with the late king of France, who took no step to oppose the revolution till it was too late. This self-confidence is to be found, more or less, in every Englishman; it however differs much from the pride of the Indians and Persians.

Their third defect is a passion for acquiring money and their attachment to worldly affairs.

The Sepoy Rebellion

The great subcontinent of India was governed and administered by the British East India Company (although independent and semi-independent states continued to exist). From the last quarter of the eighteenth century the British increasingly interfered in Indian affairs, and though many improvements were introduced, native discontent continued to grow.

The immediate cause of the Sepoy Rebellion in Bengal in 1857 was a strange but very effective rumor. New rifles had been introduced in the Indian army, which was made up mainly of Sepoys, or natives. In order to use the cartridges, the ends had to be bitten off. Word got about among the Hindus that the cartridges were greased with cow fat, and among the Moslems that they were greased with pig fat. Since the cow was sacred to the Hindus and the pig profane to the Moslems, the army broke out in mutiny. Actually animal fat had been used in the cartridges, but this was just one of a series of acts that had disturbed the Sepoys. The Rebellion, which spread beyond the army, was a violent conservative reaction against the domination of Europeans and their threat to the Indian cultural heritage. Yet many Indians remained loyal to the British and fought on their side.

The British East India Company shouldered much of the blame for India's troubles. In 1858, after order had been restored, Parliament passed an act which put India directly under the rule of the Crown. Queen Victoria proclaimed that the British would provide fair and equal government. Thereafter, the government of India increasingly became a partnership (though never really an equal one) between the British and the Indians.

A British Officer's Report

I persuaded the Sepoys to let me take the regimental color, and I took it outside, but on calling for my groom I found he had bolted with my horse. You may imagine my horror at this. I went back into the quarter guard and replaced the color, but on again coming out a trooper dismounted and took a deliberate shot at me but, missing his aim, I walked up to him and blew his brains out. Another man was then taking aim at me, when he was bayoneted by a Sepoy of my company. The firing then became general and I was compelled to run the gauntlet across the parade ground, and escaped unhurt miraculously, three bullets having passed through my hat and one through the skirt of my coat. The whole of the houses . . . were burned. Having gone as far as my weak state of health would permit and being exhausted, I took refuge in a garden under some bushes. About half an hour after, a band of robbers, looking out for plunder, detected me, robbed me of my rings, etc., and only left me my flannel waistcoat and socks. They then tore off the sleeve of my shirt and with it attempted to strangle me. . . . They left me for dead, as I had become senseless. About one hour after, I came to and managed to stagger on about a mile without shoes, where I secreted myself in a hut until daybreak, when I resumed my dreary journey, and after traveling about twelve miles, the latter part of which was in the broiling sun, without anything on my head, arrived at Aleepore.

Source: *The Annual Register*, 1857, London: F. & J. Rivington, 1858, pp. 251, 284–85.

The Sepoys Attack Cawnpore

We had but one well, in the middle of the entrenchment, and the enemy kept up their fire so incessantly both day and night that it was as much as giving a man's life blood to go and draw a bucket of water; . . . but after the second day . . . it . . . became a matter of necessity for every person to get his own water, which was usually done during the night, when the enemy could not well direct their shots. . . .

The heat was very great and what with the fight, want of room, want of proper food and care, several ladies and soldiers' wives, as also children, died with great distress. Many officers and soldiers also were sunstruck from exposure to the hot winds. The dead bodies of our people had to be thrown into a well outside the entrenchment near the new unfinished barracks, and this work was generally done at the close of each day, as nobody could venture out during the day on account of the shot and shell flying in all directions like a hail storm. . . . The distress was so great that none could offer a word of consolation to his friend or attempt to administer to the wants of each other. I have seen the dead bodies of officers and tenderly brought up young ladies of rank (colonels' and captains' daughters) put outside in the veranda in the rain, to await the time when the fatigue party usually went round to carry the dead to the well, as above, for there was scarcely room to shelter the living; the buildings were so sadly riddled that every safe corner available was considered a great object.

The enemy now commenced firing live shells well heated, with the intent of setting fire to the tents of officers in the compound, as also to the thatched barrack, which though hastily covered over with tiles, was not proof against fire. The tents therefore had all to be struck, as several had thus been burned, and at last, on the thirteenth of June, the barrack also took fire; it was about 5 P.M., and that evening was one of unspeakable distress and trial, for all the wounded and sick were in it, also the families of the soldiers. . . . The breeze being very strong, the flames spread out so quickly that it was hard matter to remove the women and children, who were all in great confusion, so that the helpless wounded and sick could not be removed and were all burned. . . .

Our barracks were so perfectly riddled as to afford little or no shelter, yet the greater portion of the people preferred to remain in them than to be exposed to the heat of the sun outside, although a great

many made themselves holes under the walls of the entrenchment. . . .
In these, with their wives and children, they were secure at least from
the shots and shells of the enemy, though not so from the effects of
the heat, and the mortality from apoplexy was considerable. At night,
however, every person had to sleep out and take the watch in . . .
turns, so that nearly the whole of the women and children also slept
under the walls of the entrenchments, near their respective relatives.
Here the live shells kept them in perpetual dread, for nearly all night
these shells were seen coming in the air and bursting in different places.

The Growth of
National Feeling in India

Indian nationalism emerged both as a reaction to and a result of
British rule. The British provided a unified government; they
trained a host of Indian civil servants; they made it possible for
Indians to get an English education and thus come in contact
with European political ideas; they built a system of communications; and they supplied a common language.

The first Indian National Congress met in 1886 to give expression to the rising spirit of Indian national feeling. The majority of the early Indian nationalists were moderates like
Dadabhai Naoroji, who was president of the Congress for three
years. The moderates put their faith in British justice and in a
slow evolution to self-government. They were highly respected
in Britain, and Dadabhai Naoroji himself was elected to the
British Parliament by a British constituency in 1892.

The extreme nationalists, like Bal Gangadhar Tilak, considered the moderates' respect for Britain both humiliating and
unjustified. They rejected British civilization and tradition, and
expressed their national feeling by a desire to revive Hinduism
and native Indian culture. Much closer to the Hindu peasant
than the moderates, they tended to have an enormous influence.

The Dissatisfaction of a Moderate

[In a memorandum written in 1880, Naoroji said:]

Europeans occupy almost all the higher places in every department of government. . . . While in India they acquire India's money, experience, and wisdom, and when they go they carry both away with them, leaving India so much poorer in material and moral wealth. Thus India is left without, and cannot have, those elders in wisdom and experience who in every country are the natural guides of the rising generations in their national and social conduct and of the destinies of their country — and a sad, sad loss this is!

Every European is isolated from the people around him. He is not their mental, moral, or social leader, or companion. For any mental or moral influence or guidance or sympathy with the people, he might just as well be living in the moon. The people know not him, and he knows not nor cares for the people. Some honorable exceptions do now and then make an effort to do some good, . . . but in the very nature of things, these efforts are always feeble . . . and of little permanent effect. . . .

The Europeans are not the natural leaders of the people. They do not belong to the people. They cannot enter into their thoughts and feelings; they cannot join or sympathize with their joys or griefs. On the contrary, every day the estrangement is increasing. Europeans deliberately and openly widen it more and more. There may be very few social institutions started by Europeans in which natives, however fit and desirous to join, are not deliberately and insultingly excluded. The Europeans are and make themselves strangers in every way. . . .

The power that is now being raised by the spread of education, though yet slow and small, is one that in time must, for weal or woe, exercise great influence. In fact, it has already begun to do so. . . . The thousands that are being sent out by the universities every year find themselves in a most [difficult] position. There is no place for them in their motherland. They may beg in the streets or break stones on the roads, for aught the rulers seem to care for their natural rights, position, and duties in their own country. . . .

The educated find themselves simply so many dummies, orna-

Source: Wm. Theodore de Bary *et al.*, editors, *Oriental Civilizations: Sources of Indian Tradition*, New York: Columbia University Press, 1958, pp. 671–73, 719–23. Reprinted by permission of the publishers.

mented with the tinsel of school education. . . . What must be the inevitable consequence? A wild, spirited horse without curb or reins will run away wild and kill and trample upon everyone that comes in his way. A misdirected force will hit anywhere and destroy anything. The power that the rulers are (so far, to their credit) raising will . . . recoil against themselves, if with this blessing of education they do not do their whole duty to the country which trusts to their righteousness and thus turn this good power to their own side. . . . The voice of the power of the rising education is, no doubt, feeble at present. Like the infant, the present dissatisfaction is only crying at the pains it is suffering. Its notions have not taken any form or shape or course yet, but it is growing. Heaven only knows what it will grow to! If the present material and moral destruction of India continues, a great convulsion must inevitably arise by which either India will be more and more crushed under the iron heel of despotism and destruction, or may succeed in shattering the destroying hand and power. Far, far is it from my earnest prayer and hope that such should be the result of the British rule.

An Extremist Calls for a Boycott

[In a speech made in 1906 to the New Party, of which he was leader, Tilak said:]

Two new words have recently come into existence with regard to our politics — Moderates and Extremists. These words have a specific relation to time, and they therefore will change with time. The Extremists of today will be Moderates tomorrow, just as the Moderates of today were Extremists yesterday. . . . We are Extremists today and our sons will call themselves Extremists and us Moderates. Every new party begins as Extremists and ends as Moderates. . . . We cannot say what will or will not happen one thousand years hence — perhaps during that long period, the whole of the white race will be swept away in another glacial period. We must therefore study the present and work out a program to meet the present condition. . . .

Your industries are ruined utterly, ruined by foreign rule; your wealth is going out of the country, and you are reduced to the lowest level which no human being can occupy. In this state of things, is there any other remedy by which you can help yourself? The remedy is not petitioning, but boycott. We say prepare your forces, organize your power, and then go to work so that they cannot refuse you what you demand. . . . Are you prepared in this way to fight if your demand is refused? If you are, . . . you will not be refused; but if you are not, nothing can be more certain than that your demand will be refused, and perhaps forever. We are not armed, and there is no necessity for arms either. We have a stronger weapon, a political weapon, in boycott. We have perceived one fact, that the whole of this administration which is carried on by a handful of Englishmen, is carried on with our assistance. We are all in subordinate service. This whole government is carried on with our assistance, and they try to keep us in ignorance of our power of cooperation between ourselves, by which what is in our own hands at present can be claimed by us and administered by us. The point is to have the entire control in our hands. . . . Self-government is our goal; we want a control over our administrative machinery. We don't want to become clerks and remain clerks. At present we are clerks and willing instruments of our own oppression in the hands of an alien government, and that government is ruling over us not by its innate strength but by keeping us in ignorance and blindness to the perception of this fact. . . . Every Englishman knows that they are a mere handful in this country, and it is the business of every one of them to fool you in believing that you are weak and they are strong. This is politics. We have been deceived by such policy so long. What the new party wants you to do is to realize the fact that your future rests entirely in your own hands. If you mean to be free, you can be free; if you do not mean to be free, you will fall and be forever fallen. . . . We shall not give them assistance to collect revenue and keep peace. We shall not assist them in fighting beyond the frontiers or outside India with Indian blood and money. We shall not assist them in carrying on the administration of justice. We shall have our own courts, and when the time comes we shall not pay taxes. Can you do that by your united efforts? If you can, you are free from tomorrow. Some gentlemen who spoke this evening referred to half a bread as against the whole bread. I sav I want the whole bread, and that immediately. But if I cannot get the whole, don't think that I have no patience.

I will take the half they give me and then try for the remainder. This is the line of thought and action in which you must train yourself. We have not raised this cry from a mere impulse. It is a reasoned impulse. Try to understand that reason and try to strengthen that impulse by your logical convictions. I do not ask you to follow us blindly. Think over the whole problem for yourselves. If you accept our advice, we feel sure we can achieve our salvation thereby. This is the advice of the new party.

Lao-tzu's Way of Life

The birth and life of Lao-tzu, the founder of Taoism, are shrouded in legend. Whether he lived around 600 B.C., or around 300 B.C., or not at all, has yet to be determined. The writings which are attributed to him, however, are one of the most enduring monuments of Chinese civilization.

Tao means "the Way." It is very difficult to define, and Taoists themselves say that it cannot be fully understood by the mind. It may be described as the ultimate reality, the unchanging beneath all change, the all-powerful, impersonal, primary force in the universe. The mystical understanding of this force brings happiness and power.

The simple life is the best approach to the Way. Lao-tzu counseled passivity, humility, spontaneity, acceptance of life, and harmony with nature. For the ruler of a state, the Way prescribed a minimum of government direction and a surrender of ambition. The goal of Taoism was an eventual return to the happy anarchy that preceded civilization. It appealed to those who wished to leave behind the follies of the world and seek happiness in nature.

The following five selections are from the writings attributed to Lao-tzu.

Rulers

Of the best rulers
  The people (only) know that they exist;
The next best they love and praise;
The next they fear;

Source: Lin Yutang, editor, *The Wisdom of China and India*, New York: Random House, Inc., 1942, pp. 591–92, 599–600, 602, 607, 624. Reprinted by permission of the publishers.

And the next they revile.

  When they do not command the people's faith,
  Some will lose faith in them,
  And then they resort to oaths!
But (of the best) when their task is accomplished, their work done,
The people all remark, "We have done it ourselves."

Warning Against the Use of Force

He who by Tao purposes to help the ruler of men
Will oppose all conquest by force of arms.
For such things are wont to rebound.
Where armies are, thorns and brambles grow.
The raising of a great host
Is followed by a year of dearth.

Therefore a good general effects his purpose and stops.
  He dares not rely upon the strength of arms;
Effects his purpose and does not glory in it;
Effects his purpose and does not boast of it;
Effects his purpose and does not take pride in it;
  Effects his purpose as a regrettable necessity;
  Effects his purpose but does not love violence.
(For) things age after reaching their prime.
That (violence) would be against Tao.
And he who is against the Tao perishes young.

Knowing Oneself

He who knows others is learned;
  He who knows himself is wise.
He who conquers others has power of muscles;
  He who conquers himself is strong.
He who is contented is rich.
  He who is determined has strength of will.
He who does not lose his center endures;
He who dies yet (his power) remains has long life.

70

Be Content

Fame or one's own self, which does one love more?
One's own self or material goods, which has more worth?
Loss (of self) or possession (of goods), which is the greater evil?

Therefore: he who loves most spends most,
      He who hoards much loses much.
The contented man meets no disgrace;
Who knows when to stop runs into no danger —
He can long endure.

The Way of Heaven

True words are not fine sounding;
      Fine-sounding words are not true.
A good man does not argue;
      He who argues is not a good man.
The wise one does not know many things;
      He who knows many things is not wise.
The Sage does not accumulate (for himself):
      He lives for other people,
      And grows richer himself;
      He gives to other people,
      And has greater abundance.
The Tao of Heaven
      Blesses, but does not harm.
The Way of the Sage
      Accomplishes, but does not contend.

The Wisdom of Confucius

The greatest single influence in Chinese civilization has been Confucius (551–479 B.C.). Whereas Taoism represents the carefree side of Chinese culture, Confucianism represents the serious and disciplined side. Confucius did not found a religion;

his philosophy was a way of life. Born into an age of civil war and treachery, he sought answers to the troubles of society in the traditions of the past. He traveled from state to state in China seeking a ruler who would implement his doctrines.

Confucius put great emphasis on the virtues inherent in good family life, such as order, benevolence, and respect. He abhorred force and violence and had implicit faith in the power of rational persuasion and moral example. Confucius wanted the ruler to set up a government of good men committed to sound principles. His goal was the establishment of universal harmony based on custom and tradition. In the second century B.C., Confucianism became the official philosophy of China and the subject of study for all aspiring statesmen. In later centuries the influence of Confucius spread throughout East Asia.

The sayings of Confucius were originally written down by students who had learned them from his immediate disciples.

Clever talk and a domineering manner have little to do with being Man-at-his-best.

Daily I examine myself on three points: Have I failed to be loyal in my work for others? Have I been false with my friends? Have I failed to pass on that which I was taught?

At fifteen I thought only of study; at thirty I began playing my role; at forty I was sure of myself; at fifty I was conscious of my position in the universe; at sixty I was no longer argumentative; and now at seventy I can follow my heart's desire without violating custom. . . .

Let the sole worry of your parents be that you might become ill.

Today, when people call a man filial they mean that he is supporting his parents. But he does as much for his dogs and horses! If he does not show respect for his parents, how is he differentiating between them and the animals? . . .

Look at the means which a man employs; consider his motives; observe his pleasures. A man simply cannot conceal himself!

Source: *The Sayings of Confucius*, translated by James R. Ware, New York: The New American Library of World Literature, Inc., 1955, pp. 21 *passim*. Copyright © 1955 by James R. Ware. Reprinted by permission of the publishers.

If, while being a student of the past, a man also understands the new things which surround us, he may be used as a teacher. . . .

Learning without thought brings ensnarement. Thought without learning totters. . . .

Shall I tell you what knowledge is? It is to know both what one knows and what one does not know. . . .

China without a recognized leader is preferable to foreigners with all their leaders. . . .

To live in the company of Men-at-their-best is the finest thing possible. How can a man be considered wise if, when he has the choice, he does not live in such surroundings? . . .

Great Man cherishes excellence; Petty Man, his own comfort. Great Man cherishes the rules and regulations; Petty Man, special favors.

He who engages solely in self-interested actions will make himself many enemies. . . .

Do not worry about not holding high position; worry rather about playing your proper role. Worry not that no one knows of you; seek to be worth knowing. . . .

As you serve your parents you should remonstrate with them only slightly. If on doing so you find that they are set in having their own way, be even more respectful and do not thwart them. Even though this overwhelm you with toil, do not become angry with them. . . .

When strict with oneself one rarely fails.

Great Man seeks to be slow of speech but quick of action.

Excellence does not remain alone; it is sure to attract neighbors.

A commander may be snatched away from his army, but will cannot be taken from the humblest man.

Civil Service Examinations in China

Confucius urged his followers to train themselves in the classical writings and to pursue careers in the service of the state. In about the middle of the second century B.C., examinations began to be used to recruit civil servants. Thereafter, in spite of setbacks, the examination system was extended. The basis of the system was a knowledge of the classics and of Confucian principles. From time to time questions of a more practical and topical nature, such as law and current events, were included. Preparation for the examinations required years of concentrated effort, and thus could usually be undertaken only by the sons of wealthy families.

In a biography of the poet-statesman Su Tungpo, Lin Yutang gives us a vivid picture of the examinations in the middle of the eleventh century A.D.

The time for the palace examinations came. Ouyang Shiu was nominated by the Emperor to be chief examiner, together with a number of distinguished scholars as judges. The approach to this most critical moment of a scholar's life was always filled with keen excitement, tense hope, and a nervous fear of failure. It was the moment to which all his years of grinding labor and hours of burning the midnight oil were supposed to lead. The candidates had to get up in the middle of the night and come to the palace at dawn, bringing their cold meals with them, for they would not be able to leave until the examinations were over. During the examinations they were shut up in cubicles under the supervision of palace guards. There was a rigorous system to prevent bribery or favoritism. The candidates' papers were recopied by official clerks before they were submitted to the examiners, to avoid recognition of their identity by their handwriting. In the recopied papers the writers' names were taken out and kept on file. While the candidates

Source: Lin Yutang, *The Gay Genius: The Biography of Su Tungpo*, New York: The John Day Company, Inc., 1947, pp. 38–40. Reprinted by permission of the publishers.

were let out after the examinations, the judges themselves were shut up within the palace and forbidden to have any contact with the people outside, usually from late January till early March, until the papers were properly graded and submitted to the Emperor. The candidates were examined first on questions of history or principles of government. There was a second examination on the classics, and finally, after the successful ones had been graded, there was one — under the direct supervision of the Emperor — on lyrics, descriptive poetry, and again, essays on politics. Emperor Jentsung was especially anxious to recruit good talent for his government and took a personal interest in these tests. He sent out the subjects for the papers by his own personal servants and sometimes, to avoid leakage, changed them at the last moment. . . .

Tungpo wrote a paper which dealt with the principle of simplicity and leniency in the administration of a country. . . . On April 8, 1057, Su passed the examinations, and on April 14, at the age of twenty, was officially decorated, . . . almost at the head of 388 successful candidates. To obtain such an honor meant that one became at once nationally known as one of the first scholars of the land.

It was typical of the brilliant young man, however, that he took some liberties with history and invented a dialogue in his paper. He was developing the theme that in giving rewards one should rather err on the side of generosity, and in punishment one should give every benefit of the doubt to an offender lest an innocent man be killed. In the time of Emperor Yao, he wrote, a man was about to be condemned to death. "Three times the Minister of Justice said, 'Let him be killed!' and three times Emperor Yao said, 'Let him be pardoned!'" The dialogue read very well, and it seemed to support an authentic story that the sage Emperor was willing to use a bad man and give him a chance to prove his talent. The judges read the story but dared not question it, because it amounted to their admitting not having read it somewhere in one of the obscure ancient texts. So Su Tungpo was passed. After the examinations one day Mei Yaochen, one of the judges, said to him:

"By the way, where does that story occur about Emperor Yao and the Minister of Justice? I can't quite recall where I read it."

"I invented it," the young scholar confessed.

"You did!" said the old judge.

"Well, that was what the sage Emperor would have done, wasn't it?" replied Su Tungpo.

To pass an examination under a certain examiner was to place a scholar under heavy obligation to him for recognition of his talent, and establish a permanent relation between the two as "master" and "disciple." The candidates went up to pay their respects to their master and the chief judges and wrote them letters of gratitude. Ouyang Shiu was the authority on literature. He could make or unmake a scholar by a word of praise or blame. A writer of the time said that the scholars did not know the fear of punishments or the joy of promotions, nor did they value the gift of life or fear the doom of death, but they did fear the opinion of Ouyang Shiu. Imagine, therefore, the effect on the young poet when Ouyang Shiu said to one of his colleagues, "On reading Su Tungpo's letter, somehow I perspired all over with joy. My old person must give place to this young man and let him rise to the top." When such a statement was made by Ouyang Shiu, the whole capital heard about it. Ouyang Shiu was also reported to have said to his own sons, "Mark my word, thirty years from now nobody will talk about me." This prediction came true, for in the first decade after Su Tungpo's death nobody was talking about Ouyang Shiu but everybody was talking about Su Tungpo and reading him in secret when his works were banned.

Kublai Khan Holds Court

The few Westerners who came into contact with the Far East during the Middle Ages were overwhelmed by the splendor and the culture they encountered. Marco Polo (c. 1254–1324), a member of a wealthy Venetian merchant family, was one of the first Europeans to become intimately acquainted with Chinese civilization. He learned the language and the customs of the land and became a favorite and a high official in the court of the Khan. He was sent on a number of diplomatic missions to various parts of the Mongol empire and had the opportunity to observe what no European had ever seen. His experiences were recorded in his memoirs, which became very popular in Europe, though people found it hard to believe that his stories were authentic.

When his Majesty holds a grand and public court, those who attend it are seated in the following order. The table of the sovereign is placed on an elevation and he takes his seat on the northern side, with his face turned toward the south; and next to him, on his left hand, sits the Empress. On his right hand are placed his sons, grandsons, and other persons connected with him by blood, upon seats somewhat lower, so that their heads are on a level with the Emperor's feet. The other princes and the nobility have their places at still lower tables; and the same rules are observed with respect to the females, the wives of the sons, grandsons, and other relatives of the Great Khan being seated on the left hand, at tables in like manner gradually lower; then follow the wives of the nobility and military officers: so that all are seated according to their respective ranks and dignities, in the places assigned to them, and to which they are entitled.

The tables are arranged in such a manner that the Great Khan, sitting on his elevated throne, can overlook the whole. It is not however to be understood that all who assemble on such occasions can be accommodated at tables. The greater part of the officers and even of the nobles, on the contrary, eat sitting upon carpets in the halls; and on the outside stand a great multitude of persons who come from different countries and bring with them many rare curiosities.

In the middle of the hall, where the Great Khan sits at table, there is a magnificent piece of furniture made in the form of a square coffer, each side of which is three paces in length, exquisitely carved in figures of animals, and gilt. It is hollow within for the purpose of receiving a capacious vase of pure gold calculated to hold many gallons. On each of its four sides stands a smaller vessel containing about a hogshead, one of which is filled with mare's milk, another with that of the camel, and so of the others, according to the kinds of beverage in use. . . .

Officers of rank are likewise appointed, whose duty it is to see that all strangers who happen to arrive at the time of the festival and are unacquainted with the etiquette of the court are suitably accommodated with places; and these stewards are continually visiting every part of the hall, inquiring of the guests if there is anything with which they are unprovided or whether any of them wish for wine, milk, meat, or other articles, in which case it is immediately brought to them by the attendants.

Source: Manuel Komroff, editor, *The Travels of Marco Polo*, New York: Liveright Publishing Corporation, pp. 134–36. Copyright 1926, © renewed 1958 by Liveright Publishing Corporation. Reprinted by permission of the publishers.

At each door of the grand hall or of whatever part the Great Khan happens to be in, stand two officers of a gigantic figure, one on each side, with staves in their hands, for the purpose of preventing persons from touching the threshold with their feet and obliging them to step beyond it. If by chance anyone is guilty of this offense, the janitors take from him his garment, which he must redeem for money; or, when they do not take the garment, they inflict on him such number of blows as they have authority for doing. But as strangers may be unacquainted with the prohibition, officers are appointed to introduce and warn them. This precaution is used because touching the threshold is regarded as a bad omen. In departing from the hall, as some of the company may be affected by the liquor, it is impossible to guard against the accident, and the order is not then strictly enforced.

The numerous persons who attend at the sideboard of his Majesty and who serve him with victuals and drink are all obliged to cover their noses and mouths with handsome veils or cloths of worked silk, in order that his victuals or his wine may not be affected by their breath. When drink is called for by him and the page-in-waiting has presented it, he retires three paces and kneels down, upon which the courtiers and all who are present in like manner make their prostration. At the same moment all the musical instruments, of which there is a numerous band, begin to play and continue to do so until he has ceased drinking, when all the company recover their posture. This reverential salutation is made as often as his Majesty drinks. . . .

When the repast is finished and the tables have been removed, persons of various descriptions enter the hall, and among these a troop of comedians and performers on different instruments. Also tumblers and jugglers, who exhibit their skill in the presence of the Great Khan, to the high amusement and gratification of all the spectators. When these sports are concluded, the people separate and each returns to his own house.

A Chinese Emperor
Rejects Western Overtures

The Chinese conducted relations between themselves and other peoples as between superiors and inferiors, for they regarded themselves, both culturally and geographically, as the very center of the world. The Western foreigners with whom they came in contact did not always behave with propriety and tended to confirm Chinese disdain for the "barbarians." Catholic missionaries, especially the Jesuits, after receiving favorable treatment in return for their military and scientific knowledge, were discredited because of theological quarrels and political intrigue. By the late eighteenth century, relations between China and the West were confined to trade in a single port — Canton.

The Chinese tended to look upon merchants as unproductive parasites. Attempts by trade-hungry Europeans to persuade the Chinese to increase trade and to treat them as equals met with no success. In 1793 Lord Macartney, heading an English delegation, arrived at the court of the Emperor Ch'ien Lung. Though Macartney refused to kowtow (prostrate himself nine times — not a dishonorable act, but symbolic of the superior-inferior relationship), he was granted an audience. The Emperor's letter to King George III illustrates China's attitude toward the West. Over the years, however, trade continued to grow in spite of Chinese restrictions.

You [George III], O King, live beyond the confines of many seas. Nevertheless, impelled by your humble desire to partake of the benefits of our civilization, you have dispatched a mission respectfully bearing your memorial. . . . I have perused your memorial: the earnest terms in which it is couched reveal a respectful humility on your part which is highly praiseworthy.

In consideration of the fact that your ambassador and his deputy

Source: Sir Frederick Whyte, K.C.S.I., *China and Foreign Powers: An Historical Review of Their Relations*, London: Oxford University Press, 1927, p. 39, Appendix I. Published under the auspices of the Royal Institute of International Affairs and reprinted by permission.

have come a long way with your memorial and tribute, I have shown them high favor and have allowed them to be introduced into my presence. To manifest my indulgence, I have entertained them at a banquet and made them numerous gifts. . . .

As to your entreaty to send one of your nationals to be accredited to my Celestial Court and to be in control of your country's trade with China, this request is contrary to all usage of my dynasty and cannot possibly be entertained. . . . If you assert that your reverence for our Celestial Dynasty fills you with a desire to acquire our civilization, our ceremonies and code of laws differ so completely from your own that even if your envoy were able to acquire the rudiments of our civilization, you could not possibly transplant our manners and customs to your alien soil. Therefore, however adept the envoy might become, nothing would be gained thereby.

Swaying the wide world, I have but one aim in view, namely, to maintain a perfect governance and to fulfill the duties of the State: strange and costly objects do not interest me. If I have commanded that the tribute offerings sent by you, O King, are to be accepted, this was solely in consideration for the spirit which prompted you to dispatch them from afar. Our dynasty's majestic virtue has penetrated into every country under heaven, and kings of all nations have offered their costly tribute by land and sea. As your ambassador can see for himself, we possess all things. I set no value on objects strange or ingenious, and have no use for your country's manufactures.

The Opening of China

Opium was introduced to China by Europeans in the seventeenth century, and the opium traffic grew rapidly in spite of imperial edicts of prohibition. In opium Europeans found a commodity which the Chinese wanted and which could be exchanged for the tea and silk that were being imported from China. The Chinese government was determined to put an end to the opium trade since the balance of payment had turned against it and had caused an outflow of gold from the Empire. Consumption of opium had also become a national vice.

It was very difficult to stop this illicit traffic. Many West-
ern nations indulged in the trade, and Chinese officials, easily
bribed, were their accomplices. The Chinese government, in
1838, decided to enforce the laws against opium. This enforce-
ment ultimately resulted in the Opium War between England
and China.

There was much more at stake than the opium trade, of
which the British had the lion's share. For a number of years the
British had been putting pressure on the Chinese to treat them
as equals and to allow an expansion of trade relations. Diplo-
macy having failed, the Opium War provided the British with
the opportunity to secure their demands by force. China, con-
fident at first that she had little to fear from a handful of foreign-
ers, soon discovered that her arms and ships were no match for
those of the Europeans.

The first selection is from a letter written in August 1839 by
Commissioner Lin Tse-hsu to Queen Victoria. It was Lin who in
the spring of 1839 seized and publicly burned the opium stocks
of the British traders at Canton — an action which led to the
outbreak of hostilities in November. The second selection is a
portion of the Treaty of Nanking (1842), which was imposed
on the Chinese after their defeat. More concessions were ex-
acted from China in later treaties.

Lin Tse-hsu's Moral Advice
to the British Monarch

A communication: magnificently our great Emperor soothes
and pacifies China and the foreign countries, regarding all with the
same kindness. If there is profit, then he shares it with the peoples of
the world; if there is harm, then he removes it on behalf of the
world. . . .

All those people in China who sell opium or smoke opium should
receive the death penalty. If we trace the crime of those barbarians who

LIN TSE-HSU'S MORAL ADVICE TO THE BRITISH MONARCH. Source: Ssu-yu Teng
and John K. Fairbank, editors, *China's Response to the West: A Documentary
Survey, 1839–1923*, Cambridge, Mass.: Harvard University Press, 1954, pp. 24–27.
Reprinted by permission of the publishers and the President and Fellows of Harvard
College.

through the years have been selling opium, then the deep harm they have wrought and the great profit they have usurped should fundamentally justify their execution according to law. . . .

Having established new regulations, we presume that the ruler of your honorable country, who takes delight in our culture and whose disposition is inclined toward us, must be able to instruct the various barbarians to observe the law with care. It is only necessary to explain to them the advantages and disadvantages and then they will know that the legal code of the Celestial Court must be absolutely obeyed with awe.

We find that your country is [far from China]. Yet there are barbarian ships that strive to come here for trade for the purpose of making a great profit. The wealth of China is used to profit the barbarians; that is to say, the great profit made by barbarians is all taken from the rightful share of China. By what right do they then in return use the poisonous drug to injure the Chinese people? Even though the barbarians may not necessarily intend to do us harm, yet in coveting profit to an extreme, they have no regard for injuring others. Let us ask, where is your conscience? I have heard that the smoking of opium is very strictly forbidden by your country; that is because the harm caused by opium is clearly understood. Since it is not permitted to do harm to your own country, then even less should you let it be passed on to the harm of other countries — how much less to China! Of all that China exports to foreign countries, there is not a single thing which is not beneficial to people. . . . Take tea and rhubarb, for example; the foreign countries cannot get along for a single day without them. If China cuts off these benefits with no sympathy for those who are to suffer, then what can the barbarians rely upon to keep themselves alive? . . . As for other foodstuffs, beginning with candy, ginger, cinnamon, and so forth, and articles for use, beginning with silk, satin, chinaware, and so on, all the things that must be had by foreign countries are innumerable. On the other hand, articles coming from the outside to China can only be used as toys. . . .

Suppose a man of another country comes to England to trade, he still has to obey the English laws; how much more should he obey in China the laws of the Celestial Dynasty?

Now we have set up regulations governing the Chinese people. He who sells opium shall receive the death penalty and he who smokes it also the death penalty. Now consider this: if the barbarians do not bring opium, then how can the Chinese people resell it and how can they smoke it? The fact is that the wicked barbarians beguile the Chinese people into a death trap. How then can we grant life only to these barbarians? He who takes the life of even one person still has to atone for it with his own life; yet is the harm done by opium limited to the taking of one life only? Therefore, in the new regulations, in regard to those barbarians who bring opium to China, the penalty is fixed at decapitation or strangulation. This is what is called getting rid of a harmful thing on behalf of mankind. . . .

The barbarian merchants of your country, if they wish to do business for a prolonged period, are required to obey our statutes respectfully and to cut off permanently the source of opium. . . . May you, O [Queen], check your wicked and sift your vicious people before they come to China, in order to guarantee the peace of your nation, to show further the sincerity of your politeness and submissiveness, and to let the two countries enjoy together the blessings of peace.

The Terms of Peace

Article I. There shall henceforward be peace and friendship between her Majesty the Queen of the United Kingdom of Great Britain and Ireland and his Majesty the Emperor of China, and between their respective subjects, who shall enjoy full security and protection for their persons and property within the dominions of the other.

Article II. His Majesty the Emperor of China agrees that British subjects, with their families and establishments, shall be allowed to reside, for the purpose of carrying on their mercantile pursuits, without molestation or restraint at the cities and towns of Canton, Amoy, Foochow-fu, Ningpo, and Shanghai. . . .

Article III. It being obviously necessary and desirable that British subjects should have some port whereat they may careen and refit their ships when required, and keep stores for the purpose, his Majesty the Emperor of China cedes to her Majesty the Queen of Great Britain, etc., the island of Hong Kong, to be possessed in perpetuity by her Bri-

THE TERMS OF PEACE. Source: *China, The Maritime Customs. III, Miscellaneous Series: No. 30, Treaties, Conventions, etc., Between China and Foreign States*, 2nd ed., Shanghai: Department of the Inspectorate General of Customs, 1917, Vol. I, pp. 352–53.

tannic Majesty, her heirs and successors, and to be governed by such laws and regulations as her Majesty the Queen of Great Britain, etc., shall see fit to direct. . . .

Article VI. The government of her Britannic Majesty having been obliged to send out an expedition to demand and obtain redress for the violent and unjust proceedings of the Chinese high authorities toward her Britannic Majesty's officer and subjects, the Emperor of China agrees to pay the sum of twelve million dollars on account of the expenses incurred, and her Britannic Majesty's Plenipotentiary voluntarily agrees, on behalf of her Majesty, to deduct from the said amount of twelve millions of dollars any sums which may have been received by her Majesty's combined forces as ransom for cities and towns in China, subsequent to the first day of August, 1841.

The Taiping Rebellion

Weakened by the deterioration of her ruling dynasty and humiliated at the hands of the British, China was torn by a number of great internal rebellions. The longest and most violent of these (1850–64) was led by a visionary who claimed to be the younger brother of Jesus sent to inaugurate a kingdom of perfect peace (taiping). His cry for social justice met with an overwhelming response among the hungry masses, and the rebels were able to conquer vast territories and even set up a rival emperor.

Conquest and success soon diminished their crusading zeal, while their strange doctrines antagonized and alienated the educated official class. The Westerners, who had initially displayed some sympathy toward the religious views of the Taipings, were soon repelled by them. The foreign governments in China, at first divided, eventually came to the assistance of the Manchu rulers against the rebels. The rebellion was crushed mainly through the efforts of provincial Chinese commanders, and the tottering Manchus were temporarily rescued.

That the Taiping Rebellion was a movement for reform and included leaders interested in modernization is illustrated in the proposals of Hung Jen-kan, who was a relative of the Taiping Emperor and who became an important member of his government in 1859. The effects of the rebellion are described by Dr. S. Wells Williams, a missionary, who was secretary of the American Legation.

Hung Jen-kan's Proposals for Reform

1. [Authority should be centralized and applied to all the people. On the other hand, the people's opinion should have ready access to the government.]

2. The promotion of the facilities of communication is aimed at convenience and speed. If someone can make a locomotive such as those made in foreign countries, . . . let him be permitted to monopolize the profit, and after a certain limit of time let other people be permitted to imitate his invention. . . . At first we should construct twenty-one main railroads in the twenty-one provinces to serve as the veins of the whole country, and when the traffic is in good circulation, the nation will be healthy. . . .

3. The promotion of ships, which should be solid, nimble, and fast. Whether fire, steam, [human] energy, or wind is to be used for power should be decided by the inventor. . . .

4. The promotion of banks. If a rich man wants to open a bank, he shall first report and deposit his deeds and other securities in the national treasury, whereupon he will be allowed to issue one million and a half [taels of] bank notes which will be inscribed with very elaborate designs, stamped with the state seals, and be exchangeable for silver or commodities, or for other bank notes and silver. . . .

5. The promotion of patents for inventing utensils and for various arts. If there are those who can make very fine, unusual, and convenient articles, they alone shall be permitted a manufacture and sales monopoly. Imitators shall be considered to have committed a crime and shall be punished. . . . As a reward for a small article there shall be a five-year period of monopoly rights and for a large one, ten years. . . . After the time limit, other persons shall be allowed to make them.

6. The promotion [i.e., exploitation] of hidden treasures. If there

HUNG JEN-KAN'S PROPOSALS FOR REFORM. Source: Ssu-yu Teng and John K. Fairbank, editors, *China's Response to the West: A Documentary Survey, 1839–1923*, Cambridge, Mass.: Harvard University Press, 1954, pp. 57–59. Reprinted by permission of the publishers and the President and Fellows of Harvard College.

are people who discover gold, silver, copper, iron, tin, coal, salt, amber, oyster shells, jade, precious stones, and other materials, they shall be required to report this to the government. They shall be appointed as the chief superintendents and be permitted to employ people to mine. . . .

7. The promotion of a postal service to transmit state documents, post offices to circulate all kinds of private letters, and newspaper offices to report frequent changes of current affairs.

8. The promotion of court investigators [to officially establish the facts, etc.]. . . .

9. The promotion of official reporting officers in all provinces. . . . They will devote their time to collecting news from the . . . provinces and a myriad of other places. . . .

12. The promotion of hospitals to relieve those who are ill and in suffering. . . . Physicians shall be installed, but they must have passed several examinations before they can be employed. . . .

14. The promotion of rural soldiers. . . . In the daytime they shall supervise all the families in cleaning the streets or roads, in order to get rid of the dirt and poisonous things that cause injury to the people. They are also to arrest those who fight and steal and to summon the bystanders to the office of the county officers to be witnesses and help render a verdict. Those who give false evidence shall be punished.

The Effects of the Rebellion

The populous mart of Hankow and its environs was taken by assault six different times during the thirty months ending in May 1855, and finally was left literally a heap of ruins. In country places the imperialists were, of the two parties, perhaps the more terrible scourge, but as the region became impoverished each side vied with the other in exhausting the people. . . .

The executions in Canton during fourteen months up to August 1856 were nearly a hundred thousand men; but the loss of life on both sides must be reckoned by millions. . . .

The destruction of life, property, and industry within the three months since [the rebels'] sally from Nanking had been unparalleled . . .

THE EFFECTS OF THE REBELLION. Source: S. Wells Williams, *The Middle Kingdom*, rev. ed., New York: Charles Scribner's Sons, 1883, Vol. II, pp. 600, 604, 606, 617, 623–24, 630–31.

and revived the stories told of the ruthless acts of Attila and Tamerlane. . . .

In Ihing, the dreadful effects of the struggle going on were seen. Utter destitution prevailed in and out of the town; people were feeding on dead bodies and ready to perish from exposure while waiting for a comrade to die.

The rebels had occupied a post near Whampoa, and their gunboats prowled through every creek in the delta, burning, destroying, capturing, and murdering without restraint. They would be followed by a band of imperialists whose excesses were sometimes even more dreadful than those of their enemies. So terrible was the plight of the wretched countrymen that the headmen of ninety-six villages near Fuhshan formed a league and armed their people to keep soldiers from either side from entering their precincts.

The condition of the people at this time was sad and desperate indeed, and their only remedy was to arm in self-defense. . . . No quarter was given on either side, and the carnage was appalling. . . . During this year (1854) the emigration to California and Australia became larger than ever before, . . . owing to the multitudes thrown out of employment who were eager in accepting the offers of the brokers to depart from the country and escape the evils they saw everywhere about them. The terrors of famine, fighting, and plundering paralyzed all industry and trade. . . .

The exhaustion and desperation consequent on these events had almost demoralized society in and around Canton, which was overcrowded with refugees, raising food to famine prices. . . . One of the insurgent practices consisted in driving great numbers of people into squares and there shooting them down by cannon placed in the approaching streets, while the houses around them were burning. The flames could be seen for two or three days from Canton, and it was estimated that during this conflict fully two hundred thousand human beings perished. . . .

Wild beasts roamed at large over the land after their departure and made their dens in the deserted towns; the pheasant's whirr resounded where the hum of busy populations had ceased, and weeds or jungle covered the ground once tilled with patient industry. Besides . . . the misery, sickness, and starvation which were endured by the survivors, it has been estimated by foreigners living at Shanghai that, during the whole period from 1851 to 1865, fully twenty million human beings were destroyed in connection with the Taiping Rebellion.

Dr. Sun Yat-sen
on the Meaning of Liberty

The Manchu dynasty was overthrown by a republican revolution in October of 1911. The guiding spirit of the new republic was Dr. Sun Yat-sen, a Christian, who had studied and traveled in Europe and America. After years of experience as a revolutionary, in 1905 he organized a group whose goal was to oust the Manchus, establish a republican form of government, and inaugurate land reforms. The program won many adherents and eventually became the basis of the Nationalist Party.

Returning from abroad when revolution broke out in 1911, Dr. Sun became the President of the Provisional Republican Government. Although he was the inspiring force of the revolution, real power was soon concentrated in the hands of a former minister of the Manchus, Yuan Shih-kai, who became the first President of the Republic. Yuan, an autocrat with little sympathy for republican institutions, crushed all opposition and exiled Dr. Sun. After Yuan's death China fell into chaos until Chiang Kai-shek was able to establish a unified government in 1928.

In a series of lectures delivered in 1924, Dr. Sun elaborated on his republican principles. His ideas on "liberty" illustrate the vast difference between the Western and Chinese interpretations of this concept.

Western revolutions began with the struggle for liberty; only after war and agitation of two or three centuries was the liberty realized from which democracy sprang. The watchword of the French Revolution was "Liberty, Equality, Fraternity." Our watchword is "People's Nationalism, People's Sovereignty, People's Livelihood." What relation do the two watchwords have to each other? According to my interpretation, our Nationalism may be said to correspond to their Liberty, because putting the People's Nationalism into effect means a struggle for the liberty of our nation. The Europeans fought for individual liberty,

Source: Dr. Sun Yat sen, *San Min Chu I: The Three Principles of the People*, translated by F. W. Price, Shanghai: China Committee, Institute of Pacific Relations, 1927, pp. 212–14. Reprinted by permission of Pacific Affairs.

but today we have a different use for liberty. Now how shall the term "liberty" be applied? If we apply it to a person, we shall become a sheet of loose sand; on no account must we give more liberty to the individual; let us secure liberty instead for the nation. The individual should not have too much liberty, but the nation should have complete liberty. When the nation can act freely, then China may be called strong. To make the nation free, we must each sacrifice his personal freedom. Students who sacrifice their personal liberty will be able to work diligently day after day and spend time and effort upon learning; when their studies are completed, their knowledge is enlarged, and their powers have multiplied, then they can do things for the nation. Soldiers who sacrifice their personal liberty will be able to obey orders, repay their country with loyalty, and help the nation to attain liberty. If students and soldiers talk liberty, they will soon have "unrestrained license," to use a Chinese phrase for liberty. Schools will have no rules and the army will have no discipline. How can you have a school without rules? What kind of army is that without discipline?

Why do we want the nation to be free? Because China under the domination of the Powers has lost her national standing. She is not merely a semi-colony; she has indeed become a hypo-colony, inferior to Burma and Annam and Korea. They are each the protectorate of one nation, the slave of one master. China is the colony of all the nations and the slave of all. In fact, we are now slaves to over ten masters; our national freedom is terribly restricted. If we want to restore China's liberty, we must unite ourselves into one unshakable body; we must use revolutionary methods to weld our state into firm unity. Without revolutionary principles we shall never succeed. Our revolutionary principles are the cement. If we can consolidate our four hundred millions and form a mighty union and make the union free, the Chinese state will be free and the Chinese people will be really free. Compare the watchword of the French Revolution with that of ours. "Liberty" in the French revolutionary watchword and "People's Nationalism" in our watchword are similar. The People's Nationalism calls for the freedom of our nation. "Equality" is similar to our "Principle of the People's Sovereignty," which aims to destroy autocracy and make all men equal. "Fraternity" originally meant *brothers* and has the same significance as the Chinese word *t'ung-pao* (compatriots). The idea in "Fraternity" is similar to our "Principle of the People's Livelihood," which plans for the happiness of our four hundred millions.

89

The Manners and Customs of Early Japan

Japanese records of the early history of Japan are primarily collections of legends and myths. The best sources of factual information for Japanese history before the sixth century A.D. are the histories of Chinese dynasties, which include information about the "barbarians" to the east. The Japanese owe an enormous cultural debt to China, including their written language and their introduction to Buddhism.

The following selections are taken from official histories of China for the years A.D. 297 and 630.

Japan, A.D. 297

The people of Wa (Japan) dwell in the middle of the ocean on the mountainous islands southeast of [the district of] Tai-fang. They formerly comprised more than one hundred communities. During the Han dynasty, (Wa) envoys appeared at the court; today, thirty of their communities maintain [relations] with us through envoys and scribes. . . .

The land of Wa is warm and mild. In winter as in summer the people live on raw vegetables and go about barefooted. They have . . . houses; father and mother, elder and younger, sleep separately. They smear their bodies with pink and scarlet, just as the Chinese use powder. They serve food on bamboo and wooden trays, helping themselves with their fingers. When a person dies, they prepare a single coffin, without an outer one. They cover the graves with earth to make a mound. When death occurs, mourning is observed for more than ten days, during which period they do not eat meat. The head mourners wail and lament, while friends sing, dance, and drink liquor. When the funeral is over, all members of the family go into the water to cleanse themselves in a bath of purification.

Source: R. Tsunoda, Wm. Theodore de Bary, D. Keene, editors, *Oriental Civilizations: Sources of Japanese Tradition*, New York: Columbia University Press, 1958, pp. 6–8; 11–12. Reprinted by permission of the publishers.

When they go on voyages across the sea to visit China, they always select a man who does not comb his hair, does not rid himself of fleas, lets his clothing get as dirty as it will, does not eat meat. . . . This man behaves like a mourner and is known as the "mourning keeper." When the voyage meets with good fortune, they all lavish on him slaves and other valuables. In case there is disease or mishap, they kill him, saying that he was not scrupulous in observing the taboos. . . .

In their meetings and in their deportment, there is no distinction between father and son or between men and women. They are fond of liquor. In their worship, men of importance simply clap their hands instead of kneeling or bowing. The people live long, some to one hundred and others to eighty or ninety years. Ordinarily, men of importance have four or five wives; the lesser ones, two or three. . . . There is no theft, and [legal action] is infrequent. In case of violation of law, the light offender loses his wife and children by confiscation; as for the grave offender, the members of his household and all his kinsmen are exterminated. There are class distinctions among the people, and some are vassals of others. Taxes are collected. There are granaries as well as markets in each province, where necessaries are exchanged under the supervision of the Wa officials. . . .

When the lowly meet men of importance on the road, they stop and withdraw to the roadside. In conveying messages to them or addressing them, they either squat or kneel, with both hands on the ground. This is the way they show respect. When responding they say "ah," which corresponds to the affirmative "yes."

The country formerly had a man as ruler. For some seventy or eighty years after that there were disturbances and warfare. Thereupon the people agreed upon a woman for their ruler. Her name was Pimiko. She occupied herself with magic and sorcery, bewitching the people. Though mature in age, she remained unmarried. She had a younger brother who assisted her in ruling the country. After she became the ruler, there were few who saw her. She had one thousand women as attendants, but only one man. He served her food and drink and acted as a medium of communication. She resided in a palace surrounded by towers and stockades, with armed guards in a state of constant vigilance. . . .

When Pimiko passed away, a great mound was raised, more than a hundred paces in diameter. Over a hundred male and female attendants followed her to the grave. Then a king was placed on the throne, but the people would not obey him. Assassination and murder followed; more than one thousand were thus slain.

A relative of Pimiko named Iyo, a girl of thirteen, was then made queen and order was restored.

Japan, A.D. 630

During the twenty years of the K'ai-huang era (581–600), the King of Wa, whose family name was Ame and personal name Tarishi-hoko, and who bore the title of Ahakomi, sent an envoy to visit the [Chinese] court. The Emperor ordered the appropriate official to make inquiries about the manners and customs [of the Wa people]. The envoy reported thus: "The King of Wa deems heaven to be his elder brother and the sun, his younger. Before break of dawn he attends the court, and, sitting cross-legged, listens to appeals. Just as soon as the sun rises, he ceases these duties, saying that he hands them over to his brother." Our just Emperor said that such things were extremely sense-less, and he admonished [the King of Wa] to alter [his ways].

There are about 100,000 households. . . . Thieves are made to make restitution in accordance with the value of the goods stolen. If the thief has no property with which to make payment, he is taken to be a slave. Other offenses are punished according to their nature — sometimes by banishment and sometimes by flogging. In the prosecution of offenses by the court, the knees of those who plead not guilty are pressed together by placing them between pieces of wood, or their heads are sawed with the stretched string of a strong bow. Sometimes pebbles are put in boiling water and both parties to a dispute made to pick them out. The hand of the guilty one is said to become inflamed. Sometimes a snake is kept in a jar, and the accused ordered to catch it. If he is guilty, his hand will be bitten. The people are gentle and peaceful. . . .

As for musical instruments, they have five-stringed lyres and flutes. Both men and women paint marks on their arms and spots on their faces and have their bodies tattooed. They catch fish by diving into the water. They have no written characters and understand only the use of notched sticks and knotted ropes. They revere Buddha.

The Advantages of
Drinking Tea

Buddhism came to Japan from China in A.D. 552. Attracting at first only a small group of nobles, it soon became the official religion of the land. Close contact with China was maintained, and many of the divisions in Chinese Buddhism were carried over to Japan. In the process of conquering Japan, Buddhism blended with the native culture and took on a characteristically Japanese flavor.

Zen Buddhism was brought to Japan at the end of the twelfth century by Eisai, a Japanese scholar who had studied in China. Zen Buddhism taught the value of meditation and concentration over that of book-learning and ritual. As a way of life it emphasized self-discipline, appreciation of beauty, austerity, and intuitive action.

The influence of Zen Buddhism on Japanese life may be seen in the Tea Ceremony. Eisai, who introduced tea from China, lauded the virtues of this beverage in order to help divert the Emperor's taste from alcohol. Zen monks later developed the Tea Ceremony, for which men gathered in quiet groups away from the cares of the world. Following a prescribed and graceful form of serving, they sipped tea while they meditated or admired a beautiful object. The Tea Ceremony, an expression of the ideals of Zen Buddhism, became a national institution in Japan.

Below, Eisai discusses the marvelous qualities of tea.

Tea is the most wonderful medicine for nourishing one's health; it is the secret of long life. On the hillsides it grows up as the spirit of the soil. Those who pick and use it are certain to attain a great age. India and China both value it highly, and in the past our country too once showed a great liking for tea. Now as then it possesses the same rare qualities, and we should make wider use of it.

Source: R. Tsunoda, Wm. Theodore de Bary, D. Keene, editors, *Oriental Civilizations: Sources of Japanese Tradition*, New York: Columbia University Press, 1958, pp. 244–46. Reprinted by permission of the publishers.

Of all the things which Heaven has created, man is the most noble. To preserve one's life so as to make the most of one's allotted span is prudent and proper, considering the high value of human life. The basis of preserving life is the cultivation of health, and the secret of health lies in the well-being of the . . . organs. Among these . . . the heart is sovereign, and to build up the heart the drinking of tea is the finest method. When the heart is weak, the other organs all suffer. It is more than two thousand years since the illustrious healer Jiva passed away in India, and in these latter degenerate days there is none who can accurately diagnose the circulation of the blood. It is more than three thousand years since the Chinese healer Shen-nung disappeared from the earth, and there is no one today who can prescribe medicines properly. With no one to consult in such matters, illness, disease, trouble, and danger follow one another in endless succession. . . .

Yet when the heart becomes sick, all organs and tastes are affected. Then, eat as one may, one will have to vomit and stop eating. But if one drinks tea, the heart will be strengthened and freed from illness. It is well to know that when the heart is ailing, the skin has a poor color, a sign that life is ebbing away. I wonder why the Japanese do not care for bitter things. In the great country of China they drink tea, as a result of which there is no heart trouble and people live long lives. Our country is full of sickly-looking, skinny persons, and this is simply because we do not drink tea. Whenever one is in poor spirits, one should drink tea. This will put the heart in order and dispel all illness. . . .

Drink lots of tea, and one's energy and spirits will be restored to full strength.

The Closing of Japan

Japan's enthusiasm for trade with Europeans was somewhat dampened by the Japanese suspicion of the motives of the foreigners. They feared the spread of Christianity, which had been introduced by St. Francis Xavier in 1549 and had made several hundred thousand converts within half a century. They suspected that the Europeans harbored political ambitions in their land. The vicious commercial and religious rivalry among the Europeans also made the Japanese uneasy.

Early in the seventeenth century the Japanese, recently united under the Tokugawa Shogunate * after a period of civil war, began to persecute Christians. The resistance of the missionaries and the Japanese converts to the commands of the Shogun turned the persecutions into a campaign of extermination which was for the most part successful. By 1640 European trade was terminated except with the Dutch, who were allowed to continue only under the most careful scrutiny.

The following selection is from the Japanese government's Act of Seclusion of 1636.

* From the end of the twelfth century to 1868 Japan was governed by shoguns, who were hereditary feudal rulers. The emperors, while still supreme in theory, were in practice limited to ceremonial functions. The Tokugawa Shogunate ruled Japan from 1603 to 1867.

1. Japanese ships shall by no means be sent abroad.

2. No Japanese shall be sent abroad. Anyone violating this prohibition shall suffer the penalty of death, and the shipowner and crew shall be held up together with the ship.

3. All Japanese residing abroad shall be put to death when they return home.

4. All Christians shall be examined by official examiners.

5. Informers against Christians shall be rewarded.

6. The arrival of foreign ships must be reported . . . and watch kept over them.

7. The Namban people (Spaniards or Portuguese) and any other people with evil titles propagating Christianity shall be incarcerated in the Omura prison as before.

8. Even ships shall not be left untouched in the matter of exterminating Christians.

9. Everything shall be done in order to see that no Christian is survived by descendants, and anyone disregarding this injunction shall be put to death, while proper punishment shall be meted out to the other members of his family according to their deeds.

10. Children born of the Namban people (Spaniards or Portu-

Source: Y. Takekoshi, *The Economic Aspects of the History of the Civilization of Japan*, London: George Allen & Unwin Ltd., 1930, Vol. II, pp. 128–29. Reprinted by permission of the publishers.

guese) in Nagasaki and people adopting these Namban children into their family shall be put to death; capital punishment shall also be meted out to those Namban descendants if they return to Japan, and their relatives in Japan, who may communicate with them, shall receive suitable punishment.

11. The samurai [warrior aristocracy of Japan] shall not purchase goods on board foreign ships directly from foreigners.

Japan—the Land of the Gods

A return to "pure" Japanese tradition and a reaction to alien culture accompanied the unity and stability achieved in the seventeenth century. The leaders of this movement exalted the ancient Japanese Shinto worship over Buddhism and Confucianism, which had been imported. They revived the study of native Japanese literature and mythology.

By the middle of the nineteenth century this movement had become ultranationalistic. Hirata Atsutane, one of its spokesmen, proclaimed the superiority of Japanese culture over all other cultures. He tried to demonstrate the antiquity of everything Japanese and insisted that Japan had invented a system of writing before China. It is interesting that he admired Western science even while he disliked the West. That Hirata's statements were not based on fact did not detract from his simple and powerful appeal. Many Japanese believed in the superiority of Japan as an article of faith.

Buddhist learning is broader in scope than Confucian, but Japanese learning is even more embracing. All the various types of learning, including Confucianism and Buddhism, are joined in Japanese learning, just as the many rivers flow into the sea, where their waters are joined. Because of the diversity and number of the different parts of Japanese learning, people are often bewildered and at a loss to evaluate it. Unless,

Source: R. Tsunoda, Wm. Theodore de Bary, D. Keene, editors, *Oriental Civilizations: Sources of Japanese Tradition*, New York: Columbia University Press, 1958, pp. 543–44. Reprinted by permission of the publishers.

therefore, we can distinguish accurately the elements which make up this vast amalgam of learning, the excellence of the true Way will remain obscure. . . . We must be aware of such matters in order to appreciate the pure and righteous Way of Japan. Japanese should study all the different kinds of learning — even though they be foreign — so that they can choose the good features of each and place them at the service of the nation. We may properly speak not only of Chinese but even of Indian and Dutch learning as Japanese learning: this fact should be understood by all Japanese who delve into foreign studies.

People all over the world refer to Japan as the Land of the Gods and call us the descendants of the gods. Indeed, it is exactly as they say: our country, as a special mark of favor from the heavenly gods, was begotten by them, and there is thus so immense a difference between Japan and all the other countries of the world as to defy comparison. Ours is a splendid and blessed country, the Land of the Gods beyond any doubt, and we, down to the most humble man and woman, are the descendants of the gods. Nevertheless, there are unhappily many people who do not understand why Japan is the Land of the Gods and we their descendants. . . . Is this not a lamentable state of affairs? Japanese differ completely from and are superior to the peoples of China, India, Russia, Holland, Siam, Cambodia, and all other countries of the world, and for us to have called our country the Land of the Gods was not mere vainglory. It was the gods who formed all the lands of the world at the Creation, and these gods were without exception born in Japan. Japan is thus the homeland of the gods, and that is why we call it the Land of the Gods. This is a matter of universal belief and is quite beyond dispute. Even in countries where our ancient traditions have not been transmitted, the peoples recognize Japan as a divine land. . . . In olden days when Korea was divided into three kingdoms, reports were heard there of how splendid, miraculous, and blessed a land Japan is, and because Japan lies to the east of Korea, they said in awe and reverence, "To the East is a divine land, called the Land of the Rising Sun." Word of this eventually spread all over the world, and now people everywhere refer to Japan as the Land of the Gods, irrespective of whether or not they know why this is true.

The Opening of Japan

Japan did not stagnate, in spite of its isolation. Throughout the eighteenth century her people were happy and prosperous. Art and literature flourished, and interest in fighting subsided. It is a curious thing that even during the long period of isolation some Japanese studied Dutch and acquainted themselves with the scientific and industrial progress of Europe.

The Western nations, especially the United States, became increasingly interested in the Pacific in the nineteenth century. Shipwrecked American sailors were given harsh treatment in Japan and were returned only through the good offices of the Dutch. The new steamships needed fueling stations in every part of the world. American whaleboats and fur-trading vessels were anxious to acquire the right to stop in Japan. For these reasons, as well as the desire for trade, the American government sent Commodore Matthew Perry to Japan in the summer of 1853 to deliver to the Japanese government a letter from the President of the United States. Perry arrived with an impressive guard and a fleet of warships. He stayed for a week and promised to return the next spring for a reply. Not all Japanese opinion was against signing an agreement. Faced with a choice of a treaty or war, the Japanese government gave in.

Officials and naval officers who were on the expedition with Perry, as well as Perry himself, kept journals and diaries of what occurred. The following is from these eyewitness accounts.

July 8, 1853. The morning seemed to confirm the reputed character of the Japanese climate, for the atmosphere was so thick and hazy that the extent of view was unfortunately very much restricted, and it was not possible to get a distinct outline of the shore until the squadron came to anchor off the city of Uraga. . . .

As the ships neared the bay, signals were made from the Commodore and instantly the decks were cleared for action, the guns placed in position and shotted, the ammunition arranged, the small arms made

Source: Matthew Perry, *Narrative of the Expedition of an American Squadron to the China Seas and Japan, Performed in the Years 1852, 1853, and 1854,* edited by Francis L. Hawks, New York: D. Appleton & Co., 1857, pp. 265–70, 273–74, 276.

ready, sentinels and men at their posts, and in short, all the usual preparations made before meeting an enemy. . . . A signal was made for all captains to go on board the flagship and receive their orders from the Commodore. This done, the vessels now continued their course. . . . When the squadron had approached within two miles of the land, a fleet of large boats amounting to more than a dozen pushed off in the direction of the ships with the seeming intention of visiting them. They were, however, not waited for and were soon left behind, much puzzled, doubtless, by the rapid progress of the steamers against the wind. . . .

At about five o'clock in the afternoon the squadron came to anchor off the city of Uraga, on the western side of the bay of Yedo. . . .

Previous to anchoring, a number of Japanese guardboats had been observed coming off from the land in pursuit, but the Commodore had given express orders, both by word and signal, forbidding the admission of anyone on board either of the ships but his own. . . .

They made several attempts to get alongside and on board of the *Saratoga*; their towlines, with which they made fast to any part of the ship, were unceremoniously cast off. They attempted to climb up by the chains but the crew was ordered to prevent them, and the sight of pikes, cutlasses, and pistols checked them, and when they found that our officers and men were very much in earnest, they desisted from their attempts to board. . . .

One of the boats came alongside of the flagship, and it was observed that a person on board had a scroll of paper in his hand which the officer of the *Susquehanna* refused to receive but which was held up to be read alongside of the *Mississippi*, when it was found to be a document in the French language which conveyed an order to the effect that the ships should go away and not anchor, at their peril. The chief functionary, as his boat reached the side of the *Susquehanna*, made signs for the gangway ladder to be let down. This was refused, but Mr. Williams, the Chinese interpreter, and Mr. Portman, the Dutch, were directed to state to him that the Commodore would not receive anyone but a functionary of the highest rank, and that he might return on shore. As there seemed to be some difficulty in making progress in the Japanese language, one on board the boat alongside said in very good English, "I can speak Dutch." Mr. Portman then commenced a conversation with him in that language, as his English seemed to have been exhausted in the first sentence. . . .

It was directed that the dignitary should be informed that the Commodore, who had been sent by his country on a friendly mission to Japan, had brought a letter from the President of the United States addressed to the Emperor, and that he wished a suitable officer might be sent on board his ship to receive a copy of the same in order that a day might be appointed for the Commodore formally to deliver the original. To this he replied that Nagasaki was the only place, according to the laws of Japan, for negotiating foreign business, and it would be necessary for the squadrons to go there. In answer to this he was told that the Commodore had come purposely to Uraga because it was near to Yedo, and that he should not go to Nagasaki; that he expected the letter to be duly and properly received where he then was; that his intentions were perfectly friendly, but that he would allow of no indignity, and would not permit the guardboats which were collecting around the ships to remain where they were, and if they were not immediately removed, the Commodore declared that he would disperse them by force. When this was interpreted to him, the functionary suddenly left his seat, went to the gangway, and gave an order which caused most of the boats to return to the shore. . . .

The policy of the Commodore, it will be seen, was to assume a resolute attitude toward the Japanese government. He had determined before reaching the coast to carry out strictly this course in all his official relations, as he believed it the best to ensure a successful issue to the delicate mission with which he had been charged. He was resolved to adopt a course entirely contrary to that of all others who had hitherto visited Japan on a similar errand — to demand as a right and not to solicit as a favor those acts of courtesy which are due from one civilized nation to another; to allow of none of those petty annoyances which had been unsparingly visited upon those who had preceded him, and to disregard the acts as well as the threats of the authorities if they in the least conflicted with his own sense of what was due to the dignity of the American flag.

The question of landing by force was left to be decided by the development of succeeding events; it was of course the very last measure to be resorted to, and the last that was desired; but in order to be prepared for the worst, the Commodore caused the ships constantly to be kept in perfect readiness and the crews to be drilled as thoroughly as they are in time of active war. He was prepared, also, to meet the Japanese on their own ground and exhibit toward them a little of their own exclusive

100

policy; if they stood on their dignity and assumed superiority, that was a game at which he could play as well as they. . . .

July 9. The first approach to the *Susquehanna* from the shore was that of a boat at early sunrise, . . . apparently containing a corps of artists who came close to the ship's side, but making no attempt to come on board, busied themselves in taking sketches of the strange vessels. The important visit of the day, however, came off at seven o'clock, when two large boats rowed alongside, one of which contained a half dozen officials. . . . The interpreter who spoke Dutch was with them and announced that the personage of highest authority in the city was present and desired to come on board. The arrival . . . was then duly announced to the Commodore, who ordered that his highness should be received by [two officers], the Commodore himself still refusing, in accordance with his policy, to receive anyone but a counselor of the Empire. The governor was attired, in character with his high position, as a noble of the third rank. He wore a rich silk robe of an embroidered pattern resembling the feathers of a peacock, with borders of gold and silver. He was duly received by the officers . . . and immediately commenced with them a conference. . . .

A boat had been sent at daylight from each ship of the squadron to survey the bay and harbor of Uraga. The governor, on observing these boats, inquired what they were doing, and when he was told that they were surveying the harbor, he said that it was against the Japanese laws to allow such examinations; to which he received for reply that the American laws command them and that Americans were as much bound to obey the American as he was the Japanese laws. "This," remarks the Commodore, "was a second and most important point gained. . . ."

At the interview, the original letter of the President together with the Commodore's letter of credence, encased in the magnificent boxes which had been prepared in Washington, were shown to his excellency, who was evidently greatly impressed with their exquisite workmanship and costliness; and he made an offer for the first time of water and refreshments, but was told that the squadron was in no need of anything. The governor was made to understand perfectly that there would be no necessity for any further discussion until the time appointed for the delivery of the answer from the Japanese government should arrive, and he left the ship fully impressed with this understanding. . . .

Everything seemed propitious [favorable], as the action of the Commodore had so far been crowned with success. He had gained his purpose in clearing the squadron of the presence of the guardboats; he had compelled the visit of the first in authority at Uraga; he had surveyed the harbor; he had refused to go to Nagasaki and kept his position in the bay of Yedo; and this last he determined to retain until he had some definite answer as to the reception of the President's letter by a person of proper rank and authority.

The Modernization of Japan

The weakness displayed by the Japanese government in the 1850's in dealing with the foreigners brought a violent reaction against the Shogun as well as the Western intruders. A number of clans rose in revolt, attacking and murdering foreigners. The hopelessness of their cause became apparent when they were crushed and humiliated by Western arms. Thereafter, those who hated the foreigners rallied around the Emperor. In 1867 they abolished the discredited Shogunate and restored the power of the Emperor as ruler of Japan. In reality, power was still concentrated in the hands of a small group.

The new Emperor and his court did not long remain anti-Western. Aware that only by learning the industrial techniques and adopting the weapons of the foreigners could Japan escape the fate of other Eastern countries, they embarked upon an extensive program of political and economic reform. With breathtaking speed, Japan rose from its weak and humiliating status to the position of a great power.

One of the architects of the new Japan was Prince Ito Hirobumi, who held many important government positions and was Prime Minister four times between 1886 and 1901. He made a careful study of Western institutions and played an important part in the modernization of Japan.

I was one of the first Japanese to visit foreign lands, and was only able to do so by stealth, escaping to Shanghai in 1863. The country was only just opened to foreign [trade], and Japanese subjects were not yet allowed to leave the country.

Source: Alfred Stead, editor, *Japan by the Japanese: A Survey of the Highest Authorities*, New York: Dodd, Mead & Co., 1904, pp. 64–66, 68.

I have always been very much in favor of the adoption of the principles of Western civilization by Japan, and I have been enabled to use my services in the direction of assisting the present progress and transformation in Japan's estate. In the thirty-four years during which I have held office, I have always tried to help, and sometimes even to force onto the antagonistic spirits measures necessary for the growth of modern Japan. From the beginning we realized fully how necessary it was that the Japanese people should not only adopt Western methods, but should also speedily become competent to do without the aid of foreign instruction and supervision. In the early days we brought many foreigners to Japan to help to introduce modern methods, but we always did it in such a way as to enable the Japanese students to take their rightful place in the nation after they had been educated. . . . We were . . . able to secure the services of many excellent men whose names are still honored in Japan although they themselves have long since left her shores.

On the occasion of my second visit to London as one of the ambassadors of our country, it was suggested to me that it would be most beneficial to establish a special engineering college in Japan, where every branch of engineering should be taught. Such a college would be quite unique, no other nation having one. The idea seemed a very good one. On my return to Japan I took the necessary steps, and with the assistance of foreign professors we founded an engineering college, now incorporated in the Tokyo University. From this institution have come the majority of engineers who are now working the resources and industries of Japan. I consider the establishment of this college as one of the most important factors in the development of Japan today.

It was most necessary that Japan should not only be educated but also provided with suitable codes of laws before there could be any question of a revision of the treaties with foreign nations, and for a considerable time all our efforts were turned in this direction.

There are two events in Japanese history that have been all-important. The first was the change of regime of government of the country and the promulgation of the constitution, and the other was the Sino-Japanese War [Chinese-Japanese War]. I spent much time away from Japan studying the constitutions of various countries, the Emperor having ordered me to undertake the arduous task of framing a draft of the new Japanese constitution. The work was very difficult and necessitated much thought. Never before had there been a constitution, in the modern sense of the word, in Japan to help me to know what were the most vital points to be provided for in the new code. The country had been so essentially a nonconstitutional and feudal one that it was difficult to sit down on the debris of its past history and prepare offhand a constitution for it; and even when I had decided as to what was most necessary, it required very great care to insure the proper working and execution of the various provisions. I had always to remember that my work was intended as a permanent measure, and therefore I had to examine all the possible effects likely to arise from it in the distant future. Above all, there was the preeminent importance to be attached to the necessity of safeguarding the sacred and traditional rights of the sovereign. . . .

The old election law . . . having been found unsatisfactory, we have introduced an improved one, one of the principal changes in which is that the voting is by secret ballot, instead of by signed ballot as at present; another important change being the insertion of provisions for more ample representation of commercial and industrial elements of the country. . . .

I have always recognized the vital importance of a supremely efficient navy and army. . . . Our program of naval expansion laid down after the Chinese War in 1895 is practically completed. . . .

Although it has been necessary first of all to develop our fleet, the army too has not been neglected. It has been more than doubled of late and has now a war footing of over 500,000 men. . . .

In Japan we have the advantage that, although the soldiers are raised by conscription, every conscript is animated by the highest sense of patriotism and pride in his country.

In commercial and industrial matters Japan is becoming well established and is making secure her hold upon the markets of the Far East. The resources of the country are very good, the coal supply especially being abundant. . . .

Besides the complete victory in the war with China and the success of treaty revision, Japan may be proud of the speediness of her material progress, because she has made a progress seldom paralleled in the modern history of the world. For instance, the system of conscription having been introduced into our country shortly after the abolition of a long-rooted feudal system, it seemed to foreigners improbable that it would be successfully carried out, but it was introduced easily and perfectly, and may serve as a demonstration of how Japan surpasses her neighboring countries, China and Korea.

Stanley "Finds" Livingstone

Doctor David Livingstone was not lost in darkest Africa when Henry M. Stanley came upon him in 1871. He was going about his work quietly as a doctor, missionary, and explorer in an area where he was known and loved. He had, on previous expeditions, crossed the Kalahari Desert, discovered Victoria Falls, followed the Zambezi River into the interior to Lake Nyasa, and in his most recent expedition was working on the shore of Lake Tanganyika. A rumor that he was lost caused the New York Herald in 1869 to commission Stanley, a journalist and adventurer, to find him. As the world waited breathlessly for news, Stanley did indeed find Livingstone.

When Livingstone died in 1873, his body was taken to England under naval escort and solemnly deposited in Westminster Abbey among the nation's heroes. Livingstone's adventures stimulated greater interest in Africa, which had already been attracting missionaries and traders.

In the following selection Stanley gives an account of his meeting with Livingstone.

At last the sublime hour has arrived! Our dreams, our hopes and anticipations are now about to be realized! Our hearts and our feelings are with our eyes as we peer into the palms and try to make out in which hut or house lives the white man with the gray beard we heard about.

"Unfurl the flags, and load your guns!"

"*Ay Wallah, ay Wallah, bana!*" respond the men, eagerly.

"One, two, three — fire!"

A volley from nearly fifty guns roars like a salute from a battery of artillery. . . .

"Now . . . hold the white man's flag up high, and let the Zanzibar flag bring up the rear. And you men keep close together and keep firing until we halt in the marketplace or before the white man's house. You have said to me often that you could smell the fish of the Tanganyika — I can smell the fish of the Tanganyika now. There are fish, and beer, and a long rest waiting for you. March!". . .

Source: Henry M. Stanley, *How I Found Livingstone*, New York: Scribner, Armstrong & Co., 1872, pp. 408–12, 415, 417–19.

We were now about three hundred yards from the village of Ujiji, and the crowds are dense about me. Suddenly I hear a voice on my right say, "Good morning, sir!"

Startled at hearing this greeting in the midst of such a crowd, I turn sharply around in search of the man and see him at my side, animated and joyous — a man dressed in a long white shirt with a turban of American sheeting around his head, and I ask, "Who are you?"

"I am Susi, the servant of Dr. Livingstone," said he, smiling. . . .

"Now, you Susi, run and tell the Doctor I am coming."

"Yes, sir," and off he darted like a madman.

By this time we were within two hundred yards of the village, and the multitude was getting denser and almost preventing our march. Flags and streamers were out; Arabs and Wangwana were pushing their way through the natives in order to greet us. . . .

Selim said to me, "I see the Doctor, sir. Oh, what an old man! He has got a white beard.". . . My heart beats fast, but I must not let my face betray my emotions, lest it shall detract from the dignity of a white man appearing under such extraordinary circumstances.

So I did that which I thought was most dignified. I pushed back the crowds, and, passing from the rear, walked down a living avenue of people until I came in front of the semicircle of Arabs, in front of which stood the white man with the gray beard. As I advanced slowly toward him I noticed he was pale, looked wearied, had a gray beard, wore a bluish cap with a faded gold band round it, had on a red-sleeved waistcoat and a pair of gray tweed trousers. I would have run to him, only I was a coward in the presence of such a mob — would have embraced him, only he being an Englishman, I did not know how he would receive me; so I did what cowardice and false pride suggested was the best thing — walked deliberately to him, took off my hat, and said, "Dr. Livingstone, I presume?"

"Yes," said he, with a kind smile, lifting his cap slightly.

I replace my hat on my head, and he puts on his cap, and we both grasp hands, and I then say aloud, "I thank God, Doctor, I have been permitted to see you."

He answered, "I feel thankful that I am here to welcome you."

Then, oblivious of the crowds, oblivious of the men who shared with me my dangers, we — Livingstone and I — turn our faces toward his [cottage]. . . .

We are seated . . . with our backs to the wall. . . .

Shortly I found myself enacting the part of an annual periodical to him. There was no need of exaggeration. . . . The world had witnessed and experienced much the last few years. The Pacific railroad had been completed; Grant had been elected President of the United States; . . . a Spanish revolution had driven Isabella from the throne of Spain; . . . Prussia had humbled Denmark and annexed Schleswig-Holstein, and her armies were now around Paris; the "Man of Destiny" [Napoleon III] was a prisoner, . . . [his wife, Eugénie], the Queen of Fashion and the Empress of the French, was a fugitive; . . . the Napoleon dynasty was extinguished by the Prussians Bismarck and Von Moltke; and France, the proud Empire, was humbled to the dust. . . .

We kept on talking and talking, and prepared food was being brought to us all that afternoon. . . .

This day, like all others, though big with happiness to me, at last was fading away. . . .

"Doctor," I said, "you had better read your letters. I will not keep you up any longer."

"Yes," he answered, "it is getting late. I will go and read my friends' letters. Good night, and God bless you."

The Destruction of Human Life in the Congo

Stanley's imagination was fired by the potential wealth of Africa. After receiving the backing of King Leopold II of Belgium and a number of financiers, he sailed back to the region of the Congo. There he set about acquiring rights to exploit the area by making "treaties" with hundreds of native chiefs. The Congo yielded great quantities of rubber, which was in great demand in Europe and America.

Leopold ruled the Congo as his own domain. The few foreigners who were allowed into the area returned with reports of unbelievable horrors inflicted on the natives by the Belgians. Finally in 1904 a commission was forced on Leopold which confirmed, on the basis of evidence from Belgian officials and others, some of the worst tales of slavery and murder. In 1908, before

Leopold died, he turned the Congo over to the Belgian government, which did away with many of the abuses.

Here are a number of eyewitness reports on the treatment of natives in the Congo during those years.

Lieutenant Tilkens writes: "Commandant Verstraeten visited my station and congratulated me warmly. He said his report would depend upon the quantity of rubber which I was able to provide. The quantity increased from 360 kilograms in September to 1500 in October, and from January onward it will amount to 4000 per month, which will bring me in a monthly premium of 500 francs. Am I not a lucky fellow?". . . He continues: "S. S. *Van Kerkhoven* is coming down the Nile and will demand 1500 porters. . . . I can hardly bear to think of them. I am asking myself how on earth I shall be able to hunt up so large a number." Then: "Marshes, hunger, exhaustion. How much blood will be shed because of this transport! Three times already I have had to make war upon the chiefs who would not help me to get the men I needed. The fellows would rather die in their own forests than as members of a transport train. If a chief refuses that means war, with modern firearms on one side against spears and javelins on the other! A chief has just been to see me, complaining: 'My village has been destroyed and my wives have been killed!' But what on earth can I do? I have often been compelled to keep these unhappy chiefs in chains until they get for me one or two hundred porters. Very often my soldiers find the villages empty of men, and then they seize the women and the children." Next, to his major: "I see the likelihood of a general rising. The natives are sick of the regime, of having to work as porters, of gathering rubber, of being forced to provide foodstuffs. Once more I have been fighting for three months with only ten days' interval. I have 152 prisoners. For two years I have been making war in this district, but have not been able to force the natives to submit; they would rather die. What am I to do? I am paid for my work. I am merely a tool in the hands of my superiors and carry out their orders as discipline demands!"

Senator Picard . . . traveled in the Congo Free State, in the "cultivated" district. . . . Here are his impressions: "The inhabitants have disappeared. Their homes have been burned; huge heaps of ashes amid

Source: Ludwig Bauer, *Leopold the Unloved*, Boston: Little, Brown and Co., 1935, pp. 263–65, 269–70.

neglected palm hedges and devastated, abandoned fields. Inhuman floggings, murders, plunderings, and carryings-off. . . ." Near Stanley Pool, on the caravan road, he notices "a continual succession of Negroes carrying loads upon their heads; worn-out beasts of burden with projecting joints, wasted features, and staring eyes, perpetually trying to keep afoot despite their exhaustion. By thousands they pass, in the service of the State, handed over by the chiefs whose slaves they are and who rob them of their wages. They totter along the road with bent knees and protruding bellies, crawling with vermin, a dreadful procession across hill and dale, dying from exhaustion by the wayside, or often succumbing even should they reach home after their wanderings. . . ."

Here are extracts from the reports of a commission of investigation which traveled through the whole State, compiled from the declarations of eyewitnesses. . . .

"Within the territories of the Abir the chief Isekifasu of Bolima was murdered. . . . There were public floggings inflicted upon six Ngombe men, each receiving a hundred lashes with a hippopotamus-hide whip. . . . Natives who tried to run away to their villages are in prison. A river can only be navigated by persons who have a passport from a rubber agent; a passport is often refused to missionaries. . . . Owing to the ruinous methods of collection, by 1904 the supply of rubber was falling off rapidly. . . . Sixteen Esanda witnesses testify to the fact that members of their families were murdered during the collection of rubber. The successor of the murdered Bolima chief Isekifasu, attended by twenty witnesses, comes and lays a hundred and ten twigs upon the table, each of them signifying a murder for rubber. The largest twigs represent chiefs, somewhat smaller ones ordinary men, short ones women, and very little ones children. The soldiers had shown him the corpses of his people saying: 'Now you'll bring us rubber!' So it goes on. . . . In one district more than two hundred murders were proved; in the next a much greater number. . . . Behind each who complains stand hundreds who do not dare to speak, or lie hundreds of slain who will never speak again. The wailings from the Congo are slow and repressed, but, irresistibly, the cry grows."

The Submission
of Lo Bengula

The African kings and chiefs, though unschooled and helpless in negotiating with the white man and defenseless against his weapons, did not always give up without a fight. Lo Bengula, King of the Matabele, was an able diplomat who, for a while, skillfully played off one European nation against another to keep his lands free. Finally, in 1888, under irresistible pressure, he surrendered the rights to exploit the rich mines on his vast lands to the agents of Cecil Rhodes. Lo Bengula never gave up trying to extricate himself from these agreements and to free his people. The submission of Lo Bengula is recorded by an eyewitness.

It was the critical moment. For a while no one spoke. The proposed Concession lay on the table. The massive bronze figure of Lo Bengula loomed large in the eyes of those standing around, and his inscrutable and bloodshot eyes sent a thrill through the assembly. Then, after an ominous pause, the King lurched suddenly forward, seized a pen, and affixed his mark. Had he been able to forecast the future, a massacre and not a treaty would have received his sanction. But the recent visit of Sir Sidney Shippard, who was accompanied by Colonel Goold-Adams and the Bishop of Bloemfontein, . . . had apparently convinced him that his true interest lay in conciliating the English rather than the Boer element in his territory. . . . Here is the . . . text of the grant:

Know all men by these presents, that whereas Charles Dunell Rudd, of Kimberley; Rochfort Maguire, of London; and Francis Robert Thompson, of Kimberley, hereinafter called the grantees, have . . . agreed . . . to pay to me, my heirs, and successors the sum of one hundred pounds sterling, British currency, on the first day of every lunar month; and, further, to deliver at my royal kraal [village] one thousand Martini-Henry breech-loading rifles, together with one hundred thou-

Source: Lewis Michell, *The Life and Times of the Rt. Hon. Cecil John Rhodes,* London: Edward Arnold, Ltd., 1912, Vol. I, pp. 255–57. Reprinted by permission of the publishers.

sand rounds of suitable ball cartridge; . . . and further, to deliver on the Zambezi River a steamboat with guns suitable for defensive purposes upon the said river, or in lieu of the said steamboat, should I so elect, to pay me the sum of five hundred pounds sterling, British currency. On the execution of these presents, I, Lo Bengula, King of Matabeleland, Mashonaland, and other adjoining territories, in exercise of my sovereign powers, . . . do hereby grant . . . unto the said grantees . . . the complete and exclusive charge over all metals and minerals situated and contained in my kingdoms, principalities, and dominions, together with full power to do all things that they may deem necessary to win and procure the same, and to hold, collect, and enjoy the profits and revenues, if any, derivable from the said metals and minerals, subject to the aforesaid payment; and whereas I have been much molested of late by divers persons seeking and desiring to obtain grants and concessions of land and mining rights in my territories, I do hereby authorize the said grantees . . . to take all necessary and lawful steps to exclude from my kingdom, principalities, and dominions all persons seeking land, metals, minerals, or mining rights therein, and I do hereby undertake to render them all such needful assistance as they may from time to time require for the exclusion of such persons, and to grant no concessions of land or mining rights from and after this date without their consent and concurrence. . . .

This, given under my hand this thirtieth day of October, in the year of our Lord 1888, at my royal kraal.

Lo Bengula X his mark
C. D. Rudd
Rochfort Maguire
F. R. Thompson

PART NINE

The Rise of Dictatorships

The Assassination of Archduke Franz Ferdinand

By 1914 Europe had become accustomed to weathering international crises and averting wars by last minute negotiations. The assassination of the heir to the Austrian throne in the Bosnian town of Sarajevo at first seemed no more than a regional affair. The Austrians, however, knew that the Bosnian assassins were part of a Serbian terrorist society, and they had reason to suspect that high-ranking Serbs had been aware of the plot. Austria, long aggravated by the threat that Serbian nationalism posed to the Empire, which contained many discontented national groups, was now determined to put an end to Serbian pretentions.

The conciliatory attitude of the Serbs toward the harsh Austrian demands did not alter Austria's plans to make war. The Germans had offered to support their Austrian allies in what they considered a local incident. Austria declared war on July 28. The Russians, who regarded themselves as the champions and protectors of all Slavic peoples, began to mobilize to help Serbia. At this point, the two great alliance systems of Europe came into play, and within a short time the major powers were at war.

An account of the assassination of the Archduke and his wife by Gavrilo Princip is given by Borijove Jevtic, one of the leaders in the band of terrorists. Jevtic was imprisoned after the assassination, but was released when no evidence could be uncovered to implicate him.

A tiny clipping from a newspaper, mailed without comment from a secret band of terrorists in Zagreb . . . to their comrades in Belgrade, was the torch which set the world afire with war in 1914. That bit of paper wrecked old, proud empires. It gave birth to new, free nations.

Source: *The New York World*, June 29, 1924. Reprinted by permission of *The World* and the North American Newspaper Alliance, Inc.

I was one of the members of the terrorist band in Belgrade which received it, and in those days I and my companions were regarded as desperate criminals. A price was on our heads. . . .

The little clipping . . . reached our meeting place . . . one night the latter part of April 1914. . . .

As everyone knows, the old Austrian-Hungarian Empire was built by conquest and intrigues, by sales and treacheries which held in subjugation many peoples who were neither Austrian nor Hungarian. It taxed them heavily; it diverted the products of their toil to serve the wealth of the master state. It interfered in their old freedom by a multiplicity of laws administered with arrogance. . . .

Several years before the war, a little group of us, thirty-five in all, living in several Bosnian and Herzogovinian cities and villages, formed the Narodna Odbrana, the Secret Society, the aim of which was to work for freedom from Austria and a union with Serbia. . . .

We were not the only organization which plotted against Austrian rule. But we were the only one which went to the length of direct action — political crimes and demonstrations to inflame the hearts of the people. The others merely distributed nationalistic and revolutionary literature and by argument sought to prepare the ground for revolution. We were the extremists. All the organizations had a loose connection with each other, but none of them knew our plans or when we would strike. . . .

Coming up to the World War period, the men who were terrorists in 1914 in Bosnia embraced all classes. Most of them were students: youth is the time for the philosophy of action. There were also teachers, tradesmen, and peasants; artisans and even men of the upper classes were ardent patriots. They were dissimilar [in] everything except hatred of the oppressor.

Such were the men into whose hands the tiny bit of newsprint was sent by friends in Bosnia that April night in Belgrade. At a small table in a very humble cafe, beneath a flickering gas jet, we sat and read it. There was no advice nor admonition sent with it. Only four letters and two numerals were sufficient to make us unanimous, without discussion, as to what we should do about it. They were contained in the fateful date, June 28.*

* **June 28:** a day all patriotic Serbs observe. On that day in 1389 the Serbian kingdom was conquered by the Turks, and in the second Balkan War Serbian armies defeated the Turks in battle on June 28.

How dared Franz Ferdinand, not only the representative of the oppressor but in his own person an arrogant tyrant, enter Sarajevo on that day? Such an entry was a studied insult. . . .

As we read that clipping in Belgrade we knew what we would do to Franz Ferdinand. We would kill him to show Austria there yet lived within its borders defiance of its rule. We would kill him to bring once more to the boiling point the fighting spirit of the revolutionaries and pave the way for revolt. We would kill him for his insult to our country. . . .

Then came the matter of arranging it. To make his death certain, twenty-two members of the organization were selected to carry out the sentence. At first we thought we would choose the men by lot. But here Gavrilo Princip intervened. Princip is destined to go down in Serbian history as one of her greatest heroes. From the moment Ferdinand's death was decided upon, he took an active leadership in its planning. Upon his advice we left the deed to members of our band who were in and around Sarajevo, under his direction and that of Gabrinović, a linotype operator on a Serbian newspaper. Both were regarded as capable of anything in the cause. . . .

The fateful morning dawned. Two hours before Franz Ferdinand arrived in Sarajevo, all the twenty-two conspirators were in their allotted positions, armed and ready. They were distributed five hundred yards apart over the whole route along which the Archduke must travel from the railroad station to the Town Hall.

When Franz Ferdinand and his retinue drove from the station they were allowed to pass the first two conspirators. The motor cars were driving too fast to make an attempt feasible and in the crowd were Serbians; throwing a grenade would have killed many innocent people.

When the car passed Gabrinović, the compositor, he threw his grenade. It hit the side of the car, but Franz Ferdinand with presence of mind threw himself back and was uninjured. Several officers riding in his attendance were injured.

The cars sped to the Town Hall and the rest of the conspirators did not interfere with them. After the reception in the Town Hall, General Potiorek, the Austrian commander, pleaded with Franz Ferdinand to leave the city, as it was seething with rebellion. The Archduke was persuaded to drive the shortest way out of the city and to go quickly. . . .

The road to the maneuvers was shaped like the letter V, making a sharp turn at the bridge over the river Nilgacka. Franz Ferdinand's car could go fast enough until it reached this spot, but here it was forced to slow down for the turn. Here Princip had taken his stand.

As the car came abreast he stepped forward from the curb, drew his automatic pistol from his coat, and fired two shots. The first struck the wife of the Archduke, the Archduchess Sofia, in the abdomen. . . . She died instantly.

The second bullet struck the Archduke close to the heart.

He uttered only one word, "Sofia" — a call to his stricken wife. Then his head fell back and he collapsed. He died almost instantly.

The officers seized Princip. They beat him over the head with the flat of their swords. They knocked him down, they kicked him, scraped the skin from his neck with the edges of their swords, tortured him, all but killed him.

Then he was taken to the Sarajevo jail. The next day he was transferred to the military prison and the roundup of his fellow conspirators proceeded, although he denied that he had worked with anyone. . . .

His only sign of regret was the statement that he was sorry he had killed the wife of the Archduke. He had aimed only at her husband and would have preferred that any other bullet should have struck General Potiorek. . . . [Princip, because he was a minor (nineteen) and could not be executed, was sentenced to twenty years of hard labor. He died in prison in 1918.]

The Germans Destroy Louvain

In 1839 Germany, along with other European nations, agreed that Belgium should be regarded as neutral in any European war. But in August 1914 the German armies swept into this tiny country on their way to France. The Belgians resisted bravely, and it took the Germans eighteen days, rather than the six they had counted on, to cross Belgium. In anger at the delay, the Germans began a campaign of destruction. In the town of Louvain the Germans threw torches into houses suspected of harboring snipers. Soon the university, the library, the churches, and thousands of homes were all ablaze. Eyewitness descriptions, such as the following, roused the indignation of neutrals.

London, August 30. I left Brussels on Thursday afternoon and have just arrived in London. For two hours on Thursday night I was in what for six hundred years had been the city of Louvain. The Germans were burning it, and to hide their work kept us locked in the railroad carriages. But the story was written against the sky, was told to us by German soldiers, . . . and we could read it in the faces of women and children being led to concentration camps and of citizens on their way to be shot.

The Germans sentenced Louvain on Wednesday to become a wilderness, and with the German system and love of thoroughness they left Louvain an empty, blackened shell. The reason for this appeal to the torch and the execution of noncombatants, as given to me on Thursday morning by General Von Lutwitz, military governor of Brussels, was this: On Wednesday, while the German military commander of the troops in Louvain was at the Hôtel de Ville [city hall] talking to the burgomaster, a son of the burgomaster with an automatic pistol shot the chief of staff and German staff surgeons.

Lutwitz claims this was the signal for the civil guard, in civilian clothes on roofs, to fire upon the German soldiers on the open square below. He said also the Belgians had quick-firing guns, brought from Antwerp. As for a week the Germans had occupied Louvain and closely guarded all approaches, the story that there was any gunrunning is absurd.

Fifty Germans were killed and wounded. For that, said Lutwitz, Louvain must be wiped out. . . .

"The Hôtel de Ville," he added, "was a beautiful building; it is a pity it must be destroyed. . . ."

Money can never restore Louvain. Great architects and artists, dead these six hundred years, made it beautiful, and their handiwork belonged to the world. With torch and dynamite the Germans have turned these masterpieces into ashes, and all the Kaiser's horses and all his men cannot bring them back again.

When by troop train we reached Louvain, the entire heart of the city was destroyed. . . . In their work the soldiers were moving from the heart of the city to the outskirts, street by street, from house to house.

In each building, so German soldiers told me, they began at the

Source: *The New York Tribune*, August 31, 1914. Copyright by *The New York Tribune*. Reprinted by permission of the publishers.

first floor, and when that was burning steadily passed to the one next. There were no exceptions — whether it was a store, chapel, or private residence, it was destroyed. The occupants had been warned to go, and in each deserted house or shop the furniture was piled, the torch was stuck under it, and into the air went the savings of years, souvenirs of children, of parents; heirlooms that had passed from generation to generation.

The people had time only to fill a pillowcase and fly. Some were not so fortunate, and by thousands, like flocks of sheep, they were rounded up and marched through the night to concentration camps. We were not allowed to speak to any citizen of Louvain, but the Germans crowded the windows, boastful, gloating, eager to interpret.

We were free to move from one end of the train to the other, and in the two hours during which it circled the burning city war was before us in its most hateful aspect. . . .

At Louvain it was war upon the defenseless, war on churches, colleges, shops of milliners and lacemakers; war brought to the bedside and fireside; against women harvesting in the fields, against children in wooden shoes at play in the streets. . . .

Outside the station in the public square the people of Louvain passed in an unending procession, women bareheaded, weeping, men carrying the children asleep on their shoulders, all hemmed in by the shadowy army of gray wolves. Once they were halted and among them were marched a line of men. They well knew their fellow townsmen. These were on their way to be shot. And better to point the moral an officer halted both processions, and climbing to a cart, explained why the men were to die. He warned others not to bring down upon themselves a like vengeance. . . .

It was all like a scene upon the stage, so unreal, so inhuman. . . .

You felt it was only a nightmare, cruel and uncivilized. And then you remembered that the German Emperor has told us what it is; it is his Holy War.

The Allies Impose Terms Upon the Germans

On November 11, 1918, at eleven o'clock in the morning, all fighting ceased on the Western Front. The war had not been going well for Germany for some time. Weary and tasting defeat, the German people revolted against Kaiser Wilhelm II, who fled to the Netherlands. It was the Chancellor of the newly created German Republic who met with Marshal Foch and his Allied associates to sign the armistice agreement.

The staggering losses in life and property suffered by the Allies and the hatred whipped up during the war against the enemy made an idealistic peace settlement unlikely, in spite of Woodrow Wilson's pronouncements. The Treaty of Versailles, drawn up without consulting the Germans, was presented to them as an ultimatum. In the Hall of Mirrors, where the German Empire had been proclaimed in 1871, the German delegates reluctantly put their signatures to the Treaty.

Excerpts from the Treaty and the reaction of the German delegates to its contents are given in the following selections.

The Treaty

Article 42. Germany is forbidden to maintain or construct any fortifications either on the left bank of the Rhine or on the right bank to the west of a line drawn 50 kilometers to the east of the Rhine.

Article 43. In the area defined above, the maintenance and the assembly of armed forces, either permanently or temporarily, and military maneuvers of any kind, as well as the upkeep of all permanent works for mobilization, are in the same way forbidden.

Article 44. In case Germany violates in any manner whatever the provisions of Articles 42 and 43, she shall be regarded as committing a hostile act against the Powers signatory of the present Treaty and as calculated to disturb the peace of the world. . . .

THE TREATY. Source: *Treaties, Conventions, International Acts, Protocols, and Agreements Between the United States of America and Other Powers, 1910–1923,* Vol. III, Washington, D.C.: Government Printing Office, 1923, pp. 3351 *passim.*

Article 80. Germany acknowledges and will respect strictly the independence of Austria, within the frontiers which may be fixed in a Treaty between that State and the principal Allied and Associated Powers. . . .

Article 81. Germany, in conformity with the action already taken by the Allied and Associated Powers, recognizes the complete independence of the Czecho-Slovak State. . . .

Article 87. Germany, in conformity with the action already taken by the Allied and Associated Powers, recognizes the complete independence of Poland. . . .

Article 119. Germany renounces in favor of the principal Allied and Associated Powers all her rights and titles over her oversea possessions. . . .

Article 160. By a date which must not be later than March 31, 1920, the German army must not comprise more than seven divisions of infantry and three divisions of cavalry. . . .

Article 198. The armed forces of Germany must not include any military or naval air forces. . . .

Article 231. The Allied and Associated Governments affirm and Germany accepts the responsibility of Germany and her allies for causing all the loss and damage to which the Allied and Associated Governments and their nationals have been subjected as a consequence of the war imposed upon them by the aggression of Germany and her allies. . . .

Article 245. Within six months after the coming into force of the present Treaty, the German government must restore to the French government the trophies, archives, historical souvenirs, or works of art carried away from France by the German authorities in the course of the war of 1870–1871 and during this last war, in accordance with a list which will be communicated to it by the French government. . . .

Article 428. As a guarantee for the execution of the present Treaty by Germany, the German territory situated to the west of the Rhine, together with the bridgeheads, will be occupied by Allied and Associated troops for a period of fifteen years from the coming into force of the present Treaty. . . .

Article 431. If before the expiration of the period of fifteen years Germany complies with all the undertakings resulting from the present Treaty, the occupying forces will be withdrawn immediately.

The German Reaction

On April 14, 1919, when it seemed as though a settlement were in sight, the German delegates were summoned to Versailles to receive the Treaty. . . .

The Treaty of Versailles was formally presented to the German representatives on May 7, 1919, by coincidence the fourth anniversary of the sinking of the *Lusitania.*

The scene was the Trianon Palace at Versailles. The day was one of surpassing loveliness, and brilliant spring sunlight flooded the room. . . .

The crowd was small, for the room was small — merely the delegates of both sides, with their assistants, and a few carefully selected press representatives. The grim-visaged Clemenceau sat at the center of the main table, Wilson at his right, Lloyd George at his left. . . .

When all were seated, the doors swung open. At the cry *"Messieurs les plenipotentiaires allemands!"* ["The German representatives"], the whole assembly rose and stood in silence while the German delegates filed in before their conquerors and sat at a table facing Clemenceau.

The Tiger [Clemenceau] rose to his feet and, his voice vibrant with the venom of 1871, almost spat out his speech with staccato precision: "It is neither the time nor the place for superfluous words. . . . The time has come when we must settle our accounts. You have asked for peace. We are ready to give you peace."

Already a secretary had quietly walked over to the table at which the Germans sat, and laid before them the thick, two hundred-odd page treaty — "The Book."

With Clemenceau still standing, the pale, black-clad Count Brockdorff-Rantzau, head of the German delegation, began reading his reply — seated.

An almost perceptible gasp swept the room, for the failure of the German to rise was taken as a studied discourtesy. Some felt that he was too nervous and shaken to stand. Others felt that he wanted to snub his "conquerors." The truth is that he planned to sit, not wishing to stand like a culprit before a judge to receive sentence. . . .

THE GERMAN REACTION. Source: Thomas A. Bailey, *Woodrow Wilson and the Lost Peace,* New York: The Macmillan Company, 1944, pp. 286, 289–90. Reprinted by permission of the publishers.

If Brockdorff-Rantzau's posture was unfortunate, his words and the intonation of his words were doubly so.

Speaking with great deliberation and without the usual courteous salutation to the presiding officer, he began by saying that the Germans were under "no illusions" as to the extent of their defeat and the degree of their "powerlessness." This was not true, for both he and his people were under great illusions.

Then he referred defiantly but inaccurately to the demand that the Germans acknowledge that "we alone are guilty of having caused the war. Such a confession in my mouth would be a lie." And the word "lie" fairly hissed from between his teeth. . . .

When the echo of Brockdorff-Rantzau's last tactless word had died away, Clemenceau spoke. His face had gone red during the harangue, but he had held himself in check with remarkable self-restraint. Harshly and peremptorily he steamrolled the proceedings to an end: "Has anybody any more observations to offer? Does no one wish to speak? If not, the meeting is closed."

The German delegates marched out, facing a battery of clicking moving picture cameras. Brockdorff-Rantzau lighted a cigarette with trembling fingers.

Lloyd George, who had snapped an ivory paper knife in his hands, remarked angrily, "It is hard to have won the war and to have to listen to that."

Thus, within a half hour was compressed one of the greatest dramas of all time.

[Though no discussion of the terms was permitted, the Germans had fifteen days in which to make a written reply. Their reply resulted in a few minor revisions. The Germans were then given a five-day ultimatum. Having no alternative, they signed the Treaty on June 28, 1919.]

On the Eve of the Russian Revolution

There was no lack of patriotic fervor in Russia when war broke out in 1914; even some radical elements offered to back the national effort. The war soon turned into an utter disaster for

Russia. Enormous military casualties, shortages of equipment at the front and food at home, and widespread profiteering combined to rouse popular discontent. The Czar did his soldiers no favor when he assumed personal command of the army. The government was left in the hands of his inept wife. She, in turn, had fallen under the influence of Rasputin, a monk who was believed to be endowed with supernatural powers. Russia was collapsing. The Czar, given ample warning of the approaching crisis, did little to avert it. Eventually even the best friends of the monarchy advised his abdication.

The state of Russia during the war and in the years before the Revolution is described by Alexander Kerensky, who later became Minister of Justice, Minister of War, and then Prime Minister in the shortlived Provisional Government of 1917.

The direct consequence of the war was a disastrous rupture of commercial relations between town and village.

The revolutionary annihilation of the internal exchange [of goods] had upset the whole economic routine of the country. Therein lay the root of all the miseries . . . which were to descend upon Russia. . . . By the autumn of 1916, the towns were experiencing a food shortage, which increased with ever-greater rapidity.

During the winter of 1916 the food shortage extended to the army, where it was due not only to the lack of commodities in the market, but also to the ever-increasing transport difficulties.

And then there was the fuel crisis. . . .

This extreme economic exhaustion in the rear had its counterpart in the extreme exhaustion of the army at the front. As early as January 1915, a colonel of the general staff, Engelhardt, a conservative member of the Duma, told the Budget Committee that "we can oppose the technical perfection of Germany only by flesh and bones; that is why we have to fill the trenches to the brim with the corpses of our soldiers."

" All we know," said Field Marshal von Hindenburg in his memoirs concerning the fighting on the Russian front, "is that from time to time we had to destroy mountains of enemy corpses which accumulated in

Source: Alexander Kerensky, *The Crucifixion of Liberty*, New York: The John Day Company, Inc., 1934, pp. 203–07. Copyright 1934 by Alexander Kerensky. Reprinted by permission of the publishers.

front of our trenches in order to be able to direct our fire against new groups of attackers. It must be left to the imagination to compute the losses. . . ." The Russian army lost two and a half million men . . . or forty per cent of the total on the Allied side. In the spring of 1915, during the tragic retreat from Galicia, the Russian guns did not reply to Mackensen's barrage of fire — we had no shells. The Russian soldiers went out to die without rifles, sometimes armed with sticks, always awaiting their turn for rifles — to be taken out of the hands of the dead or wounded. . . . Both the officers and the men of the trained peacetime regular army, especially the infantry, were slaughtered during the very first year of the war. . . .

In December 1916 the army had a million men listed as deserters. . . . Military operations sometimes had to be abandoned because the soldiers refused to leave their trenches and attack the enemy. . . .

To be sure, no one could be held responsible for those terrible social and economic upheavals which were the direct consequence of the war as such. But it is the rulers who must be held fully responsible for the internal policy of the state during a war so incredibly difficult, of such exceptional historical importance, and conducted under such unendurable economic conditions.

The first question that arises is whether the position of Russia in the World War was hopeless and helpless from the start. I say without hesitation that it was not. Wherever there was no interference from above, the Russian military and civil authorities managed to solve the most difficult war problems, and not at all badly. Local self-government bodies . . . coped splendidly with the work they had undertaken, beginning with the munition factories, down to the care of the wounded. After all was said and done, Russia had mobilized, alone, fifteen million men; she had a front which began on the Baltic and stretched across the Black Sea to Erzerum and Persia; she supported fourteen armies to hold this line. . . . During the first years of the war she bore the brunt of it; she suffered enormous losses in men, territory, fortifications, and industrial cities. And yet the technical equipment of the army, the training of its officers, and the commissariat organization in the rear were better early in 1917 than in the years 1914–15. The military strength of the country was ruined by the will of man and not by the force of circumstances. A sound organization at the front and in the country behind it was rendered impossible by the fault of the rulers and not of the ruled. The war for the very existence of Russia had to be waged simultaneously at the front and in the rear. Such was the curse of Russia — both under the Czar during Rasputin's reign, and after the fall of the monarchy, when Lenin and his adherents took over.

The March Revolution

Informed of the rioting in Petrograd, the Czar commanded his soldiers to fire on the mob and ordered the dissolution of the Duma (parliament). Neither the soldiers nor the Duma obeyed. By the time he yielded to the demand for a responsible ministry, it was already too late; his supporters had melted away. On March 15, 1917, the last of the Romanov czars, Nicholas II, was forced to abdicate his throne.

State power was in the hands of a Provisional Government until a national assembly could be elected. Composed mainly of moderates, the Provisional Government refused to comply with the desperate demands of the people for peace, food, and land. It forbade the seizure of land by the peasants, and it felt honor bound to its allies to continue the war. Its increasing unpopularity played into the hands of the extremists, who magnified its deficiencies. Lenin and the Bolsheviks overthrew the Provisional Government in November.

The following description of the March Revolution (February in the Russian calendar), which led to the establishment of the Provisional Government, was written by Leon Trotsky, who pieced the story together from a number of accounts.

The twenty-third of February was International Woman's Day. The social-democratic circles had intended to mark this day in a general manner: by meetings, speeches, leaflets. It had not occurred to anyone that it might become the first day of the Revolution. Not a single organization called for strikes on that day. What is more, even a Bolshevik organization, and a most militant one — the Vyborg borough-committee, all workers — was opposing strikes. The temper of the

Source: Leon Trotsky, *The History of the Russian Revolution*, Ann Arbor, Mich.: The University of Michigan Press, 1932, pp. 119–21, 125, 130–32, 142, 143, 146. Reprinted by permission of the publishers.

masses, according to Kayurov, one of the leaders in the workers' district, was very tense; any strike would threaten to turn into an open fight. But since the committee thought the time unripe for militant action — the Party not strong enough and the workers having too few contacts with the soldiers — they decided not to call for strikes but to prepare for revolutionary action at some indefinite time in the future. Such was the course followed by the committee on the eve of the twenty-third of February, and everyone seemed to accept it. On the following morning, however, in spite of all directives, the women textile workers in several factories went on strike, and sent delegates to the metal workers with an appeal for support. "With reluctance," writes Kayurov, "the Bolsheviks agreed to this, and they were followed by the workers — Mensheviks and Social Revolutionaries. But once there is a mass strike, one must call everybody into the streets and take the lead."

It was taken for granted that in case of a demonstration the soldiers would be brought out into the streets against the workers. What would that lead to? This was wartime; the authorities were in no mood for joking. On the other hand, a "reserve" soldier in wartime is nothing like an old soldier of the regular army. Is he really so formidable? In revolutionary circles they had discussed this much, but rather abstractly. For no one, positively no one — we can assert this categorically upon the basis of all the data — then thought that February 23 was to mark the beginning of a decisive drive against absolutism. . . .

Thus the fact is that the February Revolution was begun from below, overcoming the resistance of its own revolutionary organizations, the initiative being taken of their own accord by the most oppressed and downtrodden part of the proletariat — the women textile workers, among them no doubt many soldiers' wives. The overgrown bread lines had provided the last stimulus. . . .

On the following day the movement not only fails to diminish but doubles. About one half of the industrial workers of Petrograd are on strike on the twenty-fourth of February. The workers come to the factories in the morning; instead of going to work they hold meetings; then begin processions toward the center. New districts and new groups of the population are drawn into the movement. The slogan "Bread!" is crowded out or obscured by louder slogans: "Down with autocracy!" "Down with the war!". . . There was no fear in the crowd. "The Cossacks promise not to shoot," passed from mouth to mouth. Apparently some of the workers had talks with individual Cossacks. Later, however, cursing, half-drunken dragoons appeared on the scene. They plunged into the crowd, began to strike at heads with their lances. The demonstrators summoned all their strength and stood fast: "They won't shoot." And in fact they didn't. . . .

Throughout the entire day crowds of people poured from one part of the city to another. They were persistently dispelled by the police, stopped and crowded back by cavalry detachments, and occasionally by infantry. Along with shouts of "Down with the police!" was heard oftener and oftener a "Hurrah!" addressed to the Cossacks. That was significant. Toward the police the crowd shouted ferocious hatred. They routed the mounted police with whistles, stones, and pieces of ice. In a totally different way the workers approached the soldiers. Around the barracks, sentinels, patrols, and lines of soldiers stood groups of workingmen and women exchanging friendly words with the army men.

On the twenty-fifth, the strike spread wider. According to the government's figures, 240,000 workers participated that day. The most backward layers are following up the vanguard. . . . Orators address the crowds around the Alexander III monument. The mounted police open fire. A speaker falls wounded. Shots from the crowd kill a police inspector, wound the chief of police and several other policemen. Bottles, petards,* and hand grenades are thrown at the gendarmes. The war has taught this art. The soldiers show indifference, at times hostility, to the police. It spreads excitedly through the crowd that when the police opened fire by the Alexander III monument, the Cossacks let go a volley at the horse "pharaohs" (such was the nickname of the police) and the latter had to gallop off. This apparently was not a legend circulated for self-encouragement, since the incident, although in different versions, is confirmed from several sources. . . .

The twenty-sixth of February fell on a Sunday; the factories were closed, and this prevented measuring the strength of the mass pressure in terms of the extent of the strike. Moreover, the workers could not assemble in the factories as they had done on the preceding days, and that hindered the demonstrations. . . .

But this calmness does not last long. The workers gradually concentrate and move from all suburbs to the center. They are stopped at the bridges. They flock across the ice: it is only February and the Neva is one solid bridge of ice. The firing at their crowds on the ice is not

* **petards:** cases containing explosives.

128

enough to stop them. They find the city transformed. Posses, cordons, horse patrols everywhere. . . .

Police reports for that day testify that the fire hose was inadequate: "In the course of the disorders it was observed as a general phenomenon that the rioting mobs showed extreme defiance toward the military patrols, at whom, when asked to disperse, they threw stones and lumps of ice dug up from the street. When preliminary shots were fired into the air, the crowd not only did not disperse, but answered these volleys with laughter. . . ." The masses will no longer retreat, they resist with optimistic brilliance, they stay on the street even after murderous volleys; they cling, not to their lives, but to the pavement, to stones, to pieces of ice. The crowd is not only bitter, but audacious. This is because, in spite of the shooting, it keeps its faith in the army. It counts on victory and intends to have it at any cost.

The pressure of the workers upon the army is increasing, countering the pressure from the side of the authorities. The Petrograd garrison comes into the focus of events. The expectant period, which has lasted almost three days, during which it was possible for the main mass of the garrison to keep up friendly neutrality toward the insurrection, has come to an end. "Shoot the enemy!" the monarchy commands. "Don't shoot your brothers and sisters!" cry the workers. And not only that: "Come with us!" Thus in the streets and squares, by the bridges, at the barrack gates, is waged a ceaseless struggle — now dramatic, now unnoticeable — but always a desperate struggle, for the heart of the soldier. In this struggle, in these sharp contacts between workingmen and women and the soldiers, under the steady cracking of rifles and machine guns, the fate of the government, of the war, of the country, is being decided. [Late on the twenty-sixth and throughout the twenty-seventh the soldiers mutiny and join the revolution.]

In the early hours of the twenty-seventh, the workers thought the solution of the problem of the insurrection infinitely more distant than it really was. . . .

Chugurin was among the first to appear at the Bolshevik headquarters, a rifle in his hands, a cartridge belt over his shoulder, "all spattered up, but beaming and triumphant." Why shouldn't he beam? Soldiers with rifles in their hands are coming over to us! . . .

One after another came the joyful reports of victories. Our own armored cars have appeared! With red flags flying, they are spreading terror through the districts to all who have not yet submitted. Now it will no longer be necessary to crawl under the belly of a Cossack's horse. The Revolution is standing up to its full height.

During the twenty-seventh of February the crowd liberated without bloodshed from the many jails of the capital all political prisoners, among them the patriotic group of the Military and Industrial Committee, which had been arrested on the twenty-sixth of January, and the members of the Petrograd Committee of the Bolsheviks.

Lenin Rules in the Kremlin

Vladimir Ilyich Lenin's life was dedicated to a single purpose — revolution. A devoted follower of Marx's philosophy, he nevertheless realized that revolutions were not brought about by armchair theorists. With a will of iron and amazing energy, he set about building a trained, disciplined, and militant party of revolutionaries. For moderates or compromisers he had only contempt. He became the leader of the extremist Bolshevik wing of the Marxists in 1903. After years of exile, disappointment, and despair, his opportunity came in 1917. Against great odds Lenin won the revolution for the Bolsheviks.

Brought back to Russia in April 1917 by the Germans, who believed that he would add to the chaos, Lenin galvanized his followers against the Provisional Government. In simple and powerful slogans he offered the people what they wanted — land and peace. Departing from Marxist theory, he called for the union of worker and peasant as the means of bringing about a revolution in backward Russia. With customary disdain for democratic institutions, and with typical ruthlessness, he dispersed the freely elected Constituent Assembly in which the Bolsheviks had won only a quarter of the votes.

A description of Lenin as ruler of Russia is given below by David Shub. Shub was in close contact with Russian revolutionary leaders for several decades. After being exiled to Siberia for taking part in the Revolution of 1905–06, he escaped and came to the United States in 1908.

On the first of May Lenin stood on the Kremlin wall where Napoleon once had watched Moscow burning and gazed down at the May Day demonstration in Red Square.

"The most important thing is not to lose constant contact with the masses," he told his companion. "One must be in touch with the life of the masses." And he asked what the crowd was saying, what their mood was, was their demonstration spontaneous or artificial? . . .

Not having industrial and consumer goods in sufficient quantity to exchange with the peasants for grain, the Soviet Government on May 10, 1918, issued an order for the requisitioning of grain from "rich" peasants. A month later, on June 11, the so-called "Committees of the Poor" were created to enforce the decree in every village. An ugly atmosphere of suspicion, espionage, and betrayal was created among the peasants. Neighbor spied upon neighbor. Peasants slaughtered their cattle and refused to sow their land rather than turn over their food supplies to the government. And the countryside seethed with local uprisings, which were crushed by punitive expeditions of Cheka troops [secret police].

The complete suppression of civil liberty, the dissolution of the Constituent Assembly, the Cheka terror, and the . . . peace of Brest-Litovsk — which deprived Russia of its richest regions — brought increasing revolt from every stratum of the Russian people.

The Petrograd regiments which had overthrown Kerensky [the Provisional Government] were on the verge of a new revolt and had to be disarmed, as were other military and naval units. The Lettish [Latvian] sharpshooters became the only regular armed force on which Lenin could rely with complete certainty. . . .

In 1918 Lenin embarked on a policy of "incomplete Communism." In March the nationalization of trade was decreed. To the Seventh Party Congress he explained that the industrial workers and landless peasants had to help build Communism on the fundamental principle "From each according to his capacities, to each according to his needs."

Communism had to be predicated [based] on the elimination of the middleman. The system of private trading was to be abolished. Production would be guided by social needs, he promised.

There were special needs for nationalizing trade. The peasants, un-

Source: David Shub, *Lenin*, New York: Doubleday & Company, Inc., 1948, pp. 312–13, 330–33. Copyright 1948 by David Shub. Reprinted by permission of the publishers.

willing to sell their grain for worthless paper currency, were demanding manufactured goods. In order to secure food for the urban population, the government had to organize a barter system between village and city. Committees were formed in every town with a population of ten thousand to fix local prices of articles. The existing stocks of merchandise were registered. Trading in manufactured goods was placed under state control. But that was not enough. On October 8, 1918, the regime nationalized all domestic trade. All shops, great and small, were closed and their inventory used for barter with the peasants.

According to Trotsky, Lenin asserted in 1918, "You will see that within six months we shall establish Socialism in Russia."

Lenin also prepared the draft of a decree outlining how he proposed to force all able-bodied men and women to serve the interests of the state.

"Every toiler having worked eight hours during the day is obliged to devote three hours to military or administrative duties.

"Everyone belonging to the nobility or the well-to-do (an income of not less than five hundred rubles a month or . . . capital of not less than fifteen hundred rubles) is obliged to obtain a workbook wherein shall be recorded whether or not he has performed his share in military or administrative service. The recording is to be done by the trade union, the Soviet, or the staff of the local Red Guard. The well-to-do can obtain this book on the payment of fifty rubles.

"Nonworkers who do not belong to the wealthy classes are also required to have such a workbook, which they can obtain for five rubles. For failure to secure such a book or for false entries in it, punishment is to be meted out according to military law. . . ."

When the decree for the full nationalization of all industrial and commercial enterprises was promulgated, the Soviet state really consisted largely of a few offices in Moscow and Petrograd, whose managers had little practical experience. The "plan" existed mainly in the brain of Mikhail (Yuri) Larin.

Larin was [a Communist] who had lived for many years in Germany. . . . When [he] returned to Russia, . . . Lenin made [him] the main architect of Socialist construction. He was the author of the decree for nationalization of all industries, large and small. He created, mainly on paper, a system of central institutions for every branch of industry and commerce. All private stores were closed and the merchandise confiscated. With Russia's economy already undermined by war and civil conflict, Larin in effect destroyed the remnants.

When the non-Communist specialist Lieberman reported to Lenin on the sad state of the lumber industry as a result of Larin's decrees, Lenin interrupted him with these words:

"Of course we make mistakes, but there are no revolutions without mistakes. We learn from our mistakes, but we are glad we can correct them."

As for the latest Larin decrees Lenin remarked:

"We are engaged in making revolution. Our power may not last long, but these decrees will become part of history, and future revolutionaries will learn from them. They may learn something from Larin's decrees which you consider senseless. . . ."

The population was forbidden to produce or trade, and at the same time the state was unable not only to build new industries but to manage the existing ones. Opening a small factory or shop was prohibited under pain of being shot as a "counterrevolutionist" or speculator. But there was no trace of state-organized commerce. Economic catastrophe followed. Raw materials disappeared together with consumer goods and industrial products. The little that remained in private hands vanished from the markets. But although state factories could obtain nothing, there was an active black market where enormous speculation flourished. The result was disastrous inflation. And when the cities were unable to supply the villages with products, the peasants refused to bring their bread and meat to the cities. A great part of the city workers who had come from the villages deserted the hungry cities. The cities were emptied not only of workers, but of all who could find food in the villages. Because of the scarcity of labor and materials, hundreds of factories closed down.

To feed at least the essential workers and the administrators, the regime had to send troops to the villages to collect bread and grain by force. But the peasants resisted and armed revolts broke out. The peasants in 1918–19 were mostly ex-soldiers who had returned from the front with their rifles, machine guns, and grenades. Thus a war for bread flared in the villages. The city came to take grain but the peasant didn't want to surrender it, because the paper currency had no value. These forced requisitions drove hundreds of thousands of peasants into the arms of the counterrevolution.

The ravaged villages often joined the anti-Bolshevik forces. In the Ukraine one heard that the peasants favored the "Bolsheviks" (who took the land from nobles) but were opposed to the "Communists," who sent requisitioning squads. The peasants also replied with sabotage, refusing to produce. Crops dropped to the point where only enough was planted and harvested for local village consumption but nothing for the cities.

At one of the sessions of the Council for Labor and Defense, the above-mentioned Lieberman proposed that several tons of bread and oats be designated for the peasants who were to deliver firewood to the cities and railways. One of the commissars opposed the plan, explaining that this would entail reducing the already meager bread rations of the city workers.

Alexei Rykov then took the floor.

"We are able to get our workers and peasants accustomed to working even without bread. But unfortunately we could not get our horses accustomed to it. You may declare the horses counterrevolutionary, but you cannot ignore the fact and you must give them oats."

Turning to Dzerzhinsky, Rykov said, "Even Felix Edmundovitch can do little about it. Let him try to shoot a few dozen horses."

Lenin closed the discussion and dictated an order to issue bread and oats for the peasants.

[In March 1921 Lenin inaugurated the New Economic Policy (NEP), which attempted to cope with the economic disorganization by a temporary retreat from the socialization of industry, agriculture, and commerce.]

The Dictatorship of Stalin

After outmaneuvering his political opponents, the chief of whom was Leon Trotsky, Joseph Stalin emerged as undisputed dictator of the Soviet Union. One of the many issues on which Stalin and Trotsky differed was the extension of the revolution to other countries. Trotsky, a cosmopolitan of wide experience, believed that the Soviet Union could never become a true Communist state unless the revolution spread beyond its borders. Stalin, who was more of a nationalist, felt that his first task was to establish a strong state. His ultimate goal was no different from that of Trotsky, and he continued to support and encourage Communist groups throughout the world. In the meantime he was willing to get along with capitalist nations and to establish "Socialism in one country." In his struggle for power, Stalin had opposed a program of rapid industrialization. Once his competitors were out of the way, he initiated the Five-Year Plan for the expansion of industry. Stalin's rule, as Nikita S. Khrushchev has acknowledged, was an oppressive dictatorship in which opponents could not survive.

In the first selection Stalin discusses his policy of "Socialism in one country," and in the second he deals with the results of the First Five-Year Plan, inaugurated in 1928.

Socialism in One Country

On the question of *victory* of Socialism in our country, . . . [I said in 1925], "We can build Socialism, and we will build it together with the peasantry under the leadership of the working class. . . . Under the dictatorship of the proletariat we possess . . . all that is needed to build a complete Socialist society, overcoming all internal difficulties, for we can and must overcome them by our own efforts."

On the question of the *final* victory of Socialism . . . [I said], "The final victory of Socialism is the full guarantee against attempts at intervention, and hence against restoration [of the prerevolutionary regime], for any serious attempt at restoration can be made only with serious support from outside, only with the support of international capital. Therefore, the support of our Revolution by the workers of all countries, and still more, the victory of the workers in at least several countries, is a necessary condition for fully guaranteeing the first victorious country against attempts at intervention and restoration, a necessary condition for the final victory of Socialism."

Clear, one would think! . . .

What do we mean by the *possibility* of the victory of Socialism in one country?

We mean the possibility of solving the contradictions between the proletariat and the peasantry with the aid of the internal forces of our

Source: Joseph Stalin, *Problems of Leninism*, Moscow: Foreign Languages Publishing House, 1953, pp. 191, 192–93; 512–15.

country, the possibility of the proletariat assuming power and using that power to build a complete Socialist society in our country with the sympathy and the support of the proletarians of other countries, but without the preliminary victory of the proletarian revolution in other countries.

Without such a possibility, building Socialism is building without prospects, building without being sure that Socialism will be completely built. It is no use engaging in building Socialism without being sure that we can build it completely, without being sure that the technical backwardness of our country is not an insuperable obstacle to the complete construction of a fully Socialist society. To deny such a possibility is to display lack of faith in the cause of building Socialism, to abandon Leninism.

What do we mean by the *impossibility* of the complete, final victory of Socialism in one country without the victory of the Revolution in other countries?

We mean the impossibility of having full guarantees against intervention, and consequently against the restoration of the bourgeois order, without the victory of the Revolution in at least a number of countries. To deny this indisputable thesis is to abandon internationalism, to abandon Leninism.

The First Five-Year Plan

Let us now take up the results of the fulfillment of the Five-Year Plan. What are the results of the Five-Year-Plan in four years in the sphere of industry?

Have we achieved victory in this sphere?

Yes, we have. And not only that, but we have accomplished more than we expected, more than the hottest heads in our Party could have expected. Even our enemies do not deny this now; and certainly our friends cannot deny it.

We did not have an iron and steel industry, the foundation for the industrialization of the country. Now we have this industry.

We did not have a tractor industry. Now we have one.

We did not have an automobile industry. Now we have one.

We did not have a machine-tool industry. Now we have one.

We did not have a big up-to-date chemical industry. Now we have one.

We did not have a real and big industry for the production of modern agricultural machinery. Now we have one.

We did not have an aircraft industry. Now we have one.

In output of electric power we were last on the list. Now we rank among the first.

In output of oil products and coal we were last on the list. Now we rank among the first.

We had only one coal and metallurgical base — in the Ukraine — which we barely managed to keep going. We have not only succeeded in improving this base, but have created a new coal and metallurgical base in the East which is the pride of our country.

We had only one center of the textile industry — in the North of our country. As a result of our efforts we will have in the very near future two new centers of the textile industry in Central Asia and Western Siberia.

And we have not only created these new great industries, but have created them on a scale and in dimensions that eclipse the scale and dimensions of European industry.

And as a result of all this the capitalist elements have been completely and irrevocably eliminated from industry, and Socialist industry has become the sole form of industry in the U.S.S.R.

And as a result of all this our country has been converted from an agrarian into an industrial country. . . .

Finally, as a result of all this the Soviet Union has been converted from a weak country, unprepared for defense, into a country mighty in defense, a country prepared for every contingency [possibility], a country capable of producing on a mass scale all modern weapons of defense and of equipping its army with them in the event of an attack from without [outside].

It is true that the output of consumer goods fell short of the demand, and this creates certain difficulties. But then we must realize and take into account where such a policy of relegating the task of industrialization to the background would have led us. . . .

We would have deprived ourselves of the possibility of supplying our agriculture with tractors and agricultural machinery, which means that we would now have no bread.

We would have deprived ourselves of the possibility of achieving victory over the capitalist elements in our country, which means that we would have raised immeasurably the chances of the restoration of capitalism.

We would not now have all the modern means of defense without which it is impossible for a country to be politically independent, without which a country becomes a target for military attacks of foreign enemies. Our position would be more or less analogous to [like] the present position of China, which has no heavy industry and no war industry of her own and which is being molested by anyone who cares to do so.

In a word, in that case we would have had military intervention; not pacts of nonaggression, but war, dangerous and fatal war, a sanguinary [bloody] and unequal war; for in such a war we would be almost unarmed in the face of an enemy who has all the modern means of attack at his disposal.

Italy in the Hands of the Fascists

Italy was unable to cope with the multitude of problems that faced it after the end of World War I. Its economy was in a hopelessly chaotic state. The meager allotment of spoils Italy obtained at the Peace Conference aroused national resentment. Good political leadership was lacking, and the old parties were not up to the task of maintaining order.

A number of new political groups were formed. One of these was the Fascist Party, organized and led by Benito Mussolini, a former Socialist. The Fascists appealed directly to the use of force. They were a party of the far right, emphasizing extreme nationalism. Mussolini was frank about his intentions to establish a dictatorship. In October 1922 he and his followers threatened to march to Rome and take over the government by force. In order to avert a revolution, King Victor Emmanuel III invited Mussolini to become Prime Minister. Before long Mussolini was in complete control of the country.

Mussolini proclaimed that Fascism was above all a doctrine of action. To correct the disorders of Italy he offered to substitute energy for complicated theories and long-winded discussions. He also promised to revive Italy's ancient glory and power. International peace he deemed neither practical nor worthwhile. To prepare for the inevitable war, Mussolini moved with determination to strengthen the economy and rebuild the army.

Mussolini scoffed at the weakness of democracy and parliamentary government. There was no room in his new order for opposition or discussion. Opponents of Fascism were given brutal treatment and sometimes murdered. Many were forced out of the country.

The first selection, on the theory of Fascism, was originally written for the Enciclopedia Italiana (1932) by Mussolini with the assistance of the philosopher Giovanni Gentile. The second selection is by Gaetano Salvemini, a well-known historian who despised the Fascist regime. He left Italy in August 1925 and was officially dismissed from his post at the University of Florence in December. For a number of years he lived in England and then in the United States, where he taught at Harvard. In 1948 he returned to Italy and resumed his position at the University of Florence.

Fascism in Theory

Fascism . . . believes neither in the possibility nor the utility of perpetual peace. It thus repudiates the doctrine of pacifism. . . . War alone brings up to its highest tension all human energy and puts the stamp of nobility upon the peoples who have the courage to meet it. All other trials are substitutes, which never really put men into the position where they have to make the great decision — the alternative of life or death. Thus a doctrine which is founded upon this harmful postulate of peace is hostile to Fascism. And thus hostile to the spirit of Fascism, though accepted for what use they can be in dealing with particular political situations, are all the international leagues and societies which, as history will show, can be scattered to the winds when

FASCISM IN THEORY. Source: Benito Mussolini, "The Political and Social Doctrine of Fascism," in *International Conciliation*, January, 1935, No. 306, pp. 7–9, 13–16, by permission of the Carnegie Endowment for International Peace.

once strong national feeling is aroused by any motive — sentimental, ideal, or practical. . . .

Fascism [is] the complete opposite of that doctrine, the base of so-called scientific and Marxian Socialism, the materialist conception of history; according to which the history of human civilization can be explained simply through the conflict of interests among the various social groups and by the change and development in the means and instruments of production. That the changes in the economic field — new discoveries of raw materials, new methods of working them, and the inventions of science — have their importance no one can deny; but that these factors are sufficient to explain the history of humanity excluding all others is an absurd delusion. Fascism, now and always, believes in holiness and in heroism; that is to say, in actions influenced by no economic motive, direct or indirect. . . . And above all Fascism denies that class war can be the preponderant force in the transformation of society. These two fundamental concepts of Socialism being thus refuted, nothing is left of it but the sentimental aspiration — as old as humanity itself — toward a social convention in which the sorrows and sufferings of the humblest shall be alleviated. But here again Fascism repudiates the conception of "economic" happiness to be realized by Socialism and, as it were, at a given moment in economic evolution to assure to everyone the maximum of well-being. . . . Fascism denies the validity of the equation, well-being $=$ happiness, which would reduce men to the level of animals, caring for one thing only — to be fat and well-fed — and would thus degrade humanity to a purely physical existence.

After Socialism, Fascism combats the whole complex system of democratic ideology and repudiates it, whether in its theoretical premises or in its practical application. Fascism denies that the majority, by the simple fact that it is a majority, can direct human society; it denies that numbers alone can govern by means of a periodical consultation, and it affirms the immutable, beneficial, and fruitful inequality of mankind, which can never be permanently leveled through the mere operation of a mechanical process such as universal suffrage. The democratic regime may be defined as from time to time giving the people the illusion of sovereignty, while the real, effective sovereignty lies in the hands of other concealed and irresponsible forces. Democracy is a regime nominally without a king, but it is ruled by many kings — more absolute, tyrannical, and ruinous than one sole king, even though a tyrant. . . . The foundation of Fascism is the conception of the State, its character, its duty, and its aim. Fascism conceives of the State as an absolute, in comparison with which all individuals or groups are relative, only to be conceived of in their relation to the State. . . . In 1929, at the first five-yearly assembly of the Fascist regime, I said:

"For us Fascists, the State is not merely a guardian, preoccupied solely with the duty of assuring the personal safety of the citizens; nor is it an organization with purely material aims, such as to guarantee a certain level of well-being and peaceful conditions of life; for a mere council of administration would be sufficient to realize such objects. Nor is it a purely political creation, divorced from all contact with the complex material reality which makes up the life of the individual and the life of the people as a whole. The State, as conceived of and as created by Fascism, is a spiritual and moral fact in itself. . . . The State is the guarantor of security both internal and external, but it is also the custodian and transmitter of the spirit of the people as it has grown up through the centuries in language, in customs, and in faith. And the State is not only a living reality of the present, it is also linked with the past and above all the future, and thus . . . it represents the . . . spirit of the nation. . . ."

The Fascist State is unique, and an original creation. It is not reactionary but revolutionary, in that it anticipates the solution of the universal political problems which elsewhere have to be settled in the political field by the rivalry of parties, the excessive power of the parliamentary regime, and the irresponsibility of political assemblies; while it meets the problems of the economic field by a system of syndicalism which is continually increasing in importance, as much in the sphere of labor as of industry, and in the moral field [it] enforces order, discipline, and obedience to that which is the determined moral code of the country. Fascism desires the State to be a strong and organic body, at the same time reposing upon broad and popular support. The Fascist State has drawn into itself even the economic activities of the nation, and through the corporative social and educational institutions created by it, its influence reaches every aspect of the national life and includes, framed in their respective organizations, all the political, economic, and spiritual forces of the nation. . . . The individual in the Fascist State is not annulled but rather multiplied, just in the same way that a soldier in a regiment is not diminished but rather increased by the number of his comrades. The Fascist State organizes the nation but leaves a sufficient margin of liberty to the individual; the latter is deprived of all useless and possibly harmful freedom but retains what is essential; the deciding power in this question cannot be the individual, but the State alone.

The Fascist State is an embodied will to power and government: the Roman tradition is here an ideal of force in action. According to Fascism, government is not so much a thing to be expressed in territorial or military terms as in terms of morality and the spirit. It must be thought of as an empire — that is to say, a nation which directly or indirectly rules other nations, without the need for conquering a single square yard of territory. For Fascism, the growth of empire, that is to say the expansion of the nation, is an essential manifestation of vitality, and its opposite a sign of decadence. Peoples which are rising, or rising again after a period of decadence, are always imperialist; any renunciation is a sign of decay and of death. Fascism is the doctrine best adapted to represent the tendencies and aspirations of a people, like the people of Italy, who are rising again after many centuries of abasement and foreign servitude. But empire demands discipline, the coordination of all forces, and a deeply felt sense of duty and sacrifice: this fact explains many aspects of the practical working of the regime, the character of many forces in the State, and the necessarily severe measures which must be taken against those who would oppose this spontaneous and inevitable movement of Italy in the twentieth century, and would oppose it by recalling the outworn ideology of the nineteenth century . . . for never before has the nation stood more in need of authority, of direction, and of order. If every age has its own characteristic doctrine, there are a thousand signs which point to Fascism as the characteristic doctrine of our time.

Fascism in Action

In the autumn of 1925 we were in Florence, . . . the favorite scene of "Black-Shirt" exploits.

On the night of Friday, September 25, the Fascists of Florence inaugurated a "manhunt" against the Freemasons. Bludgeonings devel-

FASCISM IN ACTION. Source: Gaetano Salvemini, *The Fascist Dictatorship in Italy*, New York: Holt, Rinehart and Winston, Inc., 1927, Vol. I, pp. 129–34, 147–49. Copyright © renewed 1955 by Gaetano Salvemini. Reprinted by permission of the publishers.

oped on a large scale for three days up till September 28, and went on . . . during the next day. The squads of bludgeoners were captained by the editor of the local Fascist paper . . . and by three members of the local Fascist Directorate.

In the afternoon of October 3, after four days of almost complete truce, a squad of Fascists under the leadership of Luporini, one of the three directors of the local *Fascio*, went to the house of the Freemason Bandinelli, who the previous day had been beaten by the Fascists. What happened at this point is not clear. The *Nazione* of October 6 says prudently that "certain circumstances are still doubtful; reports on this point are perhaps not very precise." But if the usual Fascist methods of persuasion are borne in mind, it may easily be imagined that the discussion soon degenerated into blows. Another Freemason, named Becciolini, who was present, drew his revolver and fired on the Fascists, killing Luporini and wounding another. He was at once thrashed, flung into a motor car, taken to the premises of the Fascist Provincial Federation, brought back again half dead to the scene of the murder and there riddled with bullets. Bandinelli's house was sacked.

Two hours after this . . . vendetta, reprisals on a large scale were set on foot against people entirely unconnected with the original incident. The Fascists cleared the streets in the center of the town, blindly bludgeoning everybody. The cafés were forcibly closed, the theaters invaded, and the performances stopped. Soon after ten P.M. the work of destruction began. The offices of thirteen lawyers and one accountant, a tailoring business, and seven shops were wrecked — nearly all in the center of the town, not far from the Prefecture and the police headquarters. . . . The furniture was thrown into the streets and set on fire. Watchers on the hills round Florence saw the columns of smoke and flame rising from the city. Many of the rioters indulged in indiscriminate looting. The *Nazione* of October 6 writes: "These shady individuals who are found on the outskirts of every great party abandoned themselves to excesses which the Fascist authorities are always the first to deplore."

An hour later operations were extended to private dwellings. . . . Still more "heroic" actions were carried out that night by other squads of Fascists. A squad known as "the Desperadoes," which for three years had terrorized the city and neighboring country, silently surrounded the house of Signor Pilati, a former Socialist Member of Parliament. Pilati had lost his right arm in the war and had received the medal for military valor. Though living in humble circumstances, he was widely respected for his kindly character, his intelligence, and his hard-working life. He and his family, knowing nothing of what was happening in Florence that night, were asleep, the windows being open on account of the heat. Silently placing a ladder against the sill, the Fascists climbed into the bedroom through the window and ordered the light to be turned on. Awaking suddenly, Pilati mechanically turned on the switch, while his wife, who was sleeping beside him, also awoke. One of the Fascists, covering Pilati with a revolver, told him he was wanted at headquarters. "Are the police here?" asked the unfortunate man. "Are you Pilati?" "Yes, I am Pilati." "Then you need not come," replied the Fascist, and emptied his revolver point-blank into Pilati's body. Pilati's wife lying by her husband's side, and their fourteen-year-old son being present, the Fascists ordered the woman not to mention names; otherwise they would kill her son. Having accomplished this exploit they then returned the way they came, while their comrades in the street fired at the windows of the neighboring houses so as to prevent the occupants from looking out and identifying the aggressors. . . .

Another squad went to the villa of Signor Consolo, a lawyer, in Via Timoteo Bertelli. Consolo had been arrested the preceding May on a charge of having helped to distribute the clandestine anti-Fascist paper *Non Mollare* ["Never Yield"] and acquitted after forty days' imprisonment. But if judges acquit, Fascists kill. During the evening Consolo's chambers had been wrecked and looted. He was at home with his wife and two children. Toward eleven o'clock somebody rang his street bell saying that there was an express letter to be delivered. Suspicious of their intentions, he refused to open the door and telephoned to the nearest police station for protection. The Fascists beat in his door. Leaving the telephone receiver on the table he hid in his children's room, between their two little beds. The telephone receiver transmitted automatically to the police station every noise that was made and every word that was said. Signora Consolo implored the Fascists who were searching for her husband to have pity. The two children started out of their sleep weeping. One of the Fascists drove Signora Consolo into a corner while three others entered the children's room. They fired eight shots. Five hit the target; three lodged in the wall. When a lorry load of police arrived from headquarters they found no one but the widow and children sobbing over the bleeding corpse. . . .

At Bergano, the secondary school teacher Fachery and the lawyer

Briolini were flogged. The Fascists looted the house of Count Secco Suardo and of Signor Gavazzeni, Member of Parliament. The first was ferociously beaten and forced to sign a declaration that no violence had been done to him. Signor Gavazzeni was dragged out of his house, beaten and spat at along the streets, and taken outside the city to a place where a gallows had been erected. The Fascists put a noose round his neck, lifted him on to a stool and kept him there for some time, as if they were about to hang him. Before letting him go, they beat him nearly to death. . . .

All the Christian-Democratic clubs of [Venice], about fifteen in all, save one, were wrecked.

At Trento, the Fascists wrecked the offices of the *Azione Cattolica* (headquarters of the Christian-Democratic organizations) and the headquarters of the . . . center of all the Christian-Democratic cooperatives of the district.

Hitler's Theories

The nature and aims of Nazism can be found in the speeches Adolf Hitler made long before he came to power. Those who treated him with disdain or indifference were soon shocked by the enthusiastic support he won for his cause. Hitler was a spellbinding orator and a masterly political organizer who combined socialism and nationalism in his appeal for mass support. The National Socialist Party vowed to avenge the humiliation of 1918 and restore Germany to prosperity and power.

At the center of Hitler's political creed was the pseudoscientific doctrine of the master race — the superior Germans needed room for expansion; the inferior Slavs would have to be exterminated or enslaved. Hitler fanned the German hatred of the Jews, using them as a scapegoat for all the ills of Germany. He well realized that his utterances did not have to be true as much as they had to be emotionally appealing. What the German people needed and wanted, he believed, was strength and leadership, and not interminable democratic discussions.

Hitler was able to win the support of many Germans, among whom were men of great power and wealth. During the economic depression and the political chaos of the early 1930's, millions flocked to his banner and looked to him for salvation. In 1932 he had the largest party in the German Reichstag (the lower house of the German legislature), though not a majority. His assumption of the Chancellorship in January 1933 was but a prelude to absolute dictatorship. Once in power, Hitler was as good as his word; and the brutality of his regime did not seem to detract from his support.

In the following selections Hitler's theories are presented in excerpts from his speeches.

Force and Struggle

In a speech delivered at Essen on November 22, 1926, Hitler said: The fundamental motif through all the centuries has been the principle that force and power are the determining factors. All development is struggle. Only force rules. Force is the first law. A struggle has already taken place between original man and his primeval world. Only through struggle have states and the world become great. If one should ask whether this struggle is gruesome, then the only answer could be: For the weak, yes, for humanity as a whole, no. . . .

Unfortunately, the contemporary world stresses internationalism instead of the innate values of race; democracy and the majority instead of the worth of the great leader. Instead of everlasting struggle the world preaches cowardly pacifism and everlasting peace. These three things, considered in the light of their ultimate consequences, are the causes of the downfall of all humanity. The practical result of conciliation among nations is the renunciation of a people's own strength and their voluntary enslavement. . . .

At Munich, March 15, 1929: If men wish to live, then they are forced to kill others. The entire struggle for survival is a conquest of the means of existence, which in turn results in the elimination of others from these same sources of subsistence. As long as there are peoples on this earth, there will be nations against nations and they will be forced to protect their vital rights in the same way as the individual is forced to protect his rights.

One is either the hammer or the anvil. We confess that it is our

FORCE AND STRUGGLE. Source: Gordon W. Prange, translator and editor, *Hitler's Words: Two Decades of National Socialism, 1923–1943,* Washington, D.C.: Public Affairs Press, 1944, pp. 4, 10–11. Reprinted by permission of the publishers.

purpose to prepare the German people again for the role of the hammer. For ten years we have preached, and our deepest concern is: How can we again achieve power? We admit freely and openly that if our movement is victorious, we will be concerned day and night with the question of how to produce the armed forces which are forbidden us by the peace treaty [Treaty of Versailles]. We solemnly confess that we consider everyone a scoundrel who does not. try day and night to figure out a way to violate this treaty, for we have never recognized this treaty. . . .

We will take every step which strengthens our arms, which augments the number of our forces, and which increases the strength of our people.

We confess further that we will dash anyone to pieces who should dare to hinder us in this undertaking. . . . Our rights will never be represented by others. Our rights will be protected only when the German Reich is again supported by the point of the German dagger.

Leadership

At Nuremberg, September 14, 1935: We will harden ourselves to such an extent that any storm will find us strong. We will never forget that the sum total of all virtues and all strength can be effective only when it is subservient to one will and to one command. . . . Nothing is possible unless one will commands, a will which has to be obeyed by others, beginning at the top and ending only at the very bottom. . . .

We must train our people so that whenever someone has been appointed to command, the others will recognize it as their duty to obey him, for it can happen that an hour later they will be called upon to command and they can do it then only if others in turn obey. This is the expression of an authoritarian state — not of a weak, babbling democracy — of an authoritarian state where everyone is proud to obey, because he knows: I will likewise be obeyed when I must take command.

LEADERSHIP. Source: *Ibid.*, pp. 126–27.

The Superiority of Aryans

At Munich, April 2, 1927: We see before us the Aryan race which is . . . the bearer of all culture, the true representative of all humanity. All inventions in the field of transportation must be credited to the members of a particular race. Our entire industrial science is without exception the work of the Nordics. All great composers from Beethoven to Richard Wagner are Aryans, even though they were born in Italy or France. Do not say that art is international. The tango, the shimmy, and the jazzband are international but they are not art. Man owes everything that is of any importance to the principle of struggle and to one race which has carried itself forward successfully. Take away the Nordic Germans and nothing remains. . . .

At Munich, November 21, 1927: From all the innumerable creatures a complete species rises and becomes the master of the rest. Such a one is man — the most brutal, the most resolute creature on earth. He knows nothing but the extermination of his enemies in the world. . . . This struggle, this battle, has not been carried on by all men in the same way. Certain species stand out, and at the top of the list is the Aryan. The Aryan has forged the weapons with which mankind has made itself master of the animal world. There is scarcely anything in existence which when traced back to its origin cannot claim an Aryan as its creator.

THE SUPERIORITY OF ARYANS. Source: *Ibid.*, pp. 5–6.

War and Expansion

At Munich, May 23, 1928: We admit that for us the future of Germany does not lie in a mechanical revision of frontiers. In such a case we would again be forced to rely upon world trade, which in turn would make us competitors of four or five other states. That is no future. The National Socialist Movement extends far beyond the deceitful level of such a . . . conception. It is the champion of that idea which claims that if we do not acquire more soil, then we shall some day perish. We pursue no policy which will not secure the existence of the people for all time. . . . I believe that I have enough energy to lead our people to war, and not for the revision of frontiers, but for the deliverance

WAR AND EXPANSION. Source: *Ibid.*, pp. 27–28.

of our people in the most distant future, so that our people acquires so much soil and territory that the sacrifice in blood can be returned to posterity in four-fold measure.

Democracy

In a speech at Hamburg on August 17, 1934 Hitler said: This parliamentary democracy of ruin has at all times destroyed peoples and states. It does not express the will of the people: it serves only the ambition and interests of conscienceless corrupters of the people, be they small or great.

The effect of this kind of government in Germany was disastrous. From the time when this parliamentary democracy had finally and completely mastered the nation there began a downfall in every sphere: not only in politics, in culture, and in morals was Germany disintegrated and weakened, but even in the sphere of economics those conditions were destroyed under which alone, in the last resort, such an enormously complex and sensitive organism can flourish. . . .

But it is clear that this political disintegration of the body of a people must necessarily mean the end of every authority. Without such an authority the economic life of a people cannot function healthily.

DEMOCRACY. Source: Norman H. Baynes, translator and editor, *The Speeches of Adolf Hitler, April 1922–August 1939*, London: Oxford University Press, under the auspices of the Royal Institute of International Affairs, 1942, Vol. I, pp. 452–53. Reprinted by permission of the publishers.

Culture

Hitler, in his conversation with Otto Strasser on May 21, 1930, is reported to have said: There is no such thing as a revolution in art: there is only one eternal art — the Greek-Nordic art, and all such terms as "Dutch art," "Italian art," "German art," are merely misleading and just as foolish as it is to treat Gothic as an individual form of art — all that is simply Nordic-Greek art and anything which deserves the name of art can always only be Nordic-Greek. . . . There is no such thing as Chinese or Egyptian art: the Chinese and Egyptian peoples were of

CULTURE. Source: *Ibid.*, Vol. I, p. 567.

mixed composition, and upon a body belonging to a people of lower race there was set a Nordic head which alone created the masterpieces which today we admire as Chinese or Egyptian art.

Freedom and Peace

May Day Speech, 1939: And with that I come to the problem of freedom in general. Freedom, yes! So far as the interest of the community of the people gives the individual freedom, it is given him. But at the point where his freedom harms the interests of the community of the people, at that point the freedom of the individual ceases and the freedom of the people steps into its place. And besides, in no state is intellectual achievement more highly valued than with us. I believe that one can see that even in the leadership. We fancy that in Germany there are, after all, men at the head of the state who in intellect can stand comparison with the representatives of other states. But high above all the freedom of the individual there is the freedom of our people, the freedom of our Reich; and the security of the German *Lebensraum* [living space] is for us the supreme law. That we love peace I do not need to stress. . . .

That I love peace appears perhaps most clearly from my work: in that lies the difference between me and these warmongers. What am I creating and what do these creatures do? I have here a great people, and for it I am responsible. I try to make this people great and happy.

FREEDOM AND PEACE. Source: *Ibid.*, Vol. II, pp. 1060–61.

The Significance of the Spanish Civil War

The Spanish Republic, created in 1931, was harassed by extremists of both the right and the left. Civil war broke out in July 1936 when a group of generals made an attempt to take over the government by force. Among the rebels General Francisco Franco soon emerged as the strongest power. The Fascist governments of Hitler and Mussolini sent enormous quantities of men and weapons to aid Franco's Nationalists; the Russians sent aid to the republican Loyalists. In the democratic countries sentiment was on the side of the Loyalists, but the policy of non-intervention adopted by Britain and France and the official neutrality of the United States prevented the Loyalists from acquiring the weapons they needed to fight the war. Thousands of young men from democratic nations, about 3,500 from the United States alone, fought alongside the Spanish Loyalists in the belief that they were defending democracy against Fascism.

Herbert L. Matthews, the author of the following selection, was in Spain during the Civil War as a correspondent for The New York Times.

So far as foreign intervention on the Loyalist side in Spain was concerned, the keynote was anti-Fascism. Are we forgetting what a real and deeply felt emotion the hatred of Fascism was in the 1930's? In the few years preceding the Spanish Civil War, Fascism had won great victories in Germany, Austria, and Abyssinia [Ethiopia] and was dangerously entrenched in Italy. A few months after the Civil War ended, the European democracies were involved in a life-and-death struggle against the Fascist powers, one that we were later to join.

The history of a period, the facts and the atmosphere in which they happened, must not and cannot honestly be rewritten simply because we now hold other ideas about the forces involved or because we possess the convenient instrument of hindsight. Such rewriting can be left to the Communists and Fascists who make their histories conform to the political conveniences of the moment. It would be dishonest to write and think of the Spanish Civil War in any other terms than what really did happen and the way that we felt them. The mistakes need correction — and Lord knows we all made plenty of them — but the truth does not change.

The Spanish Civil War did not turn out as most of us hoped. Loyalist Spain did not exemplify all the desires and ideals we harbored in those years. One way or another, there was cause for bitterness and disappointment. The good and the bad were mixed. . . . It was all a

Source: Herbert L. Matthews, *The Yoke and the Arrows*, New York: George Braziller, Inc., pp. 34–38. Copyright © 1957 by Herbert L. Matthews. Reprinted by permission of the publishers.

mess, one grand and glorious mess; but really glorious in some ways amid all the tragedy.

[Some men] cried out because they thought that the impossible could happen in Spain, that Utopia could have been built then and there. Spain had a quality in the Civil War which made people feel that way. The heartbreak had to come; a tragedy was being enacted. . . .

I, too, had that wish in the Spanish Civil War. . . .

Perhaps I was tragically wrong. I do not think so. No one will ever persuade me, for instance, that the men who came from all over the world to fight in Spain were clever or cynical or hypocritical, or that they were mere robots obeying orders (except for the few Russian leaders involved). I still say they fought against Fascism and — at the same time — for the democracy we know. I still say that a vast majority of them fought and died for the highest sort of moral principles. . . .

On the day Barcelona fell to the Navarrese, the Moors, the Germans, and Italians, Mussolini went out on the balcony of the Palazzo Venezia and cried to the throng that had been duly herded in the Square, . . . "General Franco's magnificent troops . . . have not only beaten Negrin's government, but many others of our enemies are now biting the dust."

That was fair enough, so to speak. We did, indeed, bite the dust, we Americans and British and French. If Mussolini was gloating a little too soon, it was not thanks to us but to the Spanish Republicans who fought so long and so hard against impossible odds, that Italy was too weak to join Germany when World War II started. Ciano * was constrained to tell Ribbentrop † that for three years Italy would not be again in a position to fight. . . .

It was at the last dramatic Cortes [parliament] of the Second Spanish Republic in the Castle of Figueras on February 1, 1939, that Negrin said, "Countries do not live only by victories, but by the examples which their people have known how to give in tragic times.". . .

Had Premier Negrin and the Popular Front, with its predominant Socialists and Republicans, won, Spain, I am still convinced, would not have gone Communist. That was one of the mistakes the democracies made. If Britain and France had fought at Munich-time in 1938,‡ while the Spanish Civil War was still on, they would have had Repub-

* **Galeazzo Ciano:** the Italian Foreign Minister.
† **Joachim von Ribbentrop:** the German Foreign Minister.
‡ **Munich-time:** a reference to the appeasement of Hitler. See page 178.

lican Spain at their side, a democratic Spain in our sense of the word. Instead, the Allies (including the United States) had to contend with a hostile Spain that maintained a formal neutrality but helped the Axis.

It is too soon for history to pass a final judgment. I am not pretending that my opinion or that of any contemporary can be final. . . .

As a war it was lost by democracy, won by reaction. Those who fought for freedom lost in terms of men, materials, territory, and power. As a page of Spanish and world history, it had a brightness that can never be lost, although that brightness seems hopelessly dimmed — and even denied — by so many Spaniards today. . . .

There was only one thing that could be safely predicted in those days. Back in 1937, as with many others who were in the midst of events, it was easy for me to call attention to the similarity of the Japanese aggression in China and the Nazi-Fascist aggressions and to make the obvious prediction that the lines would meet.

"The youth of the world is going to war," I wrote, "one in Africa, one in Europe, one in Asia, and who shall say there are not more to come? You who stroll along the Great White Way * thinking complacently how far away it all is from peaceful America — you, too, will feel a tap on your shoulder one of these days, and will hear the call."

We have learned some lessons since Spain. Korea was wonderful proof of that. In a sense Spain was a sacrifice, but it cannot be said that it was fought in vain. It was part of the world struggle against totalitarianism. . . . The issues were somewhat confused in Spain, but it is true to say that one evil was fought there for the first time. We should not forget that until September 1939 only one people and one half of a country fought Fascism.

That was the negative side, but the Civil War was, too, in its way, a fight for liberty and democracy. As such, in a material sense, it was lost; but it can await with confidence the verdict of history.

"Countries do not live only by victories. . . ."

* **Great White Way:** Broadway, a street in New York City, so called because of its many large and elaborate neon signs.

Hunger and Unemployment in Britain

In the face of crisis the tendency of the British is to pull together. The deep antagonisms of French society were not present in England, and the Communists and Fascists were never able to attract a large following. The Liberal Party, the Conservative Party, and the Labor Party were for the most part under the control of moderate men who were committed to the democratic government and evolutionary change traditional in Britain.

The depression of the early 1930's caused immense suffering as hunger and unemployment spread throughout the country. Voluntary groups took upon themselves the lion's share of the work in alleviating distress. Although the government could have displayed more vigor and imagination in dealing with these problems, it was by no means indifferent. Britain did have a welfare program which helped mitigate some of the worst hardships. But even for those people who found enough to eat, the effect of prolonged unemployment and idleness on morale and family life was devastating.

The state of Britain during the depression is discussed by the historian Charles L. Mowat.

There were several Englands, and their differences had never been more sharply drawn. . . . One was the old England of the southern counties and the guidebooks. The second was nineteenth-century England, the industrial north, the country of coal tips and silent blast furnaces and "thousands of rows of little houses all alike." Twentieth-century England was the England of the bustling home counties, of bypasses and housing estates and suburban villas and cocktail bars gleaming with chromium trim. The fourth England was the England of the dole. Its boundaries were much the same as those of nineteenth-century England; and if one's view took in the whole of Great Britain, it would

Source: Charles L. Mowat, *Britain Between the Wars*, London: Methuen & Co., Ltd., 1955, pp. 480–87. Reprinted by permission of the author and the publishers.

include all of industrial Scotland, all of South Wales, and parts of North Wales as well.

This sad, unemployed Britain was only dimly known to many in the comfortable classes in the south, though it could be seen almost anywhere in London and in the back streets of any of the larger towns; nor could anyone long miss the seedy beggars selling matches or shoelaces, or the Welsh miners, with mufflers round their throats, singing "Land of our Fathers" by the curbside. The stricken areas were, however, a land apart: much written of, but seldom visited by outsiders, save for the devoted social workers. . . .

The appearance of the derelict towns varied little. Everywhere you saw shops closed and boarded up, houses with peeling paint and broken slates. Only the pawnshops and the cinemas flourished, only the Labor Exchange drew its shabby crowd. . . . The only sign of life was the men standing at the street corners, with nothing to do, nothing to say. . . .

The unemployed fell into three categories: those out of work for a few weeks or months at a time, or drawing partial unemployment relief (those working three days or less per week); the young men who had never had work, or who had worked as youths only until they qualified for a man's wage; and the long unemployed, those who had been out of work for a year or longer and were unlikely — particularly the older men — ever to find work again. Those long unemployed were the most to be pitied. . . . Their numbers were greatest among the men aged sixty to sixty-four (at sixty-five unemployment relief ceased), and diminished in each lower age group; they were most numerous among miners, shipbuilders, cotton-trade operatives, and therefore most numerous in the areas of greatest distress. . . .

What did the state do for these [unneeded] working people? It did not provide relief work, though it did try to stimulate employment on public works by guaranteeing loans. The government's chief policy was simply to maintain the unemployed man and his family by payments of one sort or another from public funds [the dole]. . . .

Yet, however frustrating to the individual, the dole kept people alive, and it kept them on the safe side of discontent and thoughts of revolution. . . .

It was the social and psychological effects of unemployment which left the most lasting marks. Many men out of work accepted their fate, shrugging their shoulders: "Lots worse off than them. They all say that.". . . . Some might join a . . . class, like the Durham miner who took a five-year course in English literature; others found a use for their leisure in reading or in taking part in plays or joining in the other activities of a community house or unemployed men's club. Some went for long walks, . . . others played football, even if it meant a seven-mile walk to the game. Some . . . kept poultry, others did amateur carpentry in their backyards or at the club. In summer they might pick blackberries or mushrooms, and the younger ones might go for a swim. In the mining districts men often scrabbled for coal on the tips or pilfered it from stacks of railway wagons. Many found odd jobs canvassing for newspaper subscriptions or running with betting slips; others pursued the will o' the wisp of earning some money by succumbing to shady "make and sell" schemes advertised in the personal columns in the newspapers: send 2s. 6d. for a kit for making shoe polish to sell to your friends.

To the large majority unemployment meant apathy. . . . In many families the main problem was to keep warm and to conserve low energy. This was best done by staying in bed late and going to bed early; fuel, light, and effort were all thus saved. Going to the cinema serves these purposes also, as well as providing a passing distraction from boredom. . . . For many there was nothing to do when their wives drove them out of doors but to sit in the public library or to loaf at street corners, smoking fag ends of cigarettes or the used tea leaves they stuffed into their pipes. . . .

Others, again, felt lost, hopeless. Time was heavy when there was nothing to do. "It's like as if you were dead." Friends drop away, or one is ashamed to meet them in one's old, shabby clothes. Many came to a feeling not only of uselessness but of bitterness; the youth, thwarted of his manhood, the old man, robbed of the respect of his children, deprived of his self-respect as head of the household. . . .

Yet it was the women who suffered more than the men. Unemployment brought leisure for the men, if they chose to regard it so; it brought no rest to the wives and mothers. They must scrape and scrimp to feed and clothe the family, usually on less money than before, even if what there was was now fixed and regular. Very often the children were well cared for and healthy. If anyone in the family went short on food and clothes, it was the mother. For her the bitterness was unrelieved. In Durham it took the form of a resolve: no son of mine shall go into the [coal] pits; I'll see those children dead first.

156

The Transformation of Turkey

The Ottoman Empire was referred to as "the sick man of
Europe." After World War I its long-awaited death seemed to
be at hand. The Empire had fought on the losing side, and the
victors were about to carve it up when a Turkish nationalist
movement under the leadership of Mustafa Kemal proclaimed
that the harsh terms of the Allies were absolutely unacceptable.
This display of zeal was accompanied by a demonstration of
military strength as the Turks repelled an invasion by the Greeks.
A new treaty, which provided for an independent Turkey with
a strip of land in Europe, was drawn up by the Allies and signed
at Lausanne, Switzerland, in July 1923. On October 29, the Turkish Republic was formally proclaimed. Mustafa Kemal, who
became known as Atatürk, (first among Turks) was the first
president and, in effect, dictator. He undertook an extensive
program of reform and modernization.

The following account was written by an American who
lived and taught in Turkey for a number of years.

Atatürk, though no book scholar, . . . had an uncommonly
sound knowledge of human nature; he saw that the permanent changes
he envisioned for the Turks would have to start with a sharp, even painful, break with fixed habits and a strenuous initiation into unfamiliar
ways. Otherwise, new intentions would never stand up in old surroundings under the weight of old traditions. . . . New Turks had to start
new. . . . This was one reason, besides security, for moving the nation's
capital from Istanbul to Ankara, a village in the interior of the country,
and for insisting that foreigners, too, use the old city's Turkish name,
Istanbul, instead of its Roman name, Constantinople. Thereby, citizens
and foreigners as well were fully impressed that Constantinople was no
longer the seat of empire but was simply the largest Turkish city. But
changes had to penetrate into private life. The personal symbol of Ottoman [prerevolutionary] citizenship, the red fez,* must go. . . .

* **fez:** a brimless felt cap shaped like a cone with the top flattened out, usually
with a tassel attached.

Source: Eleanor Bisbee, *The New Turks: Pioneers of the Republic, 1920–1950,*
Philadelphia: University of Pennsylvania Press, 1951, pp. 21–23, 40–41, 87–88. Reprinted by permission of the publishers.

Greeks and Venetians had introduced the fez from [Africa] and had made it familiar wherever they traded. Sultan Mahmud II had borrowed it from them when he decreed at the beginning of the nineteenth century that the fez be worn as the symbol of Ottoman citizenship by all the races, religions, and nationalities in the Empire. . . . During the century that the fez was the Ottoman headdress, its significance had narrowed as the Empire shrank. It began to signify only Moslems. The Christians in nations which were freed from Ottoman rule . . . again wore brimmed hats. . . . Moslem subjects kept the fez, and Moslems outside of the Empire wore it too. Thereafter, to the Ottoman subjects the fez more and more meant the difference between the Moslem and the Christian. . . .

The order was appalling to carry out. After a specified date no man was to appear in public unless in a brimmed hat. There weren't that many hats in the whole country. Merchants in Christian countries rushed outmoded hats from their dustiest shelves to Turkey. In the meantime, laughable or not, a man who had to appear in public bought or borrowed any style of hat or cap, sometimes even a woman's hat with a brim. That first season, until proper hats were available, was a sore trial, yet it was endured successfully. The rest of the wardrobe was changed more easily. . . .

The strongest impact of the new freedom for women and girls was really upon the young unmarried Turks. Theretofore, boys and girls in urban communities had had literally no acquaintance with one another between childhood and marriage. Customarily, a youth never saw any maiden's face except his sister's until he lifted his bride's veil at the conclusion of their marriage ceremony. She, more often than not, had also never before set eyes on him. In spite of this code, liberal families did permit glimpses. "My father," one wife told me of her own engagement, "let me go to his office when everybody else was out at noon; he allowed me to peek through a crack in the shutters, and I saw my fiancé pass on his way to lunch. I thought he was very handsome," she concluded, with a reminiscent glow in her eyes. Today's children coax reminiscences like this from their parents and grandparents. They themselves, at the most susceptible age, meet openly in university classes, social affairs, or at work.

Do not, however, picture the Turks of the Republic's first generation entering into matrimony in United States style. Conversation about marriage among Turks is full of comments utterly foreign to us. Most noticeable is, "His parents have engaged him," or "Her parents have engaged her." Someone remarks, "Mehmet's parents have engaged him to Fatma," and eager inquiries follow: "Have they met?" "Are they in love?" And often also, "Are they related?" They may be cousins. Kinship is noted even to the eighth, tenth, or farther removed cousins, and many marriages are arranged inside of a large family circle. Now and then friends commiserate: "Ahmet's desperately unhappy; his parents have engaged him but——" The "but" can mean anything from "Ahmet doesn't want to marry yet," to "He's in love with another girl.". . .

The Republic's problem with children was novel. First, there were so disproportionately many of them of primary school age. This was due less to a high birth rate than to the high death rate of adults during Turkey's five wars in barely a dozen years, 1911–23. Second, all little Turks were to grow up using a changing language in a new script, under a government new to their parents, and in preparation for unaccustomed economic and social life in a scientific age also strange to most of their parents. And nearly all of these little Turks were from illiterate families whose adult members needed essentially the same education. . . . Centralized schools were out of the question for villages far apart, where the fastest transportation on trails, even when passable, would very likely be donkeys. The Turks, therefore, started to educate villagers to educate each other. From the farms, the Ministry of Education called, and still calls, certain farmers who own their own land, have completed their military service, and can read and write. In groups of ten they are assigned to selected farms for one year of instruction by certified teachers. Book learning occupies their mornings, and their afternoons are devoted to manual skills and farming methods. Farmers who pass the final examinations return to their villages as instructors in reading, writing, arithmetic, citizenship, elementary nature study, and better farming. . . .

Such temporary measures have made a significant dent in the overwhelming problem of primary education while permanent institutes to train village teachers are being established.

Gandhi's "Fast Unto Death"

Indian nationalism found in Mohandas K. Gandhi a saintly and magnetic leader. Gandhi, a lawyer by profession, was educated in England. The Mahatma (or the Great Soul) as he was called, rejected British civilization and sought to return India to a pre-industrial state. His fight for the independence of India was pursued with unusual and compelling weapons — passive resistance and the boycott.

A new constitutional reform for India which the British had proposed in 1932 provided that the Untouchables vote as a separate group to elect their own representatives. This separation had in fact been advocated by their leader, Dr. Ambedkar, so that the Untouchables would not be outnumbered by the caste Hindus in voting. Gandhi was convinced that Hindu feelings could be aroused to the plight of the Untouchables only if they remained within the Hindu fold. In September 1932, while he was in prison for civil disobedience, he vowed he would fast unto death unless this voting provision was changed. Conferences between the British and the leader of the Untouchables were immediately arranged. The unsatisfactory clause was removed and after five days Gandhi broke his fast. Gandhi's life was saved, but Dr. Ambedkar believed that by surrendering to Gandhi's wishes he had betrayed his own people.

The first selection describes the fast; the second, by Jawaharlal Nehru, discusses its effect throughout the country.

The Fast

At 11:30 A.M. he had his last meal of lemon juice and honey with hot water. The fateful hour approached. The little group prepared themselves for the ordeal by singing a beautiful song. . . . The jail bell at last struck twelve and with its last stroke was finally sealed a decision as fixed as the polestar and as irrevocable as fate. Gandhi's "tussle with God" had commenced. . . .

THE FAST. Source: Homer A. Jack, editor, *The Gandhi Reader: A Source Book of His Life and Writings*, Bloomington, Ind.: Indiana University Press, 1956, pp. 282–86. Reprinted by permission of the publishers.

Great anxiety was felt when Gandhi commenced his fast whether he would be able to stand the physical strain of it for any length of time. For one thing, he was not the same man as he was when he undertook his twenty-one days' fast at Delhi in 1924. He was eight years older now, which means a great deal to one who is already over sixty. Moreover, it was one thing to fast at Dilkash, near the Ridge, a free man, under the loving custodianship of a Charlie Andrews and the expert care of doctors . . . who knew his constitution and personal habits intimately, and quite another thing to fast in a segregated special yard in the Yeravda Prison under the surveillance of the jail authorities, who perhaps knew how to deal with a recalcitrant prisoner refusing to take food, but certainly had no experience of long fasts or of fasting men of Gandhi's type. In fairness to them it must be admitted that so far as personal solicitude for Gandhi was concerned they, from the very highest, left nothing to be desired. But they were handicapped by the red-tapism of jail regulations. . . .

On the morning of the twenty-first he was removed to a special segregated yard. There, under the thick shade of a low mango tree, on a white iron cot on which [were] spread a jail mattress and a jail bedsheet, he remained for the greater part of the day. His two companions . . . were there with him. Around the cot were placed a number of chairs for visitors. Near the cot, on one side, was a stool on which was to be found a . . . collection of odds and ends: books, papers, writing material, bottles of water, soda-bicarb, and salt. From time to time he would pour out some water from one of the bottles, in which he would dissolve soda and salt and sip it slowly according to need and inclination. . . .

Gandhi was as buoyant and cheerful as ever, and outwardly hardly betrayed any signs of a man who is racing against time and is being rushed with every second toward the abyss of the beyond. But to a close observer it did not take long to discover how fully conscious he was of the grim reality facing him. During his Delhi fast, for instance, one could not help being struck by the way in which he economized his strength. He had reduced it to a science. But now he simply did not mind. It was a limited fast then. He knew the period that he had to pull through. The present fast was going to be a "fast unto death." If he survived it, it would not be so much because of the efficacy of the medical measures that might be adopted but because God willed it. It was predominantly a spiritual wrestle in which the physical factor played

161

only a secondary part. Although the jail authorities had allowed him to have his own nurses, one could notice that he was extremely reluctant to avail himself of their services. What mattered a few more pangs or less of physical suffering to a man who was thirsting only for the grace abounding of the Almighty, and who in any case would soon be beyond all pain? Nor could Gandhi forget even for a moment that he was still a prisoner and that whatever facilities he was allowed were by way of a privilege. And everybody who has come in close touch with Gandhi knows how disinclined temperamentally he is to avail himself of any special privileges of this kind. . . . During his Delhi fast, he used to take water with scientific precision hourly. On the present occasion he did it only in a haphazard way. The physical exertion, as also the strain caused by speaking, induced nausea at an early stage. As the fast proceeded and the body tissue burned away, his whole frame was racked by excruciating aches — those terrible aches which at Delhi had to be alleviated by frequent massage and shampoo and a variety of other means. . . .

Warning signals were not, however, lacking to remind all concerned that there was a limit beyond which flesh and blood could not go. The physical exhaustion grew with every hour that passed. The voice grew feebler. [It was] only when, now and then in the course of animated discussions, his eyes shone and the face lit up that one felt the presence of an indomitable will that had remained unaffected in spite of the ravages on the body. . . .

On the twenty-fourth, Dr. Gilder and Dr. Patel of Bombay, after examining Gandhi in consultation with the jail doctors, opined that the margin of safety would soon be passed if unnecessary interviews and the strain of negotiations that were being carried on with him were not stopped. . . .

On the twenty-sixth the prognosis became alarming. . . .

The morning and evening prayer appointments were kept as punctiliously as ever, Gandhi always sitting up in his bed for prayer. . . . From early in the morning, as soon as the jail opened, an endless round of interviews, meetings with friends and visitors, and consultations with the members of the conference that was deliberating outside would commence and continue — with a brief lull at noon, when he would have a bath . . . and steal a brief nap — till late in the night sometimes. To this was added the pressure of attending to his daily mailbag. Letters, telegrams, messages containing all sorts of suggestions, . . . and even personal requests came pouring in in increasing volume till they threatened to swamp Gandhi's little secretariat in the Yeravda Prison.

The Effect

Our peaceful and monotonous routine in jail was suddenly upset in the middle of September 1932 by a bombshell. News came that Gandhi had decided to "fast unto death.". . . What a capacity he had to give shocks to people. . . . For two days·I was in darkness with no light to show the way out, my heart sinking when I thought of some results of Gandhi's action. . . . I thought with anguish that I might not see him again. It was over a year ago that I had seen him last on board ship on the way to England. Was that going to be my last sight of him?

And then I felt annoyed with him for choosing a side issue for his final sacrifice. What would be the result on our freedom movement? Would not the larger issues fade into the background, for the time being at least? . . .

So I thought and thought, while confusion reigned in my head, with anger and hopelessness and love for him who was the cause of this upheaval. I hardly knew what to do, and I was irritable and short-tempered with everybody, most of all with myself.

And then a strange thing happened to me. I had quite an emotional crisis, and at the end of it I felt calmer and the future seemed not so dark. Bapu [Gandhi] had a curious knack of doing the right thing at the psychological moment, and it might be that this action — impossible to justify as it was from my point of view — would lead to great results, not only in the narrow field in which it was confined but in the wider aspects of our national struggle. And even if Bapu died, our struggle for freedom would go on. So whatever happened, one had to keep ready and fit for it. Having made up my mind to face even Gandhi's death without flinching, I felt calm and collected and ready to face the world and all it might offer.

Then came news of the tremendous upheaval all over the country, a magic wave of enthusiasm running through Hindu society, and untouchability appeared to be doomed. What a magician, I thought, was

THE EFFECT. Source: Jawaharlal Nehru, *Toward Freedom*, New York: The John Day Company, Inc., 1941, pp. 236–38. Reprinted by permission of the publishers.

this little man sitting in Yeravda Prison, and how well he knew how to pull the strings that move people's hearts!

A telegram from him reached me. It was the first message I had received from him since my conviction, and it did me good to hear from him after that long interval. In this telegram he said:

During all these days of agony you have been before mind's eye. I am most anxious to know your opinion. You know how I value your opinion. Saw Indu [and] Sarup's children. Indu looked happy and in possession of more flesh. Doing very well. Wire reply. Love.

It was extraordinary, and yet it was characteristic of him that in the agony of his fast and in the midst of his many preoccupations he should refer to the visit of my daughter and my sister's children to him, and even mention that Indira had put on flesh! (My sister was also in prison then, and all these children were at school in Poona.) He never forgets the seemingly little things in life which really mean so much.

Disunion and Conflict in China

China was in a state of disintegration when General Chiang Kai-shek assumed the leadership of the Kuomintang (Nationalist Party) in 1925 on the death of Dr. Sun Yat-sen. The central government exercised little authority, and independent warlords defied it with impunity. The Kuomintang itself was made up of a number of groups including Communists and Nationalists. Under Chiang's leadership the country became more unified and a broad program of reform was planned. The Communists were expelled from the Kuomintang in 1927 and mercilessly persecuted.

China was hardly in a position to offer effective resistance when the Japanese embarked on a new policy of aggression in 1931. In spite of the stubborn courage of the Chinese armies and a temporary truce between the Communists and the Nationalists, Japan overran a sizable portion of the country. Meanwhile

Chiang's reform program languished, and corruption became widespread. As discontent grew the Communists made headway, especially among the peasants.

The decline of the Chinese Nationalists from the 1930's to the Communist takeover in 1949 is analyzed by Professor John K. Fairbank of Harvard University.

In the Nationalist Revolution of the 1920's Dr. Sun and his successors learned that the road to national unity and central power lay through movements and mass mobilization which utilized doctrines of democracy and the people's livelihood. . . .

In the twenty years after they came to power, the Kuomintang leaders became conservatives increasingly concerned with the preservation of power. This is one of the oldest political phenomena in history. Beginning as revolutionists seeking to construct a new order, they became oligarchs in defense of it, or rather of their power, displaying . . . the . . . fixity of purpose and ruthlessness characteristic of self-made men. . . .

To those who saw the old China before the Kuomintang came to power and can recall the idealism, vigor, and efficiency of some of that Party's early administrators, the evils which grew up within it during the Japanese war are hard to believe. . . .

By retaining personal power, the Kuomintang leaders devitalized their organization. Politically they marked time. . . . The best men among them knew how to modernize China technologically. But they were unable to mobilize the back country in a continuing social revolution. The revolution consequently passed them by. . . .

[The grip of the Kuomintang] . . . depended partly on its prestige; and one constant aim of its Chinese Communist opponents was to undermine its moral repute through radio and press as well as by more ancient methods of rumor and propaganda. In this the Communists had the greatest help from the bad record of the government itself. In meeting China's limitless problems it committed, through the person of its corrupt administrators, infinite mistakes. The postwar takeover process, when carpetbagging generals and politicians returned to the coastal prov-

Source: John K. Fairbank, *The United States and China*, rev. ed., Cambridge, Mass.: Harvard University Press, 1958, pp. 184, 222–24, 226–27. Reprinted by permission of the publishers.

inces and Formosa, was as shameful a record of official looting as modern history has displayed. The inflation made official salaries shrink out of sight. Graft took their place. But self-seeking and corruption seem to have been intensified by the officials' loss of confidence in the government's future. . . .

The government was thus obliged to shift from a reliance on its moral prestige to an increasing reliance on naked force. . . . Men who believed in secret police, thought control, and suppression of opposition gained an ascendancy. This produced government action like the punishment of critics, not justifiable in principle but based purely on force. The result was to antagonize formerly loyal elements. This weakened the regime. This increasing weakness being perceived, further reliance was placed upon force.

Only some such theory can explain the repeated acts by which the Kuomintang right wing lost the support of the intellectual and professional classes. Time after time government use of force against intellectuals served only to weaken its position among them. The public humiliation and beating of demonstrating students, who were mostly non-Communist, turned them toward Communism. In this way, the advocates of force obliged the government to rely on nothing else. Party dictatorship, while not an absolute power, became absolutely corrupted. . . .

One long-term factor in the Communist rise to power was Japan's continuous effort at military conquest, which roused the Chinese people for patriotic political action but weakened the Nationalist government's capacity to lead them in other than military ways.

Japan's attack, from 1931 on, obliged the Kuomintang to continue militarizing in self-defense. Its resources went into its armies, it leadership into the hands of a Generalissimo, its policies became more conservative and militaristic. . . .

Meanwhile, Japan's war machine, conquering cities, . . . burning villages, squeezing the economy, bombing Free China, roused the student youth and the peasant populace for a movement of resistance and national survival which went far beyond the military sphere. Millions of persons were displaced, some fourteen million men conscripted, families broken up, vested interests destroyed, markets lost — the social order over wide areas was thoroughly disrupted. The student youth and the peasant populace were both subjected to violent social changes and so prepared for revolutionary programs of action.

166

The immediate underlying factor in the Communist rise to power was the Kuomintang's failure to lead the country in a program of creative action.

Free China had the wherewithal in men and ideas. . . . [But] the Nationalist government lacked the vitality to mobilize and lead. Intent on holding power, it distrusted the enthusiasm of private agencies and individuals. It feared change in a rapidly changing world. Its failure in political leadership gave the Communists an opportunity which they otherwise might not have had.

The Japanese Attack China

The first nation in the interwar years to demonstrate that overt aggression could bring handsome rewards without any serious penalties from the League of Nations was Japan. The Japanese were anxious to protect and expand their interests in Manchuria. The Chinese, meanwhile, were trying to find a way to undermine the Japanese position. Without consulting the cabinet, the Japanese army decided to settle the matter by force. In September 1931 an "incident" was planned which provided an excuse for a military campaign. Manchuria was soon detached from China and became Manchukuo, a Japanese puppet state. While the League appointed a commission to investigate, the Japanese continued fighting until they had the situation well under control. Had it not been for Chinese resistance and threats by the United States, they would have continued in their conquest. An existing nine-power treaty to protect the sovereignty of China was not even invoked. When the Japanese were condemned as aggressors by the League, they simply withdrew from the organization.

The following extract is from the Report of the League Commission on the Mukden Incident.

167

On the morning of Saturday, September 19, the population of Mukden woke to find their city in the hands of Japanese troops. During the night sounds of firing had been heard, but there was nothing unusual in this; it had been a nightly experience throughout the week, as the Japanese had been carrying out night maneuvers involving vigorous rifle and machine-gun firing. . . .

Appreciating the great importance of this occurrence, which as will be shown, was the first step of a movement which resulted in the military occupation of practically the whole of Manchuria, the Commission conducted an extensive enquiry into the events of that night. Of great value and interest, of course, were the official accounts of the Japanese and Chinese military leaders involved. . . .

According to the Japanese versions, Lieutenant Kawamoto, with six men under his command, was on patrol duty on the night of September 18, practicing defense exercises along the track of the South Manchuria Railway to the north of Mukden. They were proceeding southward in the direction of Mukden. The night was dark but clear and the field of vision was not wide. When they reached a point at which a small road crosses the line, they heard the noise of a loud explosion a little way behind them. They turned and ran back, and after going about two hundred yards they discovered that a portion of one of the rails on the down track had been blown out. The explosion took place at the point of junction of two rails; the end of each rail had been cleanly severed, creating a gap in the line of thirty-one inches. On arrival at the site of the explosion, the patrol was fired upon from the fields on the east side of the line. Lieutenant Kawamoto immediately ordered his men to deploy and return the fire. The attacking body, estimated at about five or six, then stopped firing and retreated northward. The Japanese patrol at once started in pursuit and, having gone about two hundred yards, they were again fired upon by a larger body, estimated at between three and four hundred. Finding himself in danger of being surrounded by this large force, Lieutenant Kawamoto then ordered one of his men to report to the Commander of No. 3 Company, who was also engaged in night maneuvers some fifteen hundred yards to the north; at the same

Source: League of Nations, *Appeal by the Chinese Government, Report of the Commission of Enquiry* (Lytton Report), Series of the League of Nations Publications, Political, Geneva, 1932, VII.12, pp. 67–71. Reprinted by permission of the Publications Board of the United Nations.

time he ordered another of his men to telephone (by means of a box telephone near the spot) to battalion headquarters at Mukden for reinforcements.

At this moment the southbound train from Changchun was heard approaching. Fearing that the train might be wrecked when it reached the damaged line, the Japanese patrol interrupted their engagement and placed detonators on the line in the hope of warning the train in time. The train, however, proceeded at full speed. When it reached the site of the explosion it was seen to sway and heel over to one side, but it recovered and passed on without stopping. As the train was due at Mukden at 10:30 P.M., where it arrived punctually, it must have been about 10 P.M., according to Lieutenant Kawamoto, when he first heard the explosion.

Fighting was then resumed. . . . Two [Japanese] companies . . . arrived a little after midnight.

Lieutenant Colonel Shimamoto at once ordered an attack on the [Chinese] barracks, . . . and by 6 A.M. the entire barracks was captured. . . .

According to the Chinese version, the Japanese attack on the barracks . . . was entirely unprovoked and came as a complete surprise. On the night of September 18, all the soldiers of the Seventh Brigade, numbering about ten thousand men, were in the north barracks. . . . As instructions had been received . . . that special care was to be taken to avoid any clash with the Japanese troops in the tense state of feeling existing at the time, the sentries at the walls of the barracks were only armed with dummy rifles. . . . The Japanese had been carrying out night maneuvers around the barracks on the nights of September 14, 15, 16, and 17. At 7 P.M. on the evening of the eighteenth, they were maneuvering at a village called Wenkuantun. At 9 P.M. Officer Liu reported that a train composed of three or four coaches, but without the usual type of locomotive, had stopped there. At 10 P.M. the sound of a loud explosion was heard, immediately followed by rifle fire. This was reported over the telephone by the Chief of Staff to the commanding officer, General Wang I-cheh, who was at his private house situated near the railway, about six or seven miles from the barracks. . . . While the Chief of Staff was still at the telephone, news was brought to him that the Japanese were attacking the barracks and that two sentries had been wounded. . . . As soon as the attack began, the Chief of Staff gave orders for the lights to be extinguished, and again reported to General Wang I-cheh by telephone. The latter replied that no resistance was to be offered. . . .

As soon as they were all assembled, the Chinese troops left the village on the early morning of the nineteenth [and] . . . made their way to a village near Kirin. . . . They left their trains thirteen miles outside Mukden, separated into nine groups, and marched round Mukden by night. To escape detection by the Japanese, General Wang I-cheh himself rode through the town disguised as a peasant. In the morning the Japanese obtained news of their presence and sent airplanes to bomb them. They were obliged to lie hidden by day, but continued their march at night. Eventually they reached a station on the Peiping–Mukden railway, and here they were able to order seven trains which brought them to Shanhaikwan by October 4.

Such are the two stories of the so-called incident of September 18 as they were told to the Commission by the participants on both sides. . . .

After a thorough consideration . . . of the accounts of the interested parties . . . and a careful weighing of the great mass of evidence, . . . the Commission has come to the following conclusions:

Tense feeling undoubtedly existed between the Japanese and Chinese military forces. The Japanese, as was explained to the Commission, . . . had a carefully prepared plan to meet the case of possible hostilities between themselves and the Chinese. On the night of September 18/19, this plan was put into operation with swiftness and precision. The Chinese . . . had no plan of attacking the Japanese troops or of endangering the lives and property of Japanese nationals at this particular time or place. They made no concerted or authorized attack . . . [and] were surprised by the Japanese attack and subsequent operations. The military operations of the Japanese troops during this night, which have been described above, cannot be regarded as measures of legitimate self-defense.

Italy Overruns Ethiopia

The lessons of Japanese aggression and German contempt for the Treaty of Versailles were not lost on Mussolini, who was bursting to win an empire for Italy. Mussolini's victim was backward Ethiopia, which had soundly defeated an invading Italian army at the end of the nineteenth century. After creating the necessary "incidents," the Italian army invaded Ethiopia in October 1935. Using tanks, planes, and poison gas, the Italians easily prevailed over the primitive Ethiopians. The League responded to Mussolini's aggression by imposing economic sanctions against Italy. These sanctions had so many loopholes and the great powers were so reluctant to offend Mussolini that he was able to complete his conquest unhindered.

On June 30, 1936, the Emperor Haile Selassie made a moving appeal for help before the League of Nations. After his country's defeat in May 1936 he lived in England. He returned to Ethiopia in 1941 with the advancing British army.

I, Haile Selassie I, Emperor of Ethiopia, am here today to claim that justice which is due to my people and the assistance promised it eight months ago, when fifty nations asserted that aggression had been committed in violation of international treaties. . . .

There is no precedent for a head of state himself speaking in this Assembly, but there is also no precedent for a people being the victim of such injustice and of being at present threatened by abandonment to an aggressor.

Also, there has never before been an example of any government proceeding with the systematic extermination of a nation by barbarous means, in violation of the most solemn promises made to all the nations of the earth that there should be no resort to a war of conquest, and that there should not be used against innocent human beings terrible poison and harmful gases.

It is to defend a people struggling for its age-old independence that the head of the Ethiopian Empire has come to Geneva to fulfill this supreme duty after having himself fought at the head of his armies. . . .

Source: *The New York Times,* July 1, 1936. Copyright by *The New York Times.* Reprinted by permission of the publisher.

It is my duty here to inform the governments assembled at Geneva — responsible as they are for the lives of men, women, and children — of the deadly peril which threatens them, by describing to them the fate which has been suffered by Ethiopia. It is not only upon the warriors that the Italian government has made war. It has above all attacked populations far removed from hostilities in order to terrorize and exterminate them. . . .

The appeals of my Delegates addressed to the League of Nations had remained without answer. . . . I decided myself to come and bear witness against the crime perpetrated against my people and to give Europe warning of the doom that awaits it if it should bow before the accomplished fact. . . .

In October 1935 the . . . nations who are listening to me today gave me assurance that the aggressor would not triumph, that the resources of the covenant [of the League of Nations] would be employed to insure the reign of right and the failure of violence. I ask those . . . nations not to forget today the policy upon which they embarked eight months ago and on the faith of which I directed the resistance of my people against the aggressor whom they denounced to the world. . . .

Counting on the faith due to treaties, I made no preparation for war. . . . My confidence had been confirmed by repeated declarations made in the Council to the effect that aggression must not be rewarded and that force would end by being compelled to bow before right. . . .

What is to become of the promises made to me? . . .

I assert that the problem submitted to the Assembly today is much wider than merely a question of settlement of Italian aggression; it is collective security, it is the very existence of the League. . . . In a word, it is international morality that is at stake. . . .

Of the powers who have promised to guarantee the collective security of small states and who raise the threat that they may one day suffer the fate of Ethiopia, I ask: What measures do you intend to take? Representatives of the world, I have come to Geneva to discharge in your midst the most painful of duties for the head of a state. What reply have I to take back to my people?

German Troops Occupy the Rhineland

Once Hitler had secured himself as absolute dictator of Germany he was able to turn his attention to issues of foreign policy. With daring and skill and with an instinctive talent for sizing up his opponents, he proceeded to defy and destroy the Treaty of Versailles. German reparation payments were stopped. When the League of Nations refused to allow Germany to rearm, Hitler withdrew from the League (October 1933) and later announced that Germany was rearming (March 1935). While Britain, France, and Italy were involved in the Ethiopian crisis, he repudiated the Locarno nonaggression pacts and sent German troops to occupy the demilitarized Rhineland (March 1936). Hitler knew that his armies were not yet strong enough to resist France and so ordered a retreat in the event of a French attack. He gambled on his hunch that the democracies would shrink from taking action against him. As it turned out, France, unable to count on British support, would not move alone. The English government made official protestations, but actually felt that Hitler was not altogether unjustified in remilitarizing German territory.

After each act of aggression Hitler was always quick to assure the world that he would ask for nothing more. Until Britain and France declared war in September 1939 his technique of frightening and reassuring his opponents was remarkably successful.

The following account of the remilitarization of the Rhineland is by William L. Shirer, an American journalist and a correspondent for The New York Times.

Berlin, March 8, 1936. Hitler has got away with it! France is not marching. Instead it is appealing to the League! No wonder the faces of Hitler and Göring and Blomberg and Fritsch were all smiles this

Source: William L. Shirer, *Berlin Diary*, New York: Alfred A. Knopf, Inc., pp. 55–56, 58. Copyright 1940, 1941 by William L. Shirer. Reprinted by permission of the publishers.

noon as they sat in the royal box at the State Opera and for the second time in two years celebrated in a most military fashion Heroes Memorial Day, which is supposed to mark the memory of the two million Germans slain in the last war.

Oh, the stupidity (or is it paralysis?) of the French! I learned today on absolute authority that the German troops which marched into the demilitarized zone of the Rhineland yesterday had strict orders to beat a hasty retreat if the French army opposed them in any way. They were not prepared or equipped to fight a regular army. That probably explains Blomberg's white face yesterday. Apparently Fritsch (Commander in Chief of the Reichswehr) and most of the generals opposed the move, but Blomberg, who has a blind faith in the Führer and his judgment, talked them into it. It may be that Fritsch, who loves neither Hitler nor the Nazi regime, consented to go along on the theory that if the coup failed, that would be the end of Hitler; if it succeeded, then one of his main military problems was solved. . . .

And the French are appealing to Geneva! I called our London office to see what the British are going to do. They laughed and read me a few extracts from the Sunday press. Garvin's Sunday *Observer* and Rothermere's *Sunday Dispatch* are delighted at Hitler's move. The British are now busy restraining the French! The Foreign Office here, which kept open tonight to watch the reaction from Paris and London, is in high spirits. No wonder!

The Meeting Between Hitler and the Austrian Chancellor

Hitler's most cherished ambition was to unite Austria with Germany. Such a union had been opposed by the victorious powers after World War I, although there had been some sentiment for it in Austria. Hitler worked on this sentiment and directed the activities of the Austrian Nazis who supported him. An attempted Nazi take-over of the Austrian government in 1934 ended in failure. Hitler nevertheless continued his propaganda barrage. He eventually found an ally in Mussolini, and he be-

came increasingly convinced that the democracies would not fight to protect Austrian independence.

In February 1938 Hitler invited Austrian Chancellor Kurt von Schuschnigg to his retreat in Berchtesgaden. There Schuschnigg was browbeaten into giving major concessions to the Austrian Nazis. Not long after he returned, he was forced to resign under threat of invasion by Hitler. The new Austrian Chancellor was a Nazi who took his orders directly from the Führer. The German army was now invited to march into Austria to help "restore order," and the union of Austria and Germany was brought about in March 1938. The usual protests were made by the democracies, and Hitler gave the usual assurance that he had no further territorial ambitions.

Hitler's behavior toward Schuschnigg, as recounted by the Austrian Chancellor, provides some insight into the character of the Führer.

The twelfth of February, 1938, the day of my interview with Adolf Hitler at his mountain retreat . . . will forever remain one of the darkest and most fateful days in the annals of Austria. . . .

It was the beginning of the end. . . .

The following conversation . . . I have written down from memory; it covers only the essential — or at least the significant — passages.

I: This room, with its wonderful view, has doubtless been the scene of many a decisive conference. . . .

Hitler: Yes, in this room my thoughts ripen. But we did not get together to speak of the fine view or of the weather.

I: First of all, Herr Reichskanzler, I would like to thank you that you have given me the opportunity for this meeting. I would like to assure you that we take the treaty between our two countries which we signed in July 1936 very seriously, and that we are most anxious to remove all of the remaining misunderstandings and difficulties. In any case, we have done everything to prove that we intend to follow a policy friendly toward Germany in accordance with our mutual agreement.

Hitler: So you call this a friendly policy, Herr Schuschnigg? On the contrary, you have done everything to avoid a friendly policy. For in-

Source: Kurt von Schuschnigg, *Austrian Requiem*, translated by Franz von Hildebrand, New York: G. P. Putnam's Sons, 1946, pp. 3, 12–17. Reprinted by permission of the publishers.

stance, you quite complacently remained a member of the League of Nations, in spite of the fact that the Reich withdrew from the League. And you call that a friendly policy?

I: Nobody asked Austria to withdraw from the League of Nations. We could not assume that such a step was expected of us, for at the time of our agreement, in July 1936, Germany had long since left the League without ever stipulating that Austria do the same. We were rather of the opinion that our presence in the League could be useful to our common cause. . . .

Hitler: Anyway, it is self-evident that you had to leave the League. Besides, Austria has never done anything that would be of any help to Germany. The whole history of Austria is just one uninterrupted act of high treason. That was so in the past and is no better today. . . .

I: Herr Reichskanzler, I am fully aware of your attitude toward the Austrian question and toward the history of my country. And you will understand that my opinion in these questions differs basically from yours. For us Austrians our entire history is an essential and inseparable part of German history. Austria's contribution in this respect is considerable.

Hitler: Absolutely zero — I am telling you — absolutely zero. Every national idea was sabotaged by Austria throughout history; and indeed, all this sabotage was the chief activity of the Hapsburgs and the Catholic Church.

I: All the same, Herr Reichskanzler, many an Austrian contribution cannot possibly be separated from the general picture of German culture. . . .

Hitler: That's as may be. I am telling you once more that things cannot go on in this way. I have a historic mission, and this mission I will fulfill because Providence has destined me to do so. I thoroughly believe in this mission; it is my life. And I believe in God; I am a religious man. . . . Consider what I have achieved. Today there are no parties, no classes, no dissensions in the German people. They all want the same thing. There is but one will. True, I had thought I could bring this about in another manner. I wanted to unite the nation in the two great churches — the Catholic and a united Protestant church — and solve my task with their help. But this appeared impracticable because the churches refused to cooperate. Therefore I decided that my task would be achieved without the churches — and if necessary despite the churches. Who is not with me will be crushed. . . . Wherever I go I need the police only to keep the masses back, to save them from being trampled, to curb their boundless enthusiasm — but not for my protection.

I: Herr Reichskanzler, I am quite willing to believe that. . . .

Hitler: . . . I am telling you that I am going to solve the so-called Austrian problem one way or the other. Do you imagine that I don't know that you are fortifying your border against the Reich?

I: That is not true.

Hitler: Oh, no? You have made rather ridiculous efforts to mine the bridges and roads leading to the Reich.

I: If such a thing were done I should have heard about it. . . .

Hitler: I have only to give an order, and in one single night all your ridiculous defense mechanisms are blown to bits. You don't seriously believe that you can stop me or even delay me for half an hour, do you? Who knows? Perhaps you will wake up one morning in Vienna to find us there — just like a spring storm. And then you'll see something. I would very much like to save Austria from such a fate, because such an action would mean blood. After the army, my SA and the Austrian Legion would move in, and nobody could stop their just revenge — not even I. Do you want to make another Spain of Austria? I would like to avoid all that — if possible.

I: I shall investigate the matter and will have any defense work on the German border stopped. I am fully aware that you can invade Austria but, Herr Reichskanzler, whether we like it or not, that would mean bloodshed. We are not alone in this world, and such a step would probably mean war.

Hitler: It is easy enough to talk of war while we are sitting here in our comfortable easy chairs. But war means endless misery for millions. Do you want to take this responsibility upon yourself, Herr Schuschnigg? Don't think for one moment that anybody on earth is going to thwart my decisions. Italy? I see eye to eye with Mussolini; the closest ties of friendship bind me to Italy. And England? England will not move one finger for Austria. . . . And France? Well, three years ago we marched on the Rhineland with a handful of battalions; that was the time I risked everything. If France had stopped us then we would have had to retreat perhaps sixty kilometers or so, and even then we could have stopped them there. But now it is too late for France. The world must know that it is unbearable for a great power like Germany to have every little state on her borders believe that it can provoke her.

Appeasement at Munich

Hitler barely had time to digest Austria before he turned his glance toward Czechoslovakia. For some years, aroused by German propaganda and the activities of Nazi sympathizers, the three million Germans in Czechoslovakia had clamored for union with Germany. While Hitler prepared his army for war, his aim was to frighten his enemies into conceding peacefully all that he wanted. The Czechs, relying on their French allies and British friends, refused to be intimidated by Hitler. The British and the French, meanwhile, sought out Hitler and, over the protests of the Czechs, signed an agreement at Munich on September 30, 1938. The Munich Pact gave portions of Czechoslovakia to Germany and left the Czechs a crippled economy and an ineffective system of defense. All parties to the Munich Pact (which included Italy) gave vows of eternal peace. Not until Hitler gobbled up the remainder of Czechoslovakia in the spring of 1939 was the policy of appeasement discredited and abandoned. When German troops invaded Poland on September 1, 1939, Britain and France declared war.

The following debate took place in the British House of Commons after Prime Minister Neville Chamberlain returned triumphantly from Munich bringing "peace in our time." Clement Attlee was at that time the Leader of the Opposition (the British Labor Party).

The Prime Minister (Mr. Chamberlain): . . . Before I come to describe the Agreement which was signed at Munich in the small hours of Friday morning last, I would like to remind the House of two things which I think it is very essential not to forget when those terms are being considered. The first is this: We did not go there to decide whether the predominantly German areas in the Sudetenland should be passed over to the German Reich. That had been decided already. Czechoslovakia had accepted the Anglo-French proposals. What we had to consider was the method, the conditions, and the time of the transfer of the territory. The second point to remember is that time was

Source: House of Commons, *Parliamentary Debates*, Fifth Series, Vol. 339, October 3, 1938, columns 40–66. Reprinted by permission.

one of the essential factors. All the elements were present on the spot for the outbreak of a conflict which might have precipitated the catastrophe. We had populations inflamed to a high degree; we had extremists on both sides ready to work up and provoke incidents; we had considerable quantities of arms which were by no means confined to regularly organized forces. Therefore it was essential that we should quickly reach a conclusion, so that this painful and difficult operation of transfer might be carried out at the earliest possible moment and concluded as soon as was consistent with orderly procedure, in order that we might avoid the possibility of something that might have rendered all our attempts at peaceful solution useless. . . .

Before giving a verdict upon this arrangement, we should do well to avoid describing it as a personal or a national triumph for anyone. The real triumph is that it has shown that representatives of four great powers can find it possible to agree on a way of carrying out a difficult and delicate operation by discussion instead of by force of arms, and thereby they have averted a catastrophe which would have ended civilization as we have known it. The relief [over] our escape from this great peril of war has, I think, everywhere been mingled in this country with a profound feeling of sympathy — [Honorable Members: "Shame."] I have nothing to be ashamed of. Let those who have hang their heads. We must feel profound sympathy for a small and gallant nation in the hour of their national grief and loss.

Mr. Bellenger: It is an insult to say it.

The Prime Minister: I say in the name of this House and of the people of this country that Czechoslovakia has earned our admiration and respect for her restraint, for her dignity, for her magnificent discipline in face of such a trial as few nations have ever been called upon to meet. . . .

I pass from that subject, and I would like to say a few words in respect of the various other participants, besides ourselves, in the Munich Agreement. After everything that has been said about the German Chancellor today and in the past, I do feel that the House ought to recognize the difficulty for a man in that position to take back such emphatic declarations as he had already made amid the enthusiastic cheers of his supporters, and to recognize that in consenting, even though it were only at the last moment, to discuss with the representatives of other Powers those things which he had declared he had already decided once for all, was a real and a substantial contribution on

179

his part. With regard to Signor Mussolini, his contribution was certainly notable and perhaps decisive. It was on his suggestion that the final stages of mobilization were postponed for twenty-four hours to give us an opportunity of discussing the situation. . . .

Ever since I assumed my present office my main purpose has been to work for the pacification of Europe, for the removal of those suspicions and those animosities which have so long poisoned the air. The path which leads to appeasement is long and bristles with obstacles. The question of Czechoslovakia is the latest and perhaps the most dangerous. Now that we have got past it, I feel that it may be possible to make further progress along the road to sanity.

In our relations with other countries everything depends upon there being sincerity and good will on both sides. I believe that there are sincerity and good will on both sides in this declaration. . . .

Mr. Attlee: We all feel relief that war has not come this time. Every one of us has been passing through days of anxiety; we cannot, however, feel that peace has been established, but that we have nothing but an armistice in a state of war. We have been unable to go in for carefree rejoicing. We have felt that we are in the midst of a tragedy. We have felt humiliation. This has not been a victory for reason and humanity. It has been a victory for brute force. At every stage of the proceedings there have been time limits laid down by the owner and ruler of armed force. The terms have not been terms negotiated; they have been terms laid down as ultimata. We have seen today a gallant, civilized, and democratic people betrayed and handed over to a ruthless despotism. We have seen something more. We have seen the cause of democracy, which is, in our view, the cause of civilization and humanity, receive a terrible defeat. . . .

The events of these last few days constitute one of the greatest diplomatic defeats that this country and France have ever sustained. There can be no doubt that it is a tremendous victory for Herr Hitler. Without firing a shot, by the mere display of military force, he has achieved a dominating position in Europe which Germany failed to win after four years of war. He has overturned the balance of power in Europe. . . .

Herr Hitler has successfully asserted the law of the jungle. He has claimed to do what he will by force and in doing so has struck at the roots of the life of civilized peoples. In doing this to one nation he threatens all, and if he does this, and he has with impunity, there is no longer any peace in the world . . . although there may be a pause in actual warfare. The whole of Europe is now under the constant menace of armed force. That is why many people cannot feel very happy about the present situation. They feel that there has been an immense victory for force and wrong. Ever since the last war people have realized that if peace is to be preserved there must be something above the will of the individual ruler of an armed state. That is the whole basis of the League of Nations. . . .

I say we are witnessing a degeneration of the world due to two things. The first thing is the failure to deal with the political and economic questions arising out of the follies of the Peace Treaties, and arising out of the widespread injustice and maladjustments of the economic system. The other thing is the failure to deal with force, the failure to restrain aggression. . . . Aggression in Manchuria, Abyssinia [Ethiopia], Spain, Austria, and Czechoslovakia — these are milestones that mark the road to the abyss. . . .

The real [heart] of it is that, having decided to leave the League system which we practiced and in which we believed and to embark on a policy of alliances and power politics, instead of strengthening the people whose natural interests were with ours, we have had nothing but constant flirtations with this and that dictator. The Prime Minister has been the dupe of the dictators, and I say that today we are in a dangerous position. . . .

We are left isolated. . . . We shall be left alone with France; all our potential allies have gone; and France, which in my view has the greatest responsibility for this debacle of policy, finds herself in the position of a second-class state.

And what have we got in place of the alliances and covenants and collective security and all the rest of it which buttressed this country in the past? We are left with two promises, one from Signor Mussolini and one from Herr Hitler. That is really all that we have got. We have to walk by faith — the faith of the Prime Minister in Signor Mussolini and his faith in Herr Hitler. The Prime Minister has said how difficult it was for Herr Hitler to recede from a statement which he had once made. I have five pages of statements made by Herr Hitler, from every one of which he has receded. I need not go through them; you know them — pages of them; but the Prime Minister says against all experience that he has faith in Herr Hitler's promise, grounded on two or three interviews — a pretty flimsy support for this country.

I ask, what is to happen next? What reason have we to think that

Herr Hitler will stop now? Suppose he does not. What will happen? . . .

The real question that faces us in this debate is not just a review of the past, not just our apprehensions of the present; it is what can we do for the future of the human race?

The Fall of France

The collapse of France in June 1940, after only a few weeks of feeble resistance, shocked and depressed the democratic world. Hitler, by then, was master of Poland, Denmark, Norway, Holland, Belgium, and it seemed only a matter of time before Britain would succumb as well.

France had for years been torn by internal political strife. A few of her statesmen were sympathetic to the Nazi cause. Some Frenchmen who saw the German war machine in action accepted defeat as inevitable and wanted to make the best terms possible. There were even those, like Pierre Laval, who thought that France should join Germany in attacking Britain. After the defeat, French resistance against Germany was carried on in England under the leadership of General Charles de Gaulle and in France by an ever-growing underground.

The chaos brought on by the war and by the signing of the armistice between France and Germany is described by William L. Shirer.

Paris, June 20, 1940. The men who went down to Orléans and Blois yesterday tell a horrible tale. Along the road they saw what they estimated to be 200,000 refugees — people of all classes, rich and poor, lying along the roadside or by the edge of the forests, starving — without food, without water, no shelter, nothing.

They are just a few of the millions who fled Paris and the other cities and towns before the German invaders. They fled, tearing in fright

Source: William L. Shirer, *Berlin Diary*, New York: Alfred A. Knopf, Inc., pp. 417–25. Copyright 1940, 1941 by William L. Shirer. Reprinted by permission of the publishers.

along the roads with their belongings on their backs or on bikes or in baby carriages, and their children atop them. Soon the roads were clogged. Troops also were trying to use them. Soon the Germans came over, bombing the roads. Soon there were dead and dying. And no food, no water, no shelter, no care. . . .

Paris, June 21. On the exact spot in the little clearing in the Forest of Compiègne, where at 5:00 A.M. on November 11, 1918, the armistice which ended the World War was signed, Adolf Hitler today handed his armistice terms to France. To make German revenge complete, the meeting of the German and French plenipotentiaries took place in Marshal Foch's private car, in which Foch laid down the armistice terms to Germany twenty-two years ago. Even the same table in the rickety old *wagon-lit* [sleeping car] was used. And through the windows we saw Hitler occupying the very seat on which Foch had sat at that table when he dictated the other armistice.

The humiliation of France, of the French, was complete. . . .

The armistice negotiations began at 3:15 P.M. A warm June sun beat down on the great elm and pine trees and cast pleasant shadows on the wooded avenues as Hitler, with the German plenipotentiaries at his side, appeared. He alighted from his car in front of the French monument to Alsace-Lorraine which stands at the end of an avenue about two hundred yards from the clearing where the armistice car waits on exactly the same spot it occupied twenty-two years ago. . . .

Through my glasses I saw the Führer stop, glance at the monument, observe the Reich flags with their big swastikas in the center. Then he strode slowly toward us, toward the little clearing in the woods. I observed his face. It was grave, solemn, yet brimming with revenge. There was also in it, as in his springy step, a note of the triumphant conqueror, the defier of the world. There was something else, difficult to describe, in his expression, a sort of scornful, inner joy at being present at this great reversal of fate — a reversal he himself had wrought.

Now he reaches the little opening in the woods. He pauses and looks slowly around. The clearing is in the form of a circle some two hundred yards in diameter and laid out like a park. Cypress trees line it all round — and behind them, the great elms and oaks of the forest. This has been one of France's national shrines for twenty-two years. From a discreet position on the perimeter of the circle we watch.

Hitler pauses and gazes slowly around. In a group just behind him are the German plenipotentiaries. . . .

The time is now 3:18 P.M. Hitler's personal flag is run up on a small standard in the center of the opening.

Also in the center is a great granite block which stands some three feet above the ground. Hitler, followed by the others, walks slowly over to it, steps up, and reads the inscription engraved in great high letters on that block. It says: HERE ON THE ELEVENTH OF NOVEMBER 1918 SUC-CUMBED THE CRIMINAL PRIDE OF THE GERMAN EMPIRE . . . VANQUISHED BY THE FREE PEOPLES WHICH IT TRIED TO ENSLAVE.

Hitler reads it and Göring reads it. They all read it, standing there in the June sun and the silence. I look for the expression on Hitler's face. I am but fifty yards from him and see him through my glasses as though he were directly in front of me. I have seen that face many times at the great moments of his life. But today! It is afire with scorn, anger, hate, revenge, triumph. He steps off the monument and con-trives to make even this gesture a masterpiece of contempt. He glances back at it, contemptuous, angry — angry, you almost feel, because he cannot wipe out the awful, provoking lettering with one sweep of his high Prussian boot. He glances slowly around the clearing, and now, as his eyes meet ours, you grasp the depth of his hatred. But there is triumph there, too — revengeful, triumphant hate. Suddenly, as though his face were not giving quite complete expression to his feelings, he throws his whole body into harmony with his mood. He swiftly snaps his hands on his hips, arches his shoulders, plants his feet wide apart. It is a magnificent gesture of defiance, of burning contempt for this place now and all that it has stood for in the twenty-two years since it wit-nessed the humbling of the German Empire. . . .

It is now 3:23 P.M. and the Germans stride over to the armistice car. For a moment or two they stand in the sunlight outside the car, chatting. Then Hitler steps up into the car, followed by the others. We can see nicely through the car windows. Hitler takes the place occupied by Marshal Foch when the 1918 armistice terms were signed. The oth-ers spread themselves around him. Four chairs on the opposite side of the table from Hitler remain empty. The French have not yet appeared. But we do not wait long. Exactly at 3:30 P.M. they alight from a car. . . .

It is a grave hour in the life of France. The Frenchmen keep their eyes straight ahead. Their faces are solemn, drawn. They are the picture of tragic dignity.

They walk stiffly to the car, where they are met by two German officers. . . . The Germans salute. The French salute. The atmosphere is what Europeans call "correct." There are salutes, but no handshakes.

Now we get our picture through the dusty windows of that old . . . car. Hitler and the other German leaders rise as the French enter the drawing room. Hitler gives the Nazi salute, the arm raised. Ribbentrop and Hess do the same. I cannot see M. Noël to notice whether he salutes or not.

Hitler, as far as we can see through the windows, does not say a word to the French or to anybody else. He nods to General Keitel at his side. We see General Keitel adjusting his papers. Then he starts to read. He is reading the preamble to the German armistice terms. The French sit there with marblelike faces and listen intently. Hitler and Göring glance at the green tabletop.

The reading of the preamble lasts but a few minutes. Hitler, we soon observe, has no intention of remaining very long, of listening to the reading of the armistice terms themselves. At 3:42 P.M., twelve minutes after the French arrive, we see Hitler stand up, salute stiffly, and then stride out of the drawing room, followed by Göring, Brauchitsch, Raeder, Hess, and Ribbentrop. The French, like figures of stone, remain at the green-topped table. General Keitel remains with them. He starts to read them the detailed conditions of the armistice.

Hitler and his aides stride down the avenue toward the Alsace-Lorraine monument, where their cars are waiting. As they pass the guard of honor, the German band strikes up the two national anthems, "Deutschland, Deutschland über Alles" and the "Horst Wessel" song. The whole ceremony in which Hitler has reached a new pinnacle in his meteoric career and Germany avenged the 1918 defeat is over in a quarter of an hour.

Churchill Assumes
Direction of the War

Winston Churchill was the symbol of British pluck and stubbornness in the face of almost certain disaster. During the interwar years he had tried in vain to rouse his complacent fellow

185

countrymen to the dangers of the Nazi menace. Neither his Conservative Party nor the people paid much heed to his warnings.

Confidence in Prime Minister Chamberlain's leadership began to decline when appeasement failed to prevent further aggression and finally resulted in war. When Hitler invaded Belgium and the Netherlands on May 10, 1940, Parliament rebelled against Chamberlain, and Churchill became Prime Minister. Leading a coalition of all parties, he gave decisive and inspiring direction in the war against Hitler. His eloquent speeches, in which he did not hide the grim truth, galvanized British resistance.

The first of the following speeches was delivered after the evacuation of the British forces from Dunkirk, May 29–June 4, 1940; the second, after the fall of France on June 22, 1940.

I have, myself, full confidence that if all do their duty, if nothing is neglected, and if the best arrangements are made, as they are being made, we shall prove ourselves once again able to defend our island home, to ride out the storm of war, and to outlive the menace of tyranny; if necessary for years, if necessary alone. At any rate, that is what we are going to try to do. That is the resolve of his Majesty's government — every man of them. That is the will of Parliament and the nation. The British Empire and the French Republic, linked together in their cause and in their need, will defend to the death their native soil, aiding each other like good comrades to the utmost of their strength. Even though large tracts of Europe and many old and famous states have fallen or may fall into the grip of the Gestapo and all the odious apparatus of Nazi rule, we shall not flag or fail. We shall go on to the end, we shall fight in France, we shall fight on the seas and oceans, we shall fight with growing confidence and growing strength in the air, we shall defend our island; whatever the cost may be, we shall fight on the beaches, we shall fight on the landing grounds, we shall fight in the fields and in the streets, we shall fight in the hills; we shall never surrender, and even if, which I do not for a moment believe, this island or a large part of it were subjugated and starving, then our Empire beyond

Source: Winston Churchill, *Blood, Sweat, and Tears*, New York: G. P. Putnam's Sons, 1941, pp. 296–97, 314. Reprinted by permission of G. P. Putnam's Sons, and McClelland & Stewart, Limited, Toronto.

the seas, armed and guarded by the British Fleet, would carry on the struggle until, in God's good time, the New World, with all its power and might, steps forth to the rescue and the liberation of the Old.

What General Weygand called the Battle of France is over. I expect that the Battle of Britain is about to begin. Upon this battle depends the survival of Christian civilization. Upon it depends our own British life and the long continuity of our institutions and our Empire. The whole fury and might of the enemy must very soon be turned on us. Hitler knows that he will have to break us in this island or lose the war. If we can stand up to him, all Europe may be free and the life of the world may move forward into broad, sunlit uplands. But if we fail, then the whole world, including the United States, including all that we have known or cared for, will sink into the abyss of a new Dark Age. . . . Let us therefore brace ourselves to our duties, and so bear ourselves that, if the British Empire and its Commonwealth last for a thousand years, men will still say, "This was their finest hour."

The Japanese Attack Pearl Harbor

Americans were stunned by the Japanese surprise attack on Pearl Harbor in Hawaii. American-Japanese relations had been tense for some time, but negotiations were still going on in Washington when news of the raid reached the United States.

America had long been an obstacle to Japanese ambitions in the Pacific. When it became evident that the United States would not back down and would cut off exports that were vital to Japan, Japan prepared for war. In September 1940 Japan had signed a pact with Germany and Italy which would bring them to Japan's aid in the event of a war with the United States. In April 1941 Japan concluded a neutrality agreement with Russia. In October the militarists under General Hideki Tojo replaced the moderates in the cabinet. The long-rehearsed attack on Pearl Harbor was put in motion at the end of November. On December 7, 1941, Japan struck. The next day the United States and the United Kingdom (as Churchill had promised) declared war on Japan. Germany and Italy, Japan's allies, then declared war on the United States.

In his Memoirs, Cordell Hull, then Secretary of State, recalls the events of December 7.

Sunday morning, December 7, 1941, I went to my office, as I had done almost every Sunday since I entered the State Department in 1933. . . .

During the morning I received a series of decoded intercepts [intercepted messages] consisting of fourteen parts of a long telegram from [the] Foreign Minister to [Ambassadors] Nomura and Kurusu. . . . There was also a short message instructing the Ambassadors to present this to our government, if possible to me, at one o'clock that afternoon. Here then was the zero hour.

The Japanese note was little more than an insult. It said that our proposal "ignores Japan's sacrifices in the four years of the China affair, menaces the Empire's existence itself, and disparages its honor and prestige." It accused us of conspiring with Great Britain and other countries "to obstruct Japan's efforts toward the establishment of peace through the creation of a new order in East Asia." It concluded by saying that, in view of the attitude of the American government, the Japanese government considered it impossible to reach an agreement through further negotiations.

The note did not declare war. Neither did it break off diplomatic relations. Japan struck without such preliminaries.

Toward noon Ambassador Nomura telephoned my office to ask for an appointment with me at one o'clock for himself and Kurusu. I granted his request.

A few minutes after one, Nomura telephoned again to ask that the appointment be postponed until 1:45. I agreed.

The Japanese envoys arrived at the Department at 2:05 and went to the diplomatic waiting room. At almost that moment the President telephoned me from the White House. His voice was steady but clipped.

Source: Cordell Hull, *The Memoirs of Cordell Hull*, New York: The Macmillan Company, 1948, Vol. II, pp. 1095–1100. Copyright 1948 by Cordell Hull. Reprinted by permission of the publishers.

He said, "There's a report that the Japanese have attacked Pearl Harbor."

"Has the report been confirmed?" I asked.

He said, "No."

While each of us indicated his belief that the report was probably true, I suggested that he have it confirmed, having in mind my appointment with the Japanese ambassadors. . . .

Nomura and Kurusu came into my office at 2:20. I received them coldly and did not ask them to sit down.

Nomura diffidently said he had been instructed by his government to deliver a document to me at one o'clock, but that difficulty in decoding the message had delayed him. He then handed me his government's note.

I asked him why he had specified one o'clock in his first request for an interview.

He replied that he did not know, but that was his instruction.

I made a pretense of glancing through the note. I knew its contents already but naturally could give no indication of this fact.

After reading two or three pages, I asked Nomura whether he had presented the document under instructions from his government.

He replied that he had.

When I finished skimming the pages, I turned to Nomura and put my eye on him.

"I must say," I said, "that in all my conversations with you during the last nine months I have never uttered one word of untruth. This is borne out absolutely by the record. In all my fifty years of public service I have never seen a document that was more crowded with infamous falsehoods and distortions — infamous falsehoods and distortions on a scale so huge that I never imagined until today that any government on this planet was capable of uttering them."

Nomura seemed about to say something. His face was impassive, but I felt he was under great emotional strain. I stopped him with a motion of my hand. I nodded toward the door. The ambassadors turned without a word and walked out, their heads down. . . .

Shortly after three o'clock I went to the White House, where I talked with the President and others for forty minutes. Mr. Roosevelt was very solemn in demeanor and conversation. The magnitude of the surprise achieved by the Japanese at Pearl Harbor was already becoming evident. But neither he nor any of us lost faith for a moment in the ability of the United States to cope with the danger. . . .

I returned to the State Department at four o'clock and called a conference of my chief advisers which lasted until six o'clock. . . .

I emphatically expressed my disappointment that our armed forces in Hawaii had been taken so completely by surprise. I repeated to my assistants that during recent weeks I had time after time warned our military and naval officials with all the vigor at my command that there was constant danger of a treacherous attack by Japan anywhere, and in all probability at many places at the same time.

Nevertheless, it was the feeling of many of us that the Japanese, in their own interest, had been exceedingly unwise in attacking Pearl Harbor, thereby instantaneously and completely uniting the American people. However, as reports came in of the tremendous damage suffered at Hawaii, this feeling became somewhat diluted. . . .

After having been at the State Department all that Sunday I went home to a somber dinner and then to the White House at 8:30. A number of other cabinet members and military officials were gathered about the President. . . .

The President continued calm, although his face was grave and he made no effort to minimize the extent of the losses we had suffered at Pearl Harbor.

The next day, Monday, I went to the Capitol to hear the President deliver his message to Congress. The Senate and House quickly voted the declaration of a state of war.

Three days later, following declarations by Hitler and Mussolini, the Senate and House voted additional declarations of a state of war with Germany and Italy.

The voices of diplomacy were now submerged by the roar of the cannon.

We had had two objectives in mind in all our relations with Japan since the outbreak of war in Europe, and especially since the fall of France. One was peace. The other, if peace could not be had, was to gain time to ready our defenses.

We failed to win peace, but we gained invaluable time.

It was not until twenty-seven months after the invasion of Poland, not until eighteen months after the fall of France, that Japan struck. Although we still needed more time to complete our defenses, neverthe-

190

less we were comparatively far better prepared on December 7, 1941, than we had been on September 1, 1939, or on June 17, 1940.

Prime Minister Churchill put it ably in his speech on December 26, 1941, to a joint session of Congress in Washington, by saying: "We have, indeed, to be thankful that so much time has been granted to us. If Germany had tried to invade the British Isles after the French collapse in June 1940, and if Japan had declared war on the British Empire and the United States at about the same date, no one can say what disaster and agonies might not have been our lot. But now, at the end of December 1941, our transformation from easygoing peace to total war efficiency has made very great progress."

The Invasion of Normandy

The tide began to turn against the advancing Axis powers in the fall of 1942. Japanese expansion was brought almost to a halt; the British took the offensive in Egypt; British and American troops landed in North Africa; the devastating German submarine campaign was weakening; the Russians were turning the tide at Stalingrad; and large-scale bombings of German cities were well under way.

One of the most extraordinary feats of planning and organization in the war was the invasion of Normandy, June 6, 1944. Hundreds of thousands of men had first to be trained and then transported across the English Channel. General Dwight D. Eisenhower was the Supreme Commander of the expedition and the coordinator of this complex operation. For several days before the invasion, German defenses were softened up by thousands of bombers, while behind the German lines the French Resistance harassed the enemy. The Germans were taken in by the tactics used to mislead them as to the point of landing. The invasion of Normandy was a magnificent success, but not without a price.

The invasion beach is described by Ernie Pyle, one of the most famous of the American war correspondents. He was later killed in the Pacific.

Owing to a last-minute alteration in the arrangements, I didn't arrive on the beachhead until the morning after D Day,* after our first wave of assault troops had hit the shore.

By the time we got there the beaches had been taken and the fighting had moved a couple of miles inland. All that remained on the beach was some sniping and artillery fire, and the occasional startling blast of a mine geysering brown sand into the air. That, plus a gigantic and pitiful litter of wreckage along miles of shoreline.

Submerged tanks and overturned boats and burned trucks and shell-shattered jeeps and sad little personal belongings were strewn all over those bitter sands. That, plus the bodies of soldiers lying in rows covered with blankets, the toes of their shoes sticking up in a line as though on drill. And other bodies, uncollected, still sprawling grotesquely in the sand or half hidden by the high grass beyond the beach. That, plus an intense, grim determination of work-weary men to get that chaotic beach organized and get all the vital supplies and the reinforcements moving more rapidly over it from the stacked-up ships standing in droves out to sea.

After it was over it seemed to me a pure miracle that we ever took the beach at all. . . .

I want to tell you what the opening of the second front in that one sector entailed, so that you can know and appreciate and forever be humbly grateful to those both dead and alive who did it for you.

Ashore, facing us, were more enemy troops than we had in our assault waves. The advantages were all theirs, the disadvantages all ours. The Germans were dug into positions they had been working on for months, although they were not entirely complete. A one-hundred-foot bluff a couple of hundred yards back from the beach had great concrete gun emplacements built right into the hilltop. These opened to the sides instead of to the front, thus making it hard for naval fire from the sea to reach them. They could shoot parallel with the shore and cover every foot of it for miles with artillery fire.

Then they had hidden machine-gun nests on the forward slopes, with cross fire taking in every inch of the beach. These nests were con-

_____
* **D Day:** the code name for the date of the invasion of Normandy.

Source: Ernie Pyle, *Brave Men*, New York: Holt, Rinehart and Winston, Inc., 1944, pp. 246–47, 250–52. Copyright 1943, 1944 by Scripps-Howard Newspaper Alliance. Copyright 1944 by Holt, Rinehart and Winston, Inc., and reprinted by their permission.

nected by networks of trenches so that the German gunners could move about without exposing themselves.

Throughout the length of the beach, running zigzag a couple of hundred yards back from the shore line, was an immense V-shaped ditch fifteen feet deep. Nothing could cross it, not even men on foot, until fills had been made. And in other places at the far end of the beach, where the ground was flatter, they had great concrete walls. These were blasted by our naval gunfire or by explosives set by hand after we got ashore.

Our only exits from the beach were several . . . valleys, each about a hundred yards wide. The Germans made the most of those funnellike traps, sowing them with buried mines. They also contained barbed-wire entanglements with mines attached, hidden ditches, and machine guns firing from the slopes.

All this was on the shore. But our men had to go through a maze nearly as deadly before they even got ashore. Underwater obstacles were terrific. Under the water the Germans had whole fields of evil devices to catch our boats. Several days after the landing we had cleared only channels through them and still could not approach the whole length of the beach with our ships. Even then some ship or boat would hit one of those mines and be knocked out of commission.

The Germans had masses of great six-pronged spiders — made of railroad iron and standing shoulder high — just beneath the surface of the water, for our landing craft to run into. They had huge logs buried in the sand, pointing upward and outward, their tops just below the water. Attached to the logs were mines.

In addition to these obstacles they had floating mines offshore, land mines buried in the sand of the beach, and more mines in checkerboard rows in the tall grass beyond the sand. And the enemy had four men on shore for every three men we had approaching the shore.

And yet we got on. . . .

I took a walk along the historic coast of Normandy in the country of France. It was a lovely day for strolling along the seashore. Men were sleeping on the sand, some of them sleeping forever. Men were floating in the water, but they didn't know they were in the water, for they were dead. . . .

The wreckage was vast and startling. The awful waste and destruction of war, even aside from the loss of human life, has always been one of its outstanding features to those who are in it. . . .

For a mile out from the beach there were scores of tanks and trucks and boats that were not visible, for they were at the bottom of the water — swamped by overloading, or hit by shells, or sunk by mines. Most of their crews were lost. . . .

On the beach itself, high and dry, were all kinds of wrecked vehicles. There were tanks that had only just made the beach before being knocked out. There were jeeps that had burned to a dull gray. There were big derricks on caterpillar treads that didn't quite make it. There were half-tracks carrying office equipment that had been made into a shambles by a single shell hit, their interiors still holding the useless equipage of smashed typewriters, telephones, office files. . . .

There were torn pistol belts and canvas water buckets, first-aid kits, and jumbled heaps of life belts. I picked up a pocket Bible with a soldier's name in it and put it in my jacket. I carried it half a mile or so and then put it back down on the beach. I don't know why I picked it up, or why I put it down again.

Soldiers carry strange things ashore with them. In every invasion there is at least one soldier hitting the beach at H hour with a banjo slung over his shoulder. The most ironic piece of equipment marking our beach — this beach first of despair, then of victory — was a tennis racket that some soldier had brought along. It lay lonesomely on the sand, clamped in its press, not a string broken. . . .

Always there are dogs in every invasion. There was a dog still on the beach, still pitifully looking for his masters.

He stayed at the water's edge, near a boat that lay twisted and half sunk at the waterline. He barked appealingly to every soldier who approached, trotted eagerly along with him for a few feet, and then, sensing himself unwanted in all the haste, he would run back to wait in vain for his own people at his own empty boat.

Over and around this long thin line of personal anguish, fresh men were rushing vast supplies to keep our armies pushing on into France. Other squads of men picked amid the wreckage to salvage ammunition and equipment that was still usable.

Men worked and slept on the beach for days before the last D Day victim was taken away for burial.

Plans for Victory and Peace

Declaration of (handwritten)

A state of harmony prevailed at a meeting of the Big Three at Yalta in the Crimea in February 1945. The war in Europe was coming to an end. Important concessions asked by the Soviet Union were granted by the United States and Britain in recognition of the Soviet Union's great sacrifices in the war, in the expectation that its assistance would be essential to defeat Japan, and in the hope that a lasting peace could be established. The Soviet Union gave little in exchange for what it received, except promises, such as free elections in Eastern Europe.

By the time the Big Three met again at Potsdam in July of the same year, the atmosphere had cooled. Germany was beaten, and the Soviet Union's actions in Eastern Europe had aroused apprehension as to its intentions. All the victors wanted to disarm Germany and to put an end to Nazi domination, but they could not agree on many issues, such as reparations. Suspicion and mistrust soon poisoned all relations between East and West.

The following selections are extracts from the Yalta and Potsdam agreements.

Yalta, February 7–12, 1945

We have considered and determined the military plans of the three allied powers for the final defeat of the common enemy. . . .

Nazi Germany is doomed. The German people will only make the cost of their defeat heavier to themselves by attempting to continue a hopeless resistance.

We have agreed on common policies and plans for enforcing the unconditional surrender terms which we shall impose together on Nazi Germany after German armed resistance has been finally crushed. These terms will not be made known until the final defeat of Germany has been accomplished. Under the agreed plan, the forces of the three powers will each occupy a separate zone of Germany. Coordinated administration and control has been provided for. . . . It has been agreed that

YALTA, FEBRUARY 7–12, 1945. Source: "The Crimea Conference," United States Department of State *Bulletin*, Vol. XII, No. 295, February 18, 1945, pp. 213–16.

France should be invited by the three powers, if she should so desire, to take over a zone of occupation and to participate as a fourth member of the control commission. . . .

It is our inflexible purpose to destroy German militarism and Nazism and to insure that Germany will never again be able to disturb the peace of the world. We are determined to disarm and disband all German armed forces; break up for all time the German General Staff that has repeatedly contrived the resurgence of German militarism; remove or destroy all German military equipment; eliminate or control all German industry that could be used for military production; bring all war criminals to just and swift punishment and exact reparation in kind for the destruction wrought by the Germans; wipe out the Nazi Party, Nazi laws, organizations, and institutions, remove all Nazi and militarist influences from public office and from the cultural and economic life of the German people; and take in harmony such other measures in Germany as may be necessary to the future peace and safety of the world. It is not our purpose to destroy the people of Germany, but only when Nazism and militarism have been extirpated will there be hope for a decent life for Germans and a place for them in the comity of nations.

We have considered the question of the damage caused by Germany to the Allied nations in this war and recognize it as just that Germany be obliged to make compensation for this damage in kind to the greatest extent possible. A commission for the compensation of damage will be established. The commission will be instructed to consider the question of the extent and methods for compensating damage caused by Germany to the Allied countries. The commission will work in Moscow.

We are resolved upon the earliest possible establishment with our allies of a general international organization to maintain peace and security. We believe that this is essential both to prevent aggression and to remove the political, economic, and social causes of war through the close and continuing collaboration of all peace-loving peoples.

We have agreed that a conference of United Nations should be called to meet at San Francisco in the United States on April 25, 1945, to prepare the charter of such an organization. . . .

The establishment of order in Europe and the rebuilding of national economic life must be achieved by processes which will enable the liberated peoples to destroy the last vestiges of Nazism and Fascism and to create democratic institutions of their own choice. This is a principle of the Atlantic Charter — the right of all peoples to choose the form of government under which they will live — the restoration of sovereign rights and self-government to those peoples who have been forcibly deprived of them by the aggressor nations.

To foster the conditions in which the liberated peoples may exercise these rights, the three governments will jointly assist the people in any European liberated state or former Axis satellite state in Europe where in their judgment conditions require (a) to establish conditions of internal peace; (b) to carry out emergency measures for the relief of distressed peoples; (c) to form interim governmental authorities broadly representative of all democratic elements in the population and pledged to the earliest possible establishment through free elections of governments responsive to the will of the people; and (d) to facilitate where necessary the holding of such elections.

Our meeting here in the Crimea has reaffirmed our common determination to maintain and strengthen in the peace to come that unity of purpose and of action which has made victory possible and certain for the United Nations in this war. We believe that this is a sacred obligation which our governments owe to our peoples and to all the peoples of the world.

Potsdam, July 17–August 2, 1945*

The conference reached an agreement for the establishment of a Council of Foreign Ministers representing the five principal powers to continue the necessary preparatory work for the peace settlements and to take up matters which from time to time may be referred to the Council by agreement of the governments participating in the Council. . . .

The Council shall normally meet in London, which shall be the permanent seat of the joint secretariat which the Council will form. . . .

* Of the Big Three at Yalta — Stalin, Roosevelt, and Churchill — only Stalin attended the entire Potsdam Conference (also called the Berlin Conference). President Truman succeeded Roosevelt, and Churchill, who attended the early sessions, was replaced by Clement Attlee, the new British Prime Minister.

POTSDAM, JULY 17–AUGUST 2, 1945. Source: "Tripartite Conference at Berlin," United States Department of State *Bulletin*, Vol. XIII, No. 319, August 5, 1945, pp. 153–55.

As its immediate important task, the Council shall be authorized to draw up, with a view to their submission to the United Nations, treaties of peace with Italy, Romania, Bulgaria, Hungary, and Finland, and to propose settlements of territorial questions outstanding on the termination of the war in Europe. The Council shall be utilized for the preparation of a peace settlement for Germany to be accepted by the government of Germany when a government adequate for the purpose is established. . . .

The Allied armies are in occupation of the whole of Germany, and the German people have begun to atone for the terrible crimes committed under the leadership of those whom in the hour of their success they openly approved and blindly obeyed.

Agreement has been reached at this conference on the political and economic principles of a coordinated Allied policy toward defeated Germany during the period of Allied control.

The purpose of this agreement is to carry out the Crimea Declaration on Germany. German militarism and Nazism will be [eliminated] and the Allies will take in agreement together, now and in the future, the other measures necessary to assure that Germany will never again threaten her neighbors or the peace of the world.

It is not the intention of the Allies to destroy or enslave the German people. It is the intention of the Allies that the German people be given the opportunity to prepare for the eventual reconstruction of their life on a democratic and peaceful basis. If their own efforts are steadily directed to this end, it will be possible for them in due course to take their place among the free and peaceful peoples of the world. . . .

All Nazi laws which provided the basis of the Hitler regime or established discrimination on grounds of race, creed, or political opinion shall be abolished. No such discriminations, whether legal, administrative, or otherwise, shall be tolerated.

War criminals and those who have participated in planning or carrying out Nazi enterprises involving or resulting in atrocities or war crimes shall be arrested and brought to judgment. Nazi leaders, influential Nazi supporters, high officials of Nazi organizations and institutions, and any other persons dangerous to the occupation or its objectives shall be arrested and interned. . . .

German education shall be so controlled as completely to eliminate Nazi and militarist doctrines and to make possible the successful development of democratic ideas.

198

The judicial system will be reorganized in accordance with the principles of democracy, of justice under law, and of equal rights for all citizens without distinction of race, nationality, or religion.

The Ordeal of Hiroshima

A new era in science and in international relations was inaugurated by a blinding flash of light radiating scorching heat. The first atomic bomb was exploded over Hiroshima on August 6, 1945, the second over Nagasaki on August 9. The death toll for both explosions was about 130,000, with many times that number wounded and in a pitiful state. Thousands of homes were destroyed, and whole areas were devastated and poisoned by radiation. The surrender of Japan followed within a few days.

The decision to drop the bomb was made by President Harry S. Truman and his advisors. An ultimatum had been sent from the Potsdam Conference to the Japanese, warning them that they would be destroyed if they did not surrender at once. The United States had already paid a high price for its victories against Japan, and it was estimated that it would suffer more than a million casualties in an invasion of the home islands of Japan. The atomic bomb was calculated to put a speedy end to the war.

The following account of the explosion over Hiroshima was written by a Japanese doctor.

August 6, 1945. The hour was early; the morning still, warm, and beautiful. Shimmering leaves, reflecting sunlight from a cloudless sky, made a pleasant contrast with shadows in my garden as I gazed absently through wide-flung doors opening to the south.

Clad in drawers and undershirt, I was sprawled on the living room floor exhausted because I had just spent a sleepless night on duty as an air warden in my hospital.

Source: Michihiko Hachiya, *Hiroshima Diary: The Journal of a Japanese Physician, August 6–September 30, 1945*, translated and edited by Warner Wells, Chapel Hill: The University of North Carolina Press, 1955, pp. 1–8. Reprinted by permission of the publishers.

Suddenly a strong flash of light startled me — and then another. So well does one recall little things that I remember vividly how a stone lantern in the garden became brilliantly lit, and I debated whether this light was caused by a magnesium flare or sparks from a passing trolley.

Garden shadows disappeared. The view where a moment before all had been so bright and sunny was now dark and hazy. Through swirling dust I could barely discern a wooden column that had supported one corner of my house. It was leaning crazily and the roof sagged danger-ously.

Moving instinctively, I tried to escape, but rubble and fallen tim-bers barred the way. By picking my way cautiously I managed to reach . . . my garden. A profound weakness overcame me, so I stopped to regain my strength. . . .

What had happened?

All over the right side of my body I was cut and bleeding. A large splinter was protruding from a mangled wound in my thigh, and some-thing warm trickled into my mouth. My cheek was torn. . . .

Where was my wife?

Suddenly thoroughly alarmed, I began to yell for her: "Yaeko-san! Yaeko-san! Where are you?"

Blood began to spurt. Had my carotid artery been cut? Would I bleed to death? Frightened and irrational, I called out again: "It's a five-hundred-ton bomb! Yaeko-san, where are you? A five-hundred-ton bomb has fallen!"

Yaeko-san, pale and frightened, her clothes torn and bloodstained, emerged from the ruins of our house holding her elbow. . . .

"We'll be all right," I exclaimed. "Only let's get out of here as fast as we can."

She nodded, and I motioned for her to follow me. . . .

We stood in the street, uncertain and afraid, until a house across from us began to sway and then . . . fell almost at our feet. Our own house began to sway, and in a minute it too collapsed in a cloud of dust. Other buildings caved in or toppled. Fires sprang up and whipped by a vicious wind began to spread.

It finally dawned on us that we could not stay there in the street, so we turned our steps toward the hospital.*. . .

We started out, but after twenty or thirty steps I had to stop. My breath became short, my heart pounded, and my legs gave way under

* Dr. Hachiya's home was only a few hundred yards from the hospital.

me. An overpowering thirst seized me, and I begged Yaeko-san to find me some water. But there was no water to be found. After a little my strength somewhat returned and we were able to go on. . . .

Our progress was interminably slow, until finally my legs refused to carry me farther. I told my wife, who was almost as badly hurt as I, to go on alone. This she objected to, but there was no choice. She had to go ahead and try to find someone to come back for me.

Yaeko-san looked into my face for a moment, and then, without saying a word, turned away and began running toward the hospital. Once she looked back and waved. . . .

Could I go on?

I tried. It was all a nightmare — my wounds, the darkness, the road ahead. My movements were ever so slow; only my mind was running at top speed.

In time I came to an open space where the houses had been removed to make a fire lane. Through the dim light I could make out ahead of me the hazy outlines of the Communications Bureau's big concrete building, and beyond it the hospital. My spirits rose because I knew that now someone would find me; and if I should die, at least my body would be found.

I paused to rest. Gradually things around me came into focus. There were the shadowy forms of people, some of whom looked like walking ghosts. . . .

All who could were moving in the direction of the hospital. I joined in the dismal parade when my strength was somewhat recovered, and at last reached the gates of the Communications Bureau.

Familiar surroundings, familiar faces. There was Mr. Iguchi and Mr. Yoshihiro and my old friend Mr. Sera, the head of the business office. They hastened to give me a hand, their expressions of pleasure changing to alarm when they saw that I was hurt. I was too happy to see them to share their concern. . . .

Later I learned that the hospital was so overrun that the Communications Bureau had to be used as an emergency hospital. . . .

My private nurse, Miss Kado, . . . set about examining my wounds without speaking a word. No one spoke. I asked for a shirt and pajamas. They got them for me, but still no one spoke. Why was everyone so quiet?

Miss Kado finished the examination, and in a moment it felt as if my chest was on fire. She had begun to paint my wounds with iodine and no amount of entreaty would make her stop. With no alternative but to endure the iodine, I tried to divert myself by looking out the window.

The hospital lay directly opposite with part of the roof and the third-floor sunroom in plain view, and as I looked up I witnessed a sight which made me forget my smarting wounds. Smoke was pouring out of the sunroom windows. The hospital was afire!

"Fire!" I shouted. "Fire! Fire! The hospital is on fire!"

My friends looked up. It was true. The hospital *was* on fire. . . .

The sky became bright, as flames from the hospital mounted. Soon the Bureau was threatened and Mr. Sera gave the order to evacuate. My stretcher was moved into a rear garden and placed beneath an old cherry tree. Other patients limped into the garden or were carried until soon the entire area became so crowded that only the very ill had room to lie down. No one talked, and the ominous silence was relieved only by a subdued rustle among so many people, restless, in pain, anxious and afraid, waiting for something else to happen. . . .

The heat finally became too intense to endure, and we were left no choice but to abandon the garden. Those who could fled; those who could not perished. Had it not been for my devoted friends, I would have died, but again they came to the rescue and carried my stretcher to the main gate on the other side of the Bureau.

Here a small group of people were already clustered, and here I found my wife. Dr. Sasada and Miss Kado joined us.

Fires sprang up on every side as violent winds fanned flames from one building to another. Soon we were surrounded. The ground we held in front of the Communications Bureau became an oasis in a desert of fire. As the flames came closer the heat became more intense, and if someone in our group had not had the presence of mind to drench us with water * from a fire hose, I doubt if anyone could have survived.

Hot as it was, I began to shiver. The drenching was too much. My heart pounded; things began to whirl until all before me blurred. . . .

I murmured weakly, "I am done."

The sound of voices reached my ears as though from a great distance and finally became louder as if close at hand. I opened my eyes; Dr. Sasada was feeling my pulse. What had happened? Miss Kado gave

---

* The water mains entered the city from the north, and since the Communications Bureau was on the northern edge of the city, its water supply was not destroyed.

me an injection. My strength gradually returned. I must have fainted. . . .

My next memory is of an open area. The fires must have receded. I was alive. My friends had somehow managed to rescue me again.

A head popped out of an air-raid dugout, and I hear the unmistakable voice of old Mrs. Saeki: "Cheer up, Doctor! Everything will be all right. The north side is burned out. We have nothing further to fear from the fire.". . .

Hiroshima was no longer a city, but a burned-over prairie. To the east and to the west everything was flattened. The distant mountains seemed nearer than I could ever remember. The hills of Ushita and the woods of Nigitsu loomed out of the haze and smoke like the nose and eyes on a face. How small Hiroshima was with its houses gone.

Nazi War Crimes

All nightmares of Nazi brutality and inhumanity were exceeded by the reality of the concentration camps. Gas chambers, cremating ovens, pits of emaciated corpses, and piles of children's shoes all bore witness to the callousness of the Germans who perpetrated these crimes. About six million Jews and several million others had been murdered. To many, death had come after suffering hunger, torture, and degradation. More unfortunate were those who had been used as guinea pigs for brutal and often pointless medical experiments. Thousands of Germans in many branches of the government and the army had carried out this policy of extermination. Never have conquerors left such a legacy of barbarism.

The records of the Nuremberg Trials, which took place after the war, reveal the nature of Nazi war crimes.

Statement of the Offense

The defendants [the Nazis] determined upon and carried out ruthless wars against countries and populations in violation of the rules

Source: *Trial of the Major War Criminals Before the International Military Tribunal, Official Text*, Nuremberg, Germany: Allied Control Authority for Germany, 1947, Vol. I, pp. 29, 43–44, 47–54.

and customs of war, including . . . murder, ill-treatment, deportation for slave labor and for other purposes of civilian populations of occupied territories, murder and ill-treatment of prisoners of war and of persons on the high seas, the taking and killing of hostages, the plunder of public and private property, the indiscriminate destruction of cities, towns, and villages, and devastation not justified by military necessity. . . . The defendants determined upon and committed crimes against humanity, both within Germany and within occupied territories, including murder, extermination, enslavement, deportation, and other inhumane acts committed against civilian populations before and during the war, and persecutions on political, racial, or religious grounds in execution of the plans for preparing and prosecuting aggressive or illegal wars. . . .

Murder and Ill-Treatment of Civilian Populations of or in Occupied Territory and on the High Seas

Throughout the period of their occupation of territories overrun by their armed forces, the defendants, for the purpose of systematically terrorizing the inhabitants, murdered and tortured civilians and ill-treated them, and imprisoned them without legal process.

The murders and ill-treatment were carried out by divers means, including shooting, hanging, gassing, starvation, gross overcrowding, systematic under-nutrition, systematic imposition of labor tasks beyond the strength of those ordered to carry them out, inadequate provision of surgical and medical services, kickings, beatings, brutality, and torture of all kinds, including the use of hot irons and pulling out of fingernails and the performance of experiments by means of operations and otherwise on living human subjects. In some occupied territories the defendants interfered in religious matters, persecuted members of the clergy and monastic orders, and expropriated church property. They conducted deliberate and systematic genocide, viz., the extermination of racial and national groups, against the civilian populations of certain occupied territories in order to destroy particular races and classes of people and national, racial, or religious groups, particularly Jews, Poles, Gypsies, and others. . . .

In the concentration camps were many prisoners who were classified *Nacht und Nebel* [Night and Fog]. These were entirely cut off from the world and were allowed neither to receive nor to send letters. They disappeared without trace and no announcement of their fate was ever made by the German authorities.

204

Such murder and ill-treatment took place in concentration camps and similar establishments set up by the defendants, particularly in the concentration camps set up at Belsen, Buchenwald, Dachau, Breendonck, Grini, Natzweiler, Ravensbruck, Vught, and Amersfoort, and in numerous cities, towns, and villages. . . .

From September 1, 1939, when the German armed forces invaded Poland, and from June 22, 1941, when they invaded the U.S.S.R., the German government and the German High Command adopted a systematic policy of murder and ill-treatment of the civilian populations of and in the Eastern countries as they were successively occupied by the German armed forces. These murders and ill-treatments were carried on continuously until the German armed forces were driven out of the said countries. . . .

The said murders and ill-treatments were carried out by divers means including all those set out above, as follows:

About 1,500,000 persons were exterminated in Maidanek and about 4,000,000 persons were exterminated in Auschwitz, among whom were citizens of Poland, the U.S.S.R., the United States of America, Great Britain, Czechoslovakia, France, and other countries.

In the Lvov region and in the city of Lvov the Germans exterminated about 700,000 Soviet people, including 70 persons in the field of arts, science, and technology, and also citizens of the United States of America, Great Britain, Czechoslovakia, Yugoslavia, and Holland, brought to this region from other concentration camps.

In the Jewish ghetto from September 7, 1941, and July 6, 1943, over 133,000 persons were tortured and shot. . . .

Beginning with June 1943 the Germans carried out measures to hide the evidence of their crimes. They exhumed and burned corpses, and they crushed the bones with machines and used them for fertilizer. . . .

In the Lithuanian S.S.R. there were mass killings of Soviet citizens, namely: in Panerai at least 100,000; in Kaunas more than 70,000; in Alitus about 60,000; at Prenai more than 3,000; in Villiampol about 8,000; in Mariampol about 7,000; in Trakai and neighboring towns 37,640.

In the Latvian S.S.R. 577,000 persons were murdered. . . .

Along with adults the Nazi conspirators mercilessly destroyed even children. They killed them with their parents, in groups, and alone. They killed them in children's homes and hospitals, burying the living in the graves, throwing them into flames, stabbing them with bayonets, poisoning them, conducting experiments upon them, extracting their blood for the use of the German army, throwing them into prison and Gestapo torture chambers and concentration camps, where the children died from hunger, torture, and epidemic diseases.

From September 6 to November 24, 1942, in the regions of Brest, Pinsk, Kobren, Dyvina, Malority, and Berezy-Kartuzsky, about 400 children were shot by German . . . units.

In the Yanov camp in the city of Lvov the Germans killed 8,000 children in two months. . . .

From Belgium between 1940 and 1944 at least 190,000 civilians were deported to Germany and used as slave labor. Such deportees were subjected to ill-treatment and many of them were compelled to work in armament factories.

From Holland between 1940 and 1944 nearly half a million civilians were deported to Germany and to other occupied countries. . . .

Murder and Ill-Treatment of Prisoners of War

The defendants murdered and ill-treated prisoners of war by denying them adequate food, shelter, clothing, and medical care and attention; by forcing them to labor in inhumane conditions; by torturing them and subjecting them to inhuman indignities. . . .

Frequently prisoners captured on the Western Front were obliged to march to the camps until they completely collapsed. Some of them walked more than 600 kilometers [372 miles] with hardly any food; they marched on for forty-eight hours running without being fed; among them a certain number died of exhaustion or of hunger; stragglers were systematically murdered. . . .

American prisoners, officers, and men were murdered in Normandy during the summer of 1944 and in the Ardennes in December 1944. American prisoners were starved, beaten, and otherwise mistreated. . . .

At Orel prisoners of war were exterminated by starvation, shooting, exposure, and poisoning.

Soviet prisoners of war were murdered en masse [in large groups] on orders from the High Command. . . . Tens of thousands of Soviet prisoners of war were tortured and murdered.

PART TEN

Hope and Distress
in the Nuclear Age

The Formation of a New International Organization

Any attempt to create an effective international organization was bound to be complicated and frustrated by conflicting national beliefs and ambitions. Nevertheless, when representatives of fifty nations gathered in San Francisco on April 25, 1945, to draw up a Charter for the United Nations, the world enjoyed a moment of hope, even in the midst of war. The Charter was signed and ratified by all the nations represented at San Francisco.

Since then the sharp differences which developed between the Soviet Union and the West, and the problems arising from the emergence of new nations, have made it difficult for the organization to function smoothly. In spite of its many problems, the United Nations has become a much more forceful international body than the earlier League of Nations.

The following selections are from the United Nations Charter.

October 24, 1945

We the peoples of the United Nations
Determined

to save succeeding generations from the scourge of war, which twice in our lifetime has brought untold sorrow to mankind, and

to reaffirm faith in fundamental human rights, in the dignity and worth of the human person, in the equal rights of men and women and of nations large and small, and

to establish conditions under which justice and respect for the obligations arising from treaties and other sources of international law can be

Source: *Documents of the United Nations Conference on International Organization, San Francisco, 1945*, London and New York: United Nations Information Organization, 1945, Vol. XV, pp. 336 *passim*.

maintained, and to promote social progress and better standards of life in larger freedom.

And for these ends

to practice tolerance and live together in peace with one another as good neighbors, and

to unite our strength to maintain international peace and security, and to insure, by the acceptance of principles and the institution of methods, that armed force shall not be used, save in the common interest, and

to employ international machinery for the promotion of the economic and social advancement of all peoples,

Have resolved to combine our efforts to accomplish these aims.

Accordingly, our respective Governments, through representatives assembled in the city of San Francisco, who have exhibited their full powers found to be in good and due form, have agreed to the present Charter of the United Nations and do hereby establish an international organization to be known as the United Nations.

Purposes and Principles

Article 1

The Purposes of the United Nations are:

1. To maintain international peace and security, and to that end: to take effective collective measures for the prevention and removal of threats to the peace, and for the suppression of acts of aggression or other breaches of the peace, and to bring about by peaceful means, and in conformity with the principles of justice and international law, adjustment or settlement of international disputes or situations which might lead to a breach of the peace;

2. To develop friendly relations among nations based on respect for the principle of equal rights and self-determination of peoples, and to take other appropriate measures to strengthen universal peace;

3. To achieve international cooperation in solving international problems of an economic, social, cultural, or humanitarian character, and in promoting and encouraging respect for human rights and for funda-

mental freedoms for all without distinction as to race, sex, language, or religion; and

4. To be a center for harmonizing the actions of nations in the attainment of these common ends.

Article 2

The Organization and its Members, in pursuit of the Purposes stated in Article 1, shall act in accordance with the following Principles.

1. The Organization is based on the principle of the sovereign equality of all its Members.

2. All Members, in order to insure to all of them the rights and benefits resulting from membership, shall fulfill in good faith the obligations assumed by them in accordance with the present Charter.

3. All Members shall settle their international disputes by peaceful means in such a manner that international peace and security, and justice are not endangered. . . .

Article 4

1. Membership in the United Nations is open to all other peace-loving states which accept the obligations contained in the present Charter and, in the judgment of the Organization, are able and willing to carry out these obligations. . . .

Article 7

1. There are established as the principal organs of the United Nations: a General Assembly, a Security Council, an Economic and Social Council, a Trusteeship, an International Court of Justice, and a Secretariat. . . .

The General Assembly

COMPOSITION

Article 9

1. The General Assembly shall consist of all the Members of the United Nations. . . .

Article 11

3. The General Assembly may call the attention of the Security Council to situations which are likely to endanger international peace and security. . . .

Article 13

1. The General Assembly shall initiate studies and make recommendations for the purpose of:

a. promoting international cooperation in the political field and encouraging the progressive development of international law and its codification;

b. promoting international cooperation in the economic, social, cultural, educational, and health fields, and assisting in the realization of human rights and fundamental freedoms for all without distinction as to race, sex, language, or religion. . . .

Article 17

1. The General Assembly shall consider and approve the budget of the Organization.

2. The expenses of the Organization shall be borne by the Members as apportioned by the General Assembly. . . .

VOTING

Article 18

1. Each member of the General Assembly shall have one vote.

2. Decisions of the General Assembly on important questions shall be made by two-thirds majority of the Members present and voting. These questions shall include: recommendations with respect to the maintenance of international peace and security, . . . the admission of new Members to the United Nations, the suspension of the rights and privileges of membership, the expulsion of Members. . . .

3. Decisions on other questions, including the determination of additional categories of questions to be decided by a two-thirds majority, shall be made by a majority of the Members present and voting.

Article 19

A Member of the United Nations which is in arrears in the payment of its financial contributions to the Organization shall have no vote in the General Assembly if the amount of its arrears equals or exceeds the amount of the contributions due from it for the preceding two full years. The General Assembly may, nevertheless, permit such a Member to vote if it is satisfied that the failure to pay is due to conditions beyond the control of the Member.

PROCEDURE

Article 20

The General Assembly shall meet in regular annual sessions and in such special sessions as occasion may require. Special sessions shall be convoked by the Secretary-General at the request of the Security Council or of a majority of the Members of the United Nations. . . .

The Security Council

COMPOSITION

Article 23

1. The Security Council shall consist of eleven Members of the United Nations. The Republic of China, France, the Union of Soviet Socialist Republics, the United Kingdom of Great Britain and Northern Ireland, and the United States of America shall be permanent members of the Security Council. The General Assembly shall elect six other Members of the United Nations to be nonpermanent members of the Security Council, due regard being specially paid in the first instance to the contribution of Members of the United Nations to the maintenance of international peace and security and to the other purposes of the Organization, and also to equitable geographical distribution.

2. The nonpermanent members of the Security Council shall be elected for a term of two years. . . .

FUNCTIONS AND POWERS

Article 24

1. In order to ensure prompt and effective action by the United Nations, its Members confer on the Security Council primary responsibility for the maintenance of international peace and security, and agree

that in carrying out its duties under this responsibility the Security Council acts on their behalf. . . .

Article 25

The Members of the United Nations agree to accept and carry out the decisions of the Security Council in accordance with the present Charter.

PROCEDURE

Article 27

1. Each member of the Security Council shall have one vote.
2. Decisions of the Security Council on procedural matters shall be made by an affirmative vote of seven members.
3. Decisions of the Security Council on all other matters shall be made by an affirmative vote of seven members including the concurring votes of the permanent members. . . .

Article 28

1. The Security Council shall be so organized as to be able to function continuously. Each member of the Security Council shall for this purpose be represented at all times at the seat of the Organization. . . .

Pacific Settlement of Disputes

Article 34

The Security Council may investigate any dispute, or any situation which might lead to international friction or give rise to a dispute, in order to determine whether the continuance of the dispute or situation is likely to endanger the maintenance of international peace and security.

Article 35

1. Any Member of the United Nations may bring any dispute, or any situation of the nature referred to in Article 34, to the attention of the Security Council or of the General Assembly.
2. A state which is not a Member of the United Nations may bring to the attention of the Security Council or of the General Assembly any

dispute to which it is a party if it accepts in advance, for the purposes of the dispute, the obligations of pacific settlement provided in the present Charter. . . .

Action with Respect to Threats to the Peace, Breaches of the Peace, and Acts of Aggression

Article 39

The Security Council shall determine the existence of any threat to the peace, breach of the peace, or act of aggression, and shall make recommendations or decide what measures shall be taken in accordance with Articles 41 and 42, to maintain or restore international peace and security. . . .

Article 41

The Security Council may decide what measures involving the use of armed force are to be employed to give effect to its decisions, and it may call upon the Members of the United Nations to apply such measures. These may include complete or partial interruption of economic relations and of rail, sea, air, postal, telegraphic, radio, and other means of communication, and the severance of diplomatic relations.

Article 42

Should the Security Council consider that measures provided for in Article 41 would be inadequate or have proved to be inadequate, it may take such action by air, sea, or land forces as may be necessary to maintain or restore international peace and security. Such action may include demonstrations, blockade, and other operations by air, sea, or land forces of Members of the United Nations.

Article 43

1. All Members of the United Nations, in order to contribute to the maintenance of international peace and security, undertake to make available to the Security Council, on its call and in accordance with a special agreement or agreements, armed forces, assistance, and facilities, including rights of passage, necessary for the purpose of maintaining international peace and security. . . .

International Economic and Social Cooperation

Article 55

With a view to the creation of conditions of stability and well-being which are necessary for peaceful and friendly relations among nations based on respect for the principle of equal rights and self-determination of peoples, the United Nations shall promote:

a. higher standards of living, full employment, and conditions of economic and social progress and development;

b. solutions of international economic, social, health, and related problems; and international cultural and educational cooperation; and

c. universal respect for, and observance of, human rights and fundamental freedoms for all without distinction as to race, sex, language, or religion.

The United States Leads the Free World

The extent of Soviet ambition became clear soon after the end of the war. By 1947 Communism had consolidated its position in Eastern Europe and was beginning to threaten Greece and Turkey. The British, who had been giving aid to both these countries, were no longer in a position to continue because of overwhelming economic problems at home. At this point President Harry S. Truman, in a speech before Congress on March 12, 1947, asked the United States to assume the responsibility of aiding free nations in their efforts to resist Communist aggression. This policy, to which Congress responded favorably, became known as the Truman Doctrine.

A few months later, on June 5, Secretary of State George C. Marshall, in a commencement address at Harvard University, discussed the gravity of the international situation. Since the elimination of poverty and hunger were considered essential for a free and stable Europe, Marshall declared that the United States was willing to aid war-torn European nations in reconstructing their economies. Russia and its satellites greeted this

215

offer with hostility. The non-Communist countries received it enthusiastically. Large appropriations were voted by Congress and the Marshall Plan went into action. When the program drew to a close at the end of 1951, the United States had spent twelve and one-half billion dollars. The Marshall Plan was an extraordinary example of international cooperation in peacetime. The rate of European recovery was impressive.

The following selections are from the speeches of Truman and Marshall.

The Truman Doctrine

Mr. President [President of the Senate], Mr. Speaker, Members of the Congress of the United States, the gravity of the situation which confronts the world today necessitates my appearance before a joint session of the Congress.

The foreign policy and the national security of this country are involved.

One aspect of the present situation which I wish to present to you at this time for your consideration and decision concerns Greece and Turkey.

The United States has received from the Greek government an urgent appeal for financial and economic assistance. . . .

I do not believe that the American people and the Congress wish to turn a deaf ear to the appeal of the Greek government.

Greece is not a rich country. Lack of sufficient natural resources has always forced the Greek people to work hard to make both ends meet. Since 1940 this industrious and peace-loving country has suffered invasion, four years of cruel enemy occupation, and bitter internal strife.

When forces of liberation entered Greece they found that the retreating Germans had destroyed virtually all the railways, roads, port facilities, communications, and merchant marine. More than a thousand villages had been burned. Eighty-five percent of the children were tubercular. Livestock, poultry, and draft animals had almost disappeared. Inflation had wiped out practically all savings.

The very existence of the Greek state is today threatened by the

THE TRUMAN DOCTRINE. Source: United States Congress, *Congressional Record*, 80th Congress, 1st Session, Washington, D.C.: Government Printing Office, 1947, Vol. XCIII, pp. 1980–81.

terrorist activities of several thousand armed men, led by Communists, who defy the government's authority at a number of points, particularly along the northern boundaries. . . .

Greece must have assistance if it is to become a self-supporting and self-respecting democracy.

The United States must supply this assistance. We have already extended to Greece certain types of relief and economic aid but these are inadequate.

There is no other country to which democratic Greece can turn.

No other nation is willing and able to provide the necessary support for a democratic Greek government.

We have considered how the United Nations might assist in this crisis. But the situation is an urgent one requiring immediate action, and the United Nations and its related organizations are not in a position to extend help of the kind that is required.

Greece's neighbor, Turkey, also deserves our attention. . . .

Since the war, Turkey has sought financial assistance from Great Britain and the United States for the purpose of effecting that modernization necessary for the maintenance of its national integrity.

That integrity is essential to the preservation of order in the Middle East.

The British government has informed us that, owing to its own difficulties, it can no longer extend financial or economic aid to Turkey.

As in the case of Greece, if Turkey is to have the assistance it needs, the United States must supply it. We are the only country able to provide that help.

I am fully aware of the broad implications involved if the United States extends assistance to Greece and Turkey, and I shall discuss these implications with you at this time.

One of the primary objectives of the foreign policy of the United States is the creation of conditions in which we and other nations will be able to work out a way of life free from coercion. This was a fundamental issue in the war with Germany and Japan. Our victory was won over countries which sought to impose their will and their way of life upon other nations. . . .

The peoples of a number of countries of the world have recently had totalitarian regimes forced upon them against their will. The government of the United States has made frequent protests against coercion and intimidation, in violation of the Yalta Agreement, in Poland,

Romania, and Bulgaria. I must also state that in a number of other countries there have been similar developments.

At the present moment in world history nearly every nation must choose between alternative ways of life. The choice is too often not a free one. . . .

I believe that we must assist free peoples to work out their own destinies in their own way.

I believe that our help should be primarily through economic and financial aid, which is essential to economic stability and orderly political processes. . . .

It would be an unspeakable tragedy if these countries which have struggled so long against overwhelming odds should lose that victory for which they sacrificed so much. Collapse of free institutions and loss of independence would be disastrous not only for them but for the world. Discouragement and possibly failure would quickly be the lot of neighboring peoples striving to maintain their freedom and independence.

Should we fail to aid Greece and Turkey in this fateful hour, the effect will be far reaching to the West as well as to the East.

We must take immediate and resolute action.

I therefore ask the Congress to provide authority for assistance to Greece and Turkey in the amount of $400,000,000 for the period ending June 30, 1948. . . .

In addition to funds, I ask the Congress to authorize the detail of American civilian and military personnel to Greece and Turkey, at the request of those countries, to assist in the tasks of reconstruction, and for the purpose of supervising the use of such financial and material assistance as may be furnished. I recommend that authority also be provided for the instruction and training of selected Greek and Turkish personnel.

Finally, I ask that the Congress provide authority which will permit the speediest and most effective use, in terms of needed commodities, supplies, and equipment, of such funds as may be authorized.

The United States contributed $341,000,000,000 toward winning World War II. This is an investment in world freedom and world peace. . . .

The seeds of totalitarian regimes are nurtured by misery and want. They spread and grow in the evil soil of poverty and strife. They reach their full growth when the hope of a people for a better life has died.

We must keep that hope alive.

The Marshall Plan

The truth of the matter is that Europe's requirements for the next three or four years of foreign food and other essential products — principally from America — are so much greater than her present ability to pay that she must have substantial additional help or face economic, social, and political deterioration of a very grave character. . . .

Aside from the demoralizing effect on the world at large and the possibilities of disturbances arising as a result of the desperation of the people concerned, the consequences to the economy of the United States should be apparent to all. It is logical that the United States should do whatever it is able to do to assist in the return of normal economic health in the world, without which there can be no political stability and no assured peace. Our policy is directed not against any country or doctrine but against hunger, poverty, desperation, and chaos. Its purpose should be the revival of a working economy in the world so as to permit the emergence of political and social conditions in which free institutions can exist. Such assistance, I am convinced, must not be on a piecemeal basis as various crises develop. Any assistance that this government may render in the future should provide a cure rather than a mere palliative [temporary remedy]. Any government that is willing to assist in the task of recovery will find full cooperation, I am sure, on the part of the United States Government. Any government which maneuvers to block the recovery of other countries cannot expect help from us. Furthermore, governments, political parties, or groups which seek to perpetuate human misery in order to profit therefrom politically or otherwise will encounter the opposition of the United States.

It is already evident that, before the United States Government can proceed much further in its efforts to alleviate the situation and help start the European world on its way to recovery, there must be some agreement among the countries of Europe as to the requirements of the situation and the part those countries themselves will take in order to give proper effect to whatever action might be undertaken by this government. It would be neither fitting nor efficacious for this government to undertake to draw up unilaterally a program designed to place Europe on its feet economically. This is the business of the Europeans.

THE MARSHALL PLAN. Source: *A Decade of American Foreign Policy, Basic Documents, 1941–49*, Senate Document 123, 81st Congress, 1st Session, Washington, D.C.: Government Printing Office, 1950, pp. 1269–70.

The initiative, I think, must come from Europe. The role of this country should consist of friendly aid in the drafting of a European program and of later support of such a program so far as it may be practical for us to do so. . . .

An essential part of any successful action on the part of the United States is an understanding on the part of the people of America of the character of the problem and the remedies to be applied. Political passion and prejudice should have no part. With foresight and a willingness on the part of our people to face up to the vast responsibility which history has clearly placed upon our country, the difficulties I have outlined can and will be overcome.

The Recovery of Europe

The vast destruction of life and property in Europe during World War II and the assumption of world leadership by the United States and Russia convinced many Europeans that their only salvation lay in burying national differences and working out some form of economic and even political association. European cooperation and economic revival were considerably advanced by Marshall Plan aid (1947–1951) and by the North Atlantic Treaty Organization (1949).

In 1951 six European nations (France, Italy, West Germany, Belgium, the Netherlands, and Luxembourg) agreed to form a European Coal and Steel Community; in 1957, after considerable success, they established a much closer union in the European Economic Community (the Common Market). Seven other nations (Austria, Denmark, Norway, Portugal, Sweden, Switzerland, and Great Britain) combined in 1959 to set up a European Free Trade Association. A major step was taken toward a greater European community when British Prime Minister Harold Macmillan announced in July 1961 that Britain wished to apply for membership in the Common Market. Other nations were expected to follow.

Negotiations between Britain and members of the Common Market seemed to progress, but were broken off abruptly in January 1963 when France vetoed British entry. Members of both EEC and EFTA continued to express the hope that some form of association of Western European nations would eventually come into being.

Stephen R. Graubard, author of the following selection, is research associate in the Center for International Affairs at Harvard University, and editor of Daedalus, the Journal of the American Academy of Arts and Sciences.

If Europe emerged from the [Second World] War uncertain about the future, the reasons were not hard to find. . . . The loss of power — military and political — seemed obvious. This loss might be remedied in time, but for the moment the United States and the Soviet Union hovered over Europe as two colossi [giants], influencing everything — the establishment of new governments, the rate of economic recovery, the stability of particular regimes. . . .

As Europeans reflected on their prospects, they faced first a loss of power, which, in more depressed moments, they chose to translate as a loss of independence. They saw the continent riven [torn apart] by new and unnatural boundaries, expressing the accidents of war more than the circumstances of nationality, history, or geography. Formerly dependent peoples in Asia and Africa rebelled against their European allegiances, or made their intentions so unmistakable that Europeans, occasionally recognizing the advantage of acting quickly, granted independence almost as soon as it was demanded. . . . In these circumstances, more than sufficient reason existed for concern and even alarm. The extraordinary thing about the postwar period was that neither developed to the extent that might have been predicted. It was as if the war itself had purged Europe of all fears. So much had been experienced — the suffering and loss had been so great — that these new blows fell almost without effect on peoples who had become habituated to [used to] adversity. . . .

Europeans had every reason to despair, but accepted none of them. . . . The concept of a single European society, which had gone out of fashion in the second half of the nineteenth century . . . returned to favor. There was no way of knowing how far the revival of European sentiment would go, or what its long-range consequences would be, but there was no denying its reality. Economic cooperation

Source: Stephen R. Graubard, "A New Europe?" in Daedalus, Vol. 93, No. 1, Winter 1964, pp. 559–65.

221

might stop with the Common Market and never proceed to political union, but this did not alter the fact that the second prospect had been raised in serious political debate throughout Europe, and that it had not been dismissed as visionary. . . . Increasingly, the idea of Europe penetrated everyone's thinking; men might define the term differently, resist it, but they refused to deny it. A consciousness of Europe, once the property of educated men, became a common possession. . . .

Geographic proximity, which for so long had seemed the condition of national war and rivalry, emerged as a factor encouraging unity. European frontiers, in the West at least, became demilitarized; the Franco-German understanding was certainly as remarkable a development as any other in a century of diplomatic change. . . .

European statesmen hurried from conference to conference, flew the oceans of the world, and indicated by their every gesture a continuing interest in maintaining control over their own destinies and in influencing that of others. The incontrovertible [undeniable] reality remained. With severely limited resources, particularly in the military sphere, Europe was incapable of defending herself. This fact could never be lost sight of. Europe's reliance on American protection was total; this situation had no historic parallel. . . .

This loss of military self-sufficiency coincided with another development, less discussed, but which could prove to be equally important. Europe, for all practical purposes, was excluded from the scientific and technological pursuits associated with the exploration of space. For the first time in centuries major discoveries were taking place in another part of the world, to which Europeans contributed in only the most insignificant manner. . . .

This issue, rarely discussed, symbolized Europe's dilemma. In the pre-1945 world, Europe's centrality, while open to challenge, was never effectively denied. Her citizens succeeded in opening up the world; her ideas dominated in science as well as in the arts; her techniques were studied and copied by all who believed in the possibility of progress. . . .

Such a dominant position, perhaps, is beyond the capacity of any society today; if so, Europe is simply experiencing what the Americans and Soviets also feel, and what is in any case inevitable, given the facts of modern technology. Dominance once enjoyed, however, is not lightly abandoned, particularly when it seems to define the whole of a society's past experience. A feeling persists in Europe, rarely expressed, that Europe must·not simply become the junior partner in a going enterprise, however magnificently managed. Europe's continuing concern is with the possibility of becoming too much the political, intellectual, and spiritual disciple of the United States. . . . This is a strange reversal of roles. Europe, in the twentieth century, is seeking the independence from the other which America so prided itself on securing in the eighteenth. . . .

Europe's experience is too deeply and permanently inscribed for illusions to exist about the possibility of starting over again. There may be a "new Europe," but Europe is not a new world. The Flemish * will not soon feel differently about the Walloons,* though any number of rational arguments may be offered to demonstrate why they should. West Germans will not easily abandon talk of the "unification" of Germany, though many abroad would wish that they might. . . .

For the moment, [Europe's] energy appears to be expended particularly in planning. Cities are being built, industries developed, and agriculture [reorganized]. Each of these activities creates opportunities and problems. As in the past, politics concerns itself largely with the situations created by immediate developments. . . .

Europe's rebuilding and decolonizing tasks have so preoccupied her, have required such vast expenditures of physical and psychic energy, that there has been little incentive to recognize that these were essentially finite [having an end] operations, which would not indefinitely make important demands on her. In the decade now opening, new preoccupations will undoubtedly assert themselves. More thought, almost certainly, will be given to relations between Western and Eastern Europe. While the Soviet's policy in this matter will be enormously influential, it may be less governing than in the past. Relations between Europe and the states of the Iberian peninsula † may change rather dramatically; this "underdeveloped" region of Europe is not necessarily destined to remain so. European-Soviet and European-American relations will almost certainly be modified, in part because of the policies pursued by the great powers, in part because of Europe's own growing consciousness of her own capabilities. It would be hazardous to guess what these changes will be, but it would be wrong to assume that ex-

* **Flemish:** the Belgians who live in the northern region of Flanders. The **Walloons** live in the southern part of Belgium. The two groups speak different languages and have different religions. There is often friction between them.
  † **Iberian peninsula:** that part of Europe in which Spain and Portugal are located.

isting relations define what they are likely to be, even in the immediate future. The question of European political unity will certainly continue to be debated. It is not impossible that it will be as unsettled a matter a decade from now as it is today [1964]. . . .

Europe, by almost any standard that is relevant, shows remarkable vitality and hope. It should not surprise anyone if in the next half century she seeks again, with something approaching her former self-confidence, to be an "example" to the world. The task, while difficult, may be precisely the one to justify the use of that now overworked phrase, the "new Europe." The present efforts, seemingly chaotic, may in time be viewed as the uncertain strivings of an old society to renew itself, by taking what is best from its recollections of a not undistinguished past.

Khrushchev Reveals the Crimes of Stalin

An anxious world watched the politics in the Kremlin after the death of Joseph Stalin in March 1953. Stalin had been one of the most successful dictators in history. He had eliminated his internal opponents, defeated his foreign enemies, and extended his rule over a vast empire. There was no one of Stalin's stature to succeed him. Out of the inevitable struggle for power that followed, Nikita S. Khrushchev emerged as ruler of Russia.

The sordid nature of the rule of Stalin was no secret. It was astonishing, nevertheless, to have Khrushchev denounce him before the Twentieth Communist Party Congress in February 1956. The brutality, the terror, and the worship of personality during Stalin's reign were all frankly and vividly revealed. The people of Russia, who must have been confused by all this, were somehow able to put away their former idol without apparent protest.

Russia under Khrushchev remains a dictatorship which does not shrink from using brute force to crush opposition, but some of the worst evils of Stalin's rule have not been revived.

Stalin acted not through persuasion, explanation, and patient cooperation with people, but by imposing his concepts and demanding absolute submission to his opinion. Whoever opposed this concept or tried to prove his viewpoint and the correctness of his position was doomed . . . to subsequent moral and physical annihilation. This was especially true during the period following the Seventeenth Party Congress [1934], when many prominent party leaders and rank and file party workers, honest and dedicated to the cause of Communism, fell victim to Stalin's despotism. . . .

Stalin originated the concept "enemy of the people." This term automatically rendered it unnecessary that the ideological errors of a man or men engaged in a controversy be proved; this term made possible the usage of the most cruel repression, violating all norms of revolutionary legality, against anyone who in any way disagreed with Stalin, against those who were only suspected of hostile intent, against those who had bad reputations. This concept "enemy of the people" actually eliminated the possibility of any kind of ideological fight or the making of one's views known on this or that issue, even those of a practical character. In the main, and in actuality, the only proof of guilt used, against all norms of current legal science, was the "confession" of the accused himself; and, as subsequent probing proved, "confessions" were acquired through physical pressures against the accused. This led to glaring violations of revolutionary legality and to the fact that many entirely innocent persons who in the past had defended the Party line became victims. . . .

Arbitrary behavior by one person encouraged and permitted arbitrariness in others. Mass arrests and deportations of many thousands of people, execution without trial and without normal investigation created conditions of insecurity, fear, and even desperation. . . .

Stalin . . . used extreme methods and mass repressions at a time when the Revolution was already victorious, when the Soviet state was strengthened, when the exploiting classes were already liquidated and Socialist relations were rooted solidly in all phases of national economy, when our Party was politically consolidated and had strengthened itself both numerically and ideologically.

Source: N. S. Khrushchev, "The Crimes of the Stalin Era: Special Report to the Twentieth Congress of the Communist Party of the Soviet Union," annotated by B. I. Nicolaevsky, in *The New Leader*, New York, 1956, pp. S13–15, 17, 20, 25, 27, 32–34, 54. © 1962 by *The New Leader*. Reprinted by permission of *The New Leader*.

It is clear that here Stalin showed in a whole series of cases his intolerance, his brutality, and his abuse of power. Instead of proving his political correctness and mobilizing the masses, he often chose the path of repression and physical annihilation, not only against actual enemies but also against individuals who had not committed any crimes against the Party and the Soviet government. . . .

Stalin's willfulness [toward] the Party and its Central Committee became fully evident after the Seventeenth Party Congress which took place in 1934. . . .

It became apparent that many Party, Soviet, and economic activists who were branded in 1937–38 as "enemies," were actually never enemies, spies, wreckers, etc., but were always honest Communists; they were only so stigmatized [accused], and often no longer able to bear barbaric tortures, they charged themselves . . . with all kinds of grave and unlikely crimes. . . .

Stalin put the Party and the NKVD [secret police] up to the use of mass terror when the exploiting classes had been liquidated in our country and when there were no serious reasons for the use of extraordinary mass terror.

This terror was actually directed not at the remnants of the defeated exploiting classes but against the honest workers of the Party and of the Soviet state; against them were made lying, slanderous, and absurd accusations concerning "two-facedness," "espionage," "sabotage," preparation of fictitious "plots," etc. . . .

The majority of the Central Committee members and candidates elected at the Seventeenth Congress and arrested in 1937 and 1938 were expelled from the party illegally. . . .

Now when the cases of some of these so-called "spies" and "saboteurs" were examined, it was found that all their cases were fabricated. Confessions of guilt of many arrested and charged with enemy activity were gained with the help of cruel and inhuman tortures. . . .

Many thousands of honest and innocent Communists have died as a result of this monstrous falsification of such "cases," as a result of the fact that all kinds of slanderous "confessions" were accepted, and as a result of the practice of forcing accusations against oneself and others. . . .

A large part of these cases are being reviewed now and a great part of them are being voided because they were baseless and falsified. . . .

Mass arrests of Party, Soviet, economic, and military workers caused tremendous harm to our country and to the cause of Socialist advancement.

Mass repressions had a negative influence on the moral-political condition of the Party, created a situation of uncertainty, contributed to the spreading of unhealthy suspicion, and sowed distrust among Communists. All sorts of slanderers and careerists were active. . . .

Stalin was a very distrustful man, sickly suspicious; we know this from our work with him. He could look at a man and say, "Why are your eyes so shifty today?" or, "Why are you turning so much today and avoiding to look me directly in the eyes?" The sickly suspicion created in him a general distrust even toward eminent party workers whom he had known for years. Everywhere and in everything he saw "enemies," "two-facers," and "spies." Possessing unlimited power, he indulged in great willfulness. . . .

Comrades! The cult of the individual acquired such monstrous size chiefly because Stalin himself, using all conceivable methods, supported the glorification of his own person. This is supported by numerous facts. One of the most characteristic examples of Stalin's self-glorification and of his lack of even elementary modesty is the edition of his *Short Biography* which was published in 1948.

This book is an expression of the most dissolute flattery, an example of making a man into a godhead, of transforming him into an infallible sage, "the greatest leader, sublime strategist of all times and nations." Finally, no other words could be found with which to lift Stalin up to the heavens.

We need not give here examples of the loathsome adulation filling this book. All we need to add is that they all were approved and edited by Stalin personally and some of them were added in his own handwriting to the draft text of the book.

Nationalization and the Welfare State in Britain

The smashing victory of the Labor Party over the Conservatives in the election of July 1945 surprised even Clement Attlee, the new Labor Prime Minister. Though Winston Churchill was the

227

great hero of the nation, the British people turned away from his party which was tainted with appeasement and depression. The Labor Party found itself with the staggering burden of finishing the war, reviving an exhausted economy, and inaugurating a great program of welfare and nationalization, all at the same time.

What Labor achieved in six years of power was a Welfare State, which was a mixture of free enterprise and socialism. The bulk of industry remained in the hands of private owners. Welfare legislation, long in existence, was extended in every area. In order to pay for the program and to strengthen the economy, austerity and rationing were continued long after the war. When the Conservative Party returned to power in 1951, it generally accepted, and even extended, the services of the Welfare State.

The author of this selection, Drew Middleton, spent many years in England as a correspondent for The New York Times.

Nationalization of industry is the most widely advertised economic result of Labor policies between 1945 and 1951. In assessing its effect on the changes in Britain since 1939, we must remember that neither was it so new nor is it so extensive as Americans believe. The British Broadcasting Corporation was created as a public corporation as long ago as 1927 [by the Conservative Party]. Today most manufacturing in Britain remains in the control of private enterprise.

Between 1945 and 1951, however, the Labor government's policy of nationalization created corporations that today operate or control industries or services. In two industries, steel and road transport, the trend toward nationalization has been reversed [by the Conservative Party]. But the following list shows the extent of nationalization in Britain today.

Coal: The Coal Industry Nationalization Act received the Royal Assent in May 1946, and on January 1, 1947, the assets of the industry were vested in the National Coal Board appointed by the Minister of Fuel and Power and responsible for the management of the industry. . . .

Gas: Under the Gas Act of 1948 the gas industry was brought under public ownership and control on May 1, 1949. . . .

Source: Drew Middleton, *These Are the British,* New York: Alfred A. Knopf, Inc., 1957, pp. 97–110. © 1957 by Drew Middleton. Reprinted by permission of the publishers.

Electricity: The Central Electricity Authority in April 1948 took over the assets of former municipal and private electricity supply systems throughout Great Britain. . . . But the industry had long been moving toward nationalization. As early as 1919 the Electricity Commissioners were established to supervise the industry and promote voluntary reorganization. . . .

Banking: The Bank of England, Britain's central bank, was established in 1694 by Act of Parliament. Its entire capital stock was acquired by the government under the Bank of England Act of 1946. . . .

Transport: On January 1, 1948, under the Transport Act passed in the preceding year, most of Britain's inland transport system came under public ownership. Nationalization embraced the railways and the hotels, road transport interests, docks and steamships owned by the railways, most of the canals, and London's passenger transport system. . . .

Airways: British governments since the twenties have been involved in civil aviation. Imperial Airways received a government grant of one million pounds as early as 1924. By 1939 the Conservative government established the British Overseas Airways Corporation by Act of Parliament. In 1946 the Labor government, under the Civil Aviation Act, set up two additional public corporations. . . .

Communications: The government took control of Cable and Wireless, Ltd., the principal overseas telegraph service, on January 1, 1947. Thus, the Post Office now operates overseas telecommunications from the United Kingdom and, of course, all internal telephonic and telegraphic systems.

These were the most important milestones on the Labor Party's progress toward nationalization. Viewed dispassionately, they were evolutionary rather than revolutionary. There had been a trend toward nationalization in electricity for some years. Objective investigators had suggested nationalization to aid the failing coal-mining industry, and during the war (1942) the Coalition government had assumed full control of the industry's operations although private ownership retained control of the mines.

We should avoid, too, the impression, popular among the uninformed in the United States and even in Britain, that nationalization meant that the workers took over management of the industries concerned. . . . On the contrary, employees protested that nationalization did not affect the management of industries, and such protests were backed by facts. In 1951, after six years of Labor Party rule, trade union representation among the full-time members of the boards of the nationalized industries was a little under twenty percent, and among the part-time members the percentage was just below fifteen percent. Five boards had no trade union representation.

The nationalization program of the Labor government between 1945 and 1951 nevertheless marked an important change in the structure of British society. The financial and economic control of some of the nation's most important industries was transferred from private to public hands. The capitalist system that had served Britain so well found its horizons limited in important fields.

There is now no important political movement in Britain to undo the work of the Labor government in the fields mentioned above. But as long as a generation survives which knew these industries under private control, harsh and persistent criticism will persist. Some of it is just. . . .

Nationalization, however, was only one means of altering the bases of British society. The historian of the future may consider that the tremendous extension of government responsibility for social welfare was a more important factor in the evolution of Britain. The Welfare State has been a target for critics on both sides of the Atlantic. Its admitted cost [and] its supposed inefficiency are denounced. British critics, however, avoid a cardinal point. The Welfare State is in Britain to stay. No government relying on the electorate for office is going to dismantle it. . . .

The system is much more extensive than most Americans realize. The government is now responsible through either central or local authorities for services that include subsistence for the needy, education and health services for all, housing, employment insurance, the care of the aged or the handicapped, the feeding of mothers and infants, sickness, maternity, and industrial injury benefits, widows' and retirement pensions, and family allowances. . . .

Again, as in the case of the nationalization of industry, we find that much of the legislation that established the Welfare State . . . is the latest step in an evolutionary process. National Insurance is the logical outgrowth of the Poor Relief Act of 1601, before there were Englishmen in America. . . .

What effect did the nationalization of industry and the establishment of the Welfare State have on British society? Obviously, the first removed from the control of the moneyed and propertied classes certain powers over the economic function of Britain. The second, because of its cost, made certain that the heavy tax rates introduced during and just before World War II would continue. These taxes were paid principally by the middle class, which, at the outset, refused in many instances to use the National Health Service.

The effect was a leveling one. The dominant class was stripped, on one hand, of some of its power to control a large section of the national economy, although, as we have seen, it managed to retain its direction of the nationalized industries. At the same time this class found that it must continue to pay year by year a high proportion of its earned income for the state's care of its less prosperous fellows. The decline in the influence, prosperity, and prestige of the old middle class was definitely accelerated by these two bold advances toward Socialism. . . .

But to balance this gradual depression of one class there was the expansion of another. The victory of the Labor Party in 1945 encouraged the working class of the nation to seek a richer, fuller life. It opened vistas of a new existence and greater opportunities.

India's Place in World Affairs

The independence of India, long demanded by Indians and willingly granted by the British Labor government in 1947, was accompanied by bloodshed as well as rejoicing. The fears of the Moslem minority led to a partition of the subcontinent into India and Pakistan. Violence broke out between Moslems and Hindus, resulting in many deaths and the transfer of huge populations from one area to another. Although India and Pakistan are now on better terms than they were in the past, suspicion and hard feelings remain, and the outstanding differences between these countries are not yet settled.

The greatest experiment in democracy in an underdeveloped country is taking place in India, where a small educated leadership is attempting to cope with almost insuperable economic and social problems in a land with an enormous and rapidly expanding population. In foreign affairs, India, by adhering to a policy of nonalignment, has attempted to play the role of a moral force between East and West.

In the fall of 1962 India was jarred out of its complacency when Communist China attacked its borders. The policy of nonalignment was not without its advantages in this crisis. Britain and the United States at once gave support to India's cause; and not long after, the Soviet Union indicated its displeasure with Communist China's action.

In the following speech made in 1949, Jawaharlal Nehru, Prime Minister of the new republic, explains India's neutrality. After Nehru's death in May 1964, his successor, Lal Bahadur Shastri, declared that Nehru's policy of nonalignment would continue and that India could not afford to become associated with any power bloc.

As I said, our general policy has been to try to cultivate friendly relations with all countries, but that is something which anyone can say. It is not a very helpful thought. It is almost outside, if I may say so, of politics. It may be just a verbal statement or a moral urge. It is hardly a political urge. Nevertheless, something can be said for it even on the political plane. We cannot perhaps be friendly always with every country. The alternative is to become very friendly with some and hostile to others. That is the normal foreign policy of a country — very friendly with close relations with some, with the consequence that you are hostile with others. . . . And ultimately your hostility provokes other people's hostility and that is the way of conflict and leads to no solution. Fortunately, India has inherited no past hostility to any other country. Why should we then start this train of hostility now with any country? Of course, if circumstances compel us it cannot be helped, but it is far better for us to try our utmost to keep clear of these hostile backgrounds. Naturally, again, we are likely to be more friendly to some countries than to others, because this may be to our mutual advantage. That is a different matter, but even so, our friendship with other countries should not, as far as possible, be such as brings us inevitably into conflict with some other country. Now, some people may think that this is a policy of hedging or just avoiding pitfalls, a middle-of-the-road policy. As I conceive it, it is nothing of the kind. It is not a middle-of-the-road

Source: Jawaharlal Nehru, *Independence and After: A Collection of Speeches, 1946–49*, New York: The John Day Company, Inc., 1950, pp. 254–60. Reprinted by permission of the publishers.

policy. It is a positive, constructive policy deliberately aiming at something and deliberately trying to avoid hostility to other countries, to any country as far as possible.

How can we achieve this? Obviously there are risks and dangers, and the first duty of every country is to protect itself. Protecting oneself unfortunately means relying on the armed forces and the like and so we build up, where necessity arises, our defense apparatus. We cannot take the risk of not doing so, although Mahatma Gandhi would have taken that risk no doubt and I dare not say that he would have been wrong. Indeed, if a country is strong enough to take that risk it will not only survive, but it will become a great country. But we are small folk and dare not take that risk. But in protecting oneself, we should do so in such a way as not to antagonize others and also as not to appear to aim at the freedom of others. That is important. Also, we should avoid in speech or writing anything which worsens the relationship of nations. Now, the urge to do or say things against countries, against their policies, and sometimes against their statesmen is very great, because other people are very offensive at times; they are very aggressive at times. If they are aggressive, we have to protect ourselves against their aggression. If there is fear of future aggression, we have to protect ourselves against that. That I can understand, but there is a distinct difference between that and shouting loudly from the house tops all the time attacking this country or that — even though that country may deserve to be criticized or attacked. . . .

May I say that I do not for an instant claim any superior vantage point for India to advise or criticize the rest of the world. I think we are merely trying not to get excited about these problems and anyhow, there is no reason why we should not try. It follows, therefore, that we should not align ourselves with what are called power blocs. We can be of far more service without doing so, and I think there is just a possibility — and I shall not put it higher than that — that at a moment of crisis our peaceful and friendly efforts might make a difference and avert that crisis. If so, it is well worth trying. When I say that we should not align ourselves with any power blocs, obviously it does not mean that we should not be closer in our relations with some countries than with others. . . .

There are two other issues in the world which, unless satisfactorily solved, may well lead to conflict and a conflict on a big scale. One is . . . the issue of domination of one country over another. Where there is continued domination, whether it is in Asia or Africa, there will be no peace either there or in the people's minds elsewhere. . . .

The second important factor is that of racial equality. That too, in some parts of the world . . . has come very much to the forefront. For example, take the question of Indians in South Africa. It is a matter which concerns us all. It is not merely a question of Indians or South Africans, but it is a matter of vital significance to the world, because that too symbolizes something in the world. If that is to continue in the world, then there is bound to be conflict and conflict on a big scale, because it is a continuous challenge to the self-respect of a vast number of people in the world, and they will not put up with it.

I am not touching upon the third matter, the basic matter that is, economic policies — it is too big a subject — except that I would like to say this in regard to it, that the only way to proceed in the world today, as far as I can see, is for each country to realize that it must not interfere with another country's economic policy. Ultimately the policies that deliver the goods will succeed, those that do not will not succeed. This policy of interfering aggressively with other countries' policies inevitably leads to trouble. . . .

May I just say one word before I close? We are striving for One World, and what with the development of communications and everything, we come closer to one another. We know a great deal more about one another than we used to. Nevertheless, I have a feeling that our knowledge of one another is often extraordinarily superficial, and we, living in our grooves, big or small, seem to imagine, each country seems to imagine, that we are more or less the center of the world . . . that our way of living is the right way of living and other people's way of living is either a bad way or a mad way, or just some kind of backward way. Now I suppose it is a common human failing to imagine that we are right and others are wrong. But of course, apart from being right or wrong, it may be both are right and both are wrong; anyhow, in so far as the people's manner of living is concerned, there may be differences, not only as between Europe, America, Asia, and Africa, but also internally in some of the continents. Now Europe and America, because they have been dominant countries with a dominant culture, have tended to think that ways of living other than theirs are necessarily inferior. Whether they are inferior or not I do not know. If they are inferior, probably their own people will change them. But this method of approach of one country to another is a very limited approach and does not indicate much wisdom, because this world is a very varied place. . . . The world is a very diverse place, and I personally see no reason why we should regiment it along one line.

Communist Rule in China

Chinese Communists and Nationalists were engaged in a bitter power struggle for the control of China even while they were united in their battle against the Japanese invaders. By 1945 the strength and popularity of General Chiang Kai-shek had seriously declined. His Kuomintang (Nationalist Party) ruled on behalf of the few rather than the masses, and it imposed its will by force. The Communists took advantage of this situation and entrenched themselves in certain areas. By the end of World War II they ruled a territory which included ninety million people.

In spite of the efforts of the United States to get Communists and Nationalists to work in harmony, civil war raged in China. The Communists won control of the mainland, and on October 1, 1949, the People's Republic of China was proclaimed. Chiang Kai-shek and his supporters fled to Formosa.

Mao Tse-tung, the ruler of Communist China, is a staunch opponent of the West. He has rejected Khrushchev's policy of "peaceful coexistence." The differences which have developed between the Soviet Union and Communist China have caused a major split in the world Communist movement.

In the first selection, written in 1949, Mao explains the meaning of "democratic dictatorship." The second selection consists of extracts from two letters which give the basis of the rift between the Soviet Union and Communist China.

"Democratic Dictatorship"

Twenty-four years have elapsed since Sun Yat-sen's death, and under the leadership of the Chinese Communist Party, Chinese revolutionary theory and practice have made tremendous strides, funda-

"DEMOCRATIC DICTATORSHIP." Source: Mao Tse-tung, *On the People's Democratic Dictatorship* . . . , Peking: Foreign Languages Press, 1952, pp. 9–15.

mentally altering the face of China. The Chinese people have by now accumulated vital and basic experiences along the following two lines:

1. At home, the masses of the people must be awakened. This means aligning the working class, the peasantry, and the . . . bourgeoisie . . . into a united front under the leadership of the working class, and from this, proceeding to the creation of a state of the people's democratic dictatorship, a state under the leadership of the working class and based on the alliance of the workers and peasants.

2. On the international plane we must unite in a common struggle with the peoples of all countries and with those nations which treat us as equals. This means allying * ourselves with the Soviet Union, with every [Communist] country, and with the proletariat and broad masses in all other countries. This means forming an international united front.

"You are leaning to one side." Exactly. The forty years' experience of Sun Yat-sen and the twenty-eight years' experience of the Chinese Communist Party have convinced us that in order to attain victory and consolidate it, we must lean to one side. According to these experiences, the Chinese people must lean either to the side of imperialism or to that of Socialism. There can be no exception. There can be no sitting on the fence; there is no third road. . . .

"You are too provocative." We are talking about how to deal with domestic and foreign reactionaries, i.e., the imperialists and their jackals and not any others. As to the reactionaries, the question of being provocative or not does not arise. It is all the same whether one is provocative or not — because they are reactionaries. Only by drawing a sharp line between reactionaries and revolutionaries, only by exposing the intrigues and plots of the reactionaries and arousing the vigilance and attention of the revolutionaries, and only by raising our own morale while deflating the enemy's prestige — only by these methods can the reactionaries be isolated, overcome, and supplanted. . . .

"Victory can be achieved even without international assistance." This is an erroneous way of thinking. In an era when imperialism still exists, it is impossible for a genuine people's revolution in any country to achieve victory without various forms of help from the international revolutionary forces. Even when victory is won, it cannot be made secure without such help. This was true of the victory of the October

* This was written when Communist China and the U.S.S.R. were more closely allied.

Revolution [in Russia] and its consolidation, as Stalin long ago told us. This was also the case in the downfall of the three imperialist countries during the Second World War and in the establishment of the [Communist] countries. This is also true of the present and the future of People's China.

"We need assistance from the British and American governments." At the present time, this is also a naïve way of thinking. The present rulers of Great Britain and the United States are still imperialists. Will they give aid to a people's state? . . .

Internationally we belong to the side of the anti-imperialist front, headed by the Soviet Union. We can only turn to this side for genuine and friendly help, not to the side of the imperialist front.

"You are dictatorial." My dear sirs, just as you say. That is just what we are. All the experiences of the Chinese people, accumulated in the course of several decades, tell us to put into effect a people's democratic dictatorship. This means that the reactionaries must be deprived of the right to voice their opinions; only the people have that right.

"Who are the 'people'?" At the present stage in China, they are the working class, the peasantry, and . . . the bourgeoisie. . . .

Under the leadership of the working class and the Communist Party these classes unite to create their own state and elect their own government so as to enforce their dictatorship over the henchmen of imperialism — the landlord class and bureaucratic capitalist class, as well as the reactionary clique of the Kuomintang, which represents these classes, and their accomplices. The people's government will suppress such individuals. It will only tolerate them if they behave themselves, but not if they prove intractable [stubborn] in speech or action. If they are intractable, they will be instantly curbed and punished. Within the ranks of the people, the democratic system is carried out by giving freedom of speech, assembly, and association. The right to vote is given only to the people, not to the reactionaries.

These two aspects, democracy for the people and dictatorship for the reactionaries, when combined constitute the people's democratic dictatorship. . . .

"Don't you want to abolish state power?" Yes, we do, but not at the present time. We cannot yet afford to. Why not? Because imperialism still exists, and within our country reactionaries and classes still exist.

Our present task is to strengthen the people's state machine — meaning principally the people's army, the people's police, and the people's courts — so that national defense can be made secure and the people's interests protected. . . .

"You are not benevolent." Exactly. We definitely do not adopt a benevolent policy towards reactionaries, or the counterrevolutionary activities of the reactionary classes. Our benevolent policy applies only to the people; it does not apply to such activities or such persons who are outside the ranks of the people.

The Rift Between the Soviet Union and Communist China

Excerpts from the Letter sent by the Central Committee of the Chinese Communist Party to the Central Committee of the Soviet Communist Party on June 14, 1963

United States imperialism is pressing its policies of aggression and war all over the world. . . .

The international proletariat must . . . establish the broadest united front against the United States imperialists. . . .

To make no distinction between enemies, friends and ourselves and to entrust the fate of the people and of mankind to collaboration with the United States imperialism is to lead people astray. . . .

The superiority of the Socialist system and the achievements of the Socialist countries in construction play an exemplary role and are an inspiration to the oppressed peoples and the oppressed nations.

But this exemplary role and inspiration can never replace the revolutionary struggles of the oppressed peoples and nations. No oppressed people or nation can win liberation except through its own stanch revolutionary struggle.

Certain persons * have one-sidedly exaggerated the role of peaceful competition between Socialist and imperialist countries in their attempt to substitute peaceful competition for the revolutionary strug-

* Khrushchev and his supporters.

THE RIFT BETWEEN THE SOVIET UNION AND COMMUNIST CHINA. Source: *The New York Times,* July 5, 1963, and July 15, 1963. © 1963 by *The New York Times.* Reprinted by permission of the publishers.

gles of the oppressed peoples and nations. According to their preaching, it would seem that imperialism will automatically collapse in the course of this peaceful competition, and that the only thing the oppressed peoples and nations have to do is to wait quietly for the advent of this day. . . .

Moreover, certain persons have concocted the strange tale that China and some other Socialist countries want "to unleash wars" and to spread Socialism by "wars between states." . . . Such tales are nothing but imperialist and reactionary slanders. To put it bluntly, the purpose of those who repeat these slanders is to hide the fact they are opposed to revolutions by the oppressed peoples and nations of the world and opposed to others supporting such revolutions. . . .

Certain persons now actually hold that it is possible to bring about "a world without weapons, without armed forces and without wars," through "general and complete disarmament" while the system of imperialism and of the exploitation of man by man still exists. This is sheer illusion. . . .

What are the facts in the world today? Is there a shadow of evidence that the imperialist countries headed by the United States are ready to carry out general and complete disarmament? Are they not each and all engaged in general and complete arms expansion? . . .

The question, then, is what is the way to secure world peace? According to the Leninist viewpoint, world peace can be won only by the struggles of the people in all countries and not by begging the imperialists for it. World peace can only be effectively defended by relying on the development of the forces of the Socialist camp, on the revolutionary struggles of the proletariat and working people of all countries. . . .

Any policy to the contrary definitely will not lead to world peace but will only encourage the ambitions of the imperialists and increase the danger of world war. . . .

The possibility of banning nuclear weapons does indeed exist. However, if the imperialists are forced to accept an agreement to ban nuclear weapons, it decidedly will not be because of their "love for humanity" but because of the pressure of the people of all countries and for the sake of their own vital interests. . . .

The emergence of nuclear weapons . . . does not and cannot alter the law of class struggle, and does not and cannot change the nature of imperialism and reaction.

It cannot, therefore, be said that with the emergence of nuclear weapons the possibility and the necessity of social and national revolutions have disappeared, or . . . the theories of proletarian revolution and the dictatorship of the proletariat and of war and peace have become outmoded and changed into stale "dogmas.". . .

It was Lenin who advanced the thesis that it is possible for the Socialist countries to practice peaceful coexistence. . . .

Since its founding, the People's Republic of China, too, has consistently pursued the policy of peaceful coexistence with countries having different social systems. . . .

However, a few years ago certain persons suddenly claimed Lenin's policy of peaceful coexistence as their own "great discovery." They maintain that they have a monopoly on the interpretation of this policy. They treat "peaceful coexistence" as if it were an all-inclusive, mystical book from heaven and attribute to it every success the people of the world achieve by struggle. What is more, they label all who disagree with their distortions of Lenin's views as opponents of peaceful coexistence, as people completely ignorant of Lenin and Leninism, and as heretics deserving to be burned at the stake.

How can the Chinese Communists agree with this view and practice? They cannot; it is impossible. . . .

Peaceful coexistence designates a relationship between countries with different social systems, and must not be interpreted as one pleases. It should never be extended to apply to the relations between oppressed and oppressor nations, between oppressed and oppressor countries, or between oppressed and oppressor classes, and [it should] never be described as the main content of the transition from capitalism to Socialism, still less should it be asserted that peaceful coexistence is mankind's road to Socialism. The reason is that it is one thing to practice peaceful coexistence between countries with different social systems. It is absolutely impermissible and impossible for countries practicing peaceful coexistence to touch even a hair of each other's social systems. The class struggle, the struggle for national liberation and the transition from capitalism to Socialism in various countries are quite another thing. They are all bitter, life-and-death revolutionary struggles which aim at changing the social system. Peaceful coexistence cannot replace the revolutionary struggles of the people. . . .

It is necessary for the Socialist countries to engage in negotiations of one kind or another with the imperialist countries. It is possible to reach certain agreements through negotiation. . . . But necessary compromises between the Socialist countries and the imperialist countries do not require the oppressed peoples and nations to follow suit and compromise with imperialism and its lackeys. No one should ever demand in the name of peaceful coexistence that the oppressed peoples and nations should give up their revolutionary struggles. . . .

Excerpts from the Open Letter of the Central Committee of the Soviet Communist Party to all Communists of the Soviet Union in reply to the Chinese Communist Party's Criticism

The Central Committee of the C.P.S.U. [Communist Party of the Soviet Union] deems it necessary to address this open letter to you to set out our position on the fundamental questions of the international Communist movement in connection with the letter of the Central Committee of the Communist Party of China of June 14, 1963. . . .

For many years the relations between our parties were good. But some time ago, serious differences came to light. . . .

What [are these] differences? . . .

Questions that bear on vital interests of the peoples are in the center of the dispute.

These are the questions of war and peace, the question of the role and development of the world Socialist system; these are the questions of the struggle against the . . . practice of the "personality cult" [under Stalin]; these are the questions of strategy and tactics of the world labor movement and the national liberation struggle. . . .

The essence of these differences lies in the diametrically [absolutely] opposite approach to problems so vital as the possibility of averting world thermonuclear war, peaceful coexistence of states with different social systems, interconnection between the struggle for peace and the development of the world revolutionary movement.

Our party . . . set before Communists as a task of extreme importance the task of struggling for peace, for averting a world thermonuclear catastrophe. . . . In modern conditions the forces of peace, of which the mighty community of Socialist states is the main bulwark, can, by their joint efforts, avert a new world war. . . .

The nuclear rocket weapons . . . changed the old notions about war. These weapons possess an unheard-of devastating force. . . .

To prevent a new world war is quite a real and feasible task. The

241

twentieth Congress of our party formed the extremely important conclusion that in our times there is no fatal inevitability of war between states. . . .

The Chinese comrades . . . do not believe in the possibility of preventing a new world war; they underestimate the forces of peace and Socialism and overestimate the forces of imperialism. . . .

The Chinese comrades obviously underestimate all the danger of thermonuclear war. "The atomic bomb is a paper tiger; it is not terrible at all," they contend. . . .

They straightforwardly say, "On the ruins of destroyed imperialism" — in other words, as a result of the unleashing of war — "a bright future will be built." If we agree to this, then indeed there is no need for the principle of peaceful coexistence, for the struggle for the strengthening of peace.

We cannot agree to such an adventuristic way; it contradicts the nature of Marxism-Leninism. . . .

The working class of the capitalist countries would be sure to ask them, "Do we ask you to trigger a war and destroy our countries while annihilating imperialists?". . .

The atomic bomb does not distinguish between the imperialists and the working people; . . . millions of workers would be destroyed for each monopolist. . . .

The true position of the C.P.C. [Chinese Communist Party] leadership is manifested very clearly in questions of war and peace, in its full underestimation and . . . deliberate ignoring of the struggle for disarmament.

The Chinese Communists object even to the very raising by Communists of this question. . . . They try to prove that general disarmament is possible only when Socialism has triumphed all over the world.

Must the Marxists sit on their hands waiting for the victory of Socialism all over the world while mankind suffocates in the clutches of the arms race . . . ?

No. This would be criminal inaction in face of the imperative call of the time. . . .

We hold that the working class, the working people of all countries, can force the imperialist governments to consent to disarmament, can prevent war. . . .

There are serious difficulties between the C.P.C. and the C.P.S.U.

and other Marxist-Leninist parties on the question of struggle against the consequences of the Stalin personality cult.

The C.P.C. leaders took upon themselves the role of the defenders of the personality cult, the propagators of Stalin's faulty ideas. They are trying to thrust upon other parties the practices, the . . . morals, the forms and methods of the leadership that were flourishing in the period of the personality cult. We must say outright that this is an unenviable role that will bring them neither honor nor glory. . . .

The atmosphere of fear, suspicion and uncertainty that poisoned the life of the people in the period of the personality cult is gone, never to return. . . .

The next important question on which we differ is that of the ways and methods of the revolutionary struggle of the working class in the countries of capitalism, the struggle for national liberation, the ways of the transition of all mankind to Socialism.

As depicted by the Chinese comrades, . . . the C.P.S.U. [and] the Marxist-Leninist parties have forgotten the revolution, even "fear" it, and, instead of revolutionary struggle, [are] concerned with things "unworthy" of a real revolutionary, such as peace, the economic development of the Socialist countries, and improvement of the living standard of their peoples. . . .

Is it true that in coming out for peace and pursuing the policy of peaceful coexistence the Communists of the Socialist countries think only of themselves and have forgotten their class brothers in the countries of capital?

Everyone who has pondered the meaning of the present struggle for peace, against thermonuclear war, realizes that by their policy of peace the Soviet Communists . . . give inestimable aid to the working class . . . of the capitalist countries. And this is not because averting nuclear war means saving from death the working class, the peoples of whole countries and even continents — though this alone is enough to justify all our policy.

The other reason is that this policy is the best way to help the international revolutionary working-class movement achieve its principal class aims; is it not a tremendous contribution to the struggle of the working class when the countries of Socialism . . . score magnificent successes in the development of economy, score ever new victories in science and technology, constantly improve the living and working conditions of the people, develop and improve Socialist democracy?

Looking at these successes and victories, every worker in a capitalist country will say: "Socialism proves by deeds that it is superior to capitalism. This system is worth fighting for."

The Recovery of Japan

Until World War II Japan had never been conquered or occupied by a foreign power. Japan's imperial dreams were shattered by its defeat. Japan was stripped of its empire and its military machine was destroyed. Many of its prominent citizens were barred from public office and influential positions because of their part in the war.

Japan's adaptability in this situation was as extraordinary as its transformation had been at the end of the nineteenth century. The Japanese maintained good relations with the Occupation whose policies were welcomed by those Japanese who had liberal tendencies. The Emperor renounced his claim to divinity, asked for cooperation with the conquerors, and accepted the new constitution, which declared that he derived his position "from the will of the people." A peace treaty was signed with the United States in 1951, and an arrangement to end the state of war with Russia was made in 1956, after which Japan was admitted into the United Nations.

Japan has tried to make amends to its former enemies in Asia, such as Burma and the Philippines. In spite of Japan's great population and the loss of territory, the recovery from the war has been rapid. Whether the new democratic government has permanently become an integral part of Japanese life still remains to be seen.

Over the years the pattern of Japanese life, social relationships, and behavior has been markedly reshaped; by extension, change has begun to affect the Japanese value system as well as the Japanese peo-

Source: Paul F. Langer, "Growing Pains of a Changing Japan," in *Current History*, November 1962, pp. 283–85. Reprinted by permission of Current History, Inc.

ple's attitudes toward their society, the government, and the outside world.

The three most important factors in this development have been the destruction of the traditional social, political, and economic order; foreign — especially American — influence in all spheres of Japanese life; and the continuing impact of swift economic change.

Take, for example, Tokyo, now the world's most populous city. The Japanese capital is one vast construction zone. . . . Giant transmitters tower over the city's roofs with their forest of television antennas. Hundreds of thousands of automobiles crowd the narrow streets where billboards and neon lights advertise everything from the newest American motion picture to the latest refrigerator off the Japanese assembly lines. Modern department stores display Japanese goods, English ties, Dior gowns, and American liquor.

This process of modernization and internationalization is, of course, not limited to Japan. But what is striking in Japan's case is the unprecedented intensity, speed, depth, and scope of the transformation.

Tokyo is a pacesetter for the rest of Japan. The change is not confined to a small and sophisticated upper stream of society; it reaches into the lower income groups as well and affects even the older generation. Japan's two top best sellers in 1961 illustrate the trend of the times: *How to Improve Your English*, which sold 1.2 million copies in less than six months, and *I'll Have a Look at Everything*, the travel account of a Japanese graduate student who after a year at Harvard had explored the lower depths of America, Europe, and the Near East on a dollar a day.

If Tokyo's traffic congestion can vie with that of New York (ten thousand cars are joining the capital's traffic snarl every month), one must recall that just a few years back only the rich and powerful drove through Tokyo's streets. To venture by automobile into the rural areas meant until recently an excursion into a vehicular no-man's-land. Today, the peaceful silence of the Japanese countryside is broken by the sputtering of Japan-made compact cars and motorcycles.

The traditional fabric of Japanese life, focused on the family and involving a complex system of duties, . . . has been severely strained; in the case of the younger generation the pattern has been almost totally discarded. The destruction of the family system, the freeing of women from restrictive legal shackles, the elimination from education of the nationalistic and militaristic state cult, the growing opportunities for economic independence, all this has freed Japan's youth from the customary parental and government control.

Rural prosperity and modernization have tended to erase the formerly sharp distinction between village and city, placing television sets, refrigerators, washing machines, and electric rice cookers [in] many rural homes. These material developments, aided by the amazing growth of Japanese mass communications, have also projected modern ideas into the most remote parts of rural Japan.

Two economic miracles have taken place in recent years in Japan. The first involves the outstanding performance of Japanese agriculture. One of the world's most densely populated countries, growing at the rate of a million people a year, has somehow succeeded in making itself virtually self-supporting in food although it has less than sixteen percent of cultivable land. This success must be attributed largely to man-made factors — among them, the increased use of fertilizer and chemicals, advanced farming techniques, rapid mechanization adapted to Japanese conditions (more than a half a million tractors are in use today), the virtual elimination of tenant farming, the diversification of Japan's eating habits, and the rise of labor productivity.

While agricultural output increases, Japan's farming population is steadily decreasing. In 1950 it still accounted for forty-five percent of the total population. In 1960 it had been reduced to thirty-seven percent. The government hopes to see this trend continue. . . .

The agricultural miracle tends to be overshadowed by the even more amazing overall growth of the Japanese economy. For several years now, mining and manufacturing have increased yearly by twenty to thirty percent. Japan now leads the world in shipbuilding, has passed Britain in steel production, and is narrowing the gap with West Germany. The introduction of foreign — mostly American — technology has raised the efficiency of Japanese industry and the quality of its products. . . . Japanese department stores are being opened in the United States. Japan is in 1962 the world's fourth-ranking industrial power. Its growth rate last year was about thirteen percent — several times that of the United States.

The resulting prosperity has not benefited every Japanese equally; even in the cities there remains some real poverty, especially among the employees of smaller firms, among unskilled workers, and among day laborers. But much of the economic gain has percolated down to the working people. . . . In 1962 Japan is therefore the first non-Western nation to approach a Western standard of living, life expectancy, and consumption. . . . The Japanese performance is all the more remarkable as it was achieved without the imposition of totalitarian economic or political controls in a country that possesses only two resources: manpower and brains.

Israel Becomes an Independent State

A dream some two thousand years old was fulfilled for many Jews when David Ben-Gurion proclaimed the independence of the State of Israel on May 14, 1948. During centuries of dispersal and persecution, Jews had found comfort in their ancient heritage and in the promise and hope of returning to the ancient land of Israel.

Modern Jewish nationalism dates from the end of the nineteenth century. With the outbreak of government-sponsored riots against Jews in Russia and persecution in other quarters, young Jews from Eastern Europe went flocking to the barren land of Palestine (at that time part of the Ottoman Empire) in the hope of building a permanent home there.

From the disruption of the Ottoman Empire during World War I until 1948, the British ruled Palestine as a Mandate from the League of Nations. In 1917 they had issued the Balfour Declaration, which promised to establish "a national home for the Jewish people" in Palestine. Increasing pressure of Jewish immigration in the interwar years aroused fear and hostility among the Arabs. Reluctant to offend the Arab world, the British restricted immigration to a trickle at a time when Nazi persecutions began driving thousands of Jews to Palestine. Hostility between Jews and the British authorities mounted after the end of World War II when the British refused to open the doors to refugees.

When the British offered to surrender their Mandate, the United Nations voted to partition Palestine between Jews and Arabs — a solution acceptable to the Jews but not to the Arabs. On the departure of the British on May 15, 1948, six Arab na-

*tions joined in an attack on Israel. Although the Arabs failed in
their attempt to destroy the new state, no permanent peace has
been established between Israel and its neighbors.*

*The following selection is from the Proclamation of Inde-
pendence of the State of Israel.*

The Land of Israel was the birthplace of the Jewish people.
Here their spiritual, religious, and national identity was formed. Here
they achieved independence and created a culture of national and universal significance. Here they wrote and gave the Bible to the world.

Exiled from the Land of Israel the Jewish people remained faith-
ful to it in all the countries of their dispersion, never ceasing to pray
and hope for their return and the restoration of their national freedom.
Impelled by this historic association, Jews strove throughout the centuries to go back to the land of their fathers and regain their state-
hood. In recent decades they returned in . . . masses. They reclaimed
the wilderness, revived their language, built cities and villages, and
established a vigorous and ever-growing community, with its own economic and cultural life. They sought peace yet were prepared to defend
themselves. They brought the blessings of progress to all inhabitants of
the country and looked forward to sovereign independence.

In the year 1897 the First Zionist Congress, inspired by Theodor
Herzl's vision of the Jewish State, proclaimed the right of the Jewish
people to national revival in their own country.

This right was acknowledged by the Balfour Declaration of November 2, 1917, and reaffirmed by the Mandate of the League of
Nations, which gave explicit international recognition to the historic
connection of the Jewish people with Palestine and their right to recon-
stitute their National Home.

The recent holocaust, which engulfed millions of Jews in Europe,
proved anew the need to solve the problem of the homelessness and
lack of independence of the Jewish people by means of the reestablish-
ment of the Jewish State, which would open the gates to all Jews and
endow the Jewish people with equality of status among the family of
nations.

The survivors of the disastrous slaughter in Europe, and also Jews

Source: State of Israel, *Government Yearbook 5711 (1950)*, pp. 43–45.

from other lands, have not desisted from their efforts to reach Eretz-Yisrael [Land of Israel], in face of difficulties, obstacles, and perils; and have not ceased to urge their right to a life of dignity, freedom, and honest toil in their ancestral land.

In the Second World War the Jewish people in Palestine made their full contribution to the struggle of the freedom-loving nations against the Nazi evil. The sacrifices of their soldiers and their war effort gained them the right to rank with the nations which founded the United Nations.

On November 29, 1947, the General Assembly of the United Nations adopted a Resolution requiring the establishment of a Jewish State in Palestine. The General Assembly called upon the inhabitants of the country to take all the necessary steps on their part to put the plan into effect. This recognition by the United Nations of the right of the Jewish people to establish their independent State is unassailable.

It is the natural right of the Jewish people to lead, as do all other nations, an independent existence in its sovereign State.

Accordingly, we, the members of the National Council, representing the Jewish people in Palestine and the World Zionist Movement, are met together in solemn assembly today, the day of termination of the British Mandate for Palestine; and by virtue of the natural and historic right of the Jewish people and of the Resolution of the General Assembly of the United Nations.

We hereby proclaim the establishment of the Jewish State in Palestine, to be called Medinath Yisrael [The State of Israel]. . . .

The State of Israel will be open to the immigration of Jews from all countries of their dispersion; will promote the development of the country for the benefit of all its inhabitants; will be based on the principles of liberty, justice, and peace as conceived by the Prophets of Israel; will uphold the full social and political equality of all its citizens, without distinction of religion, race, or sex; will guarantee freedom of religion, conscience, education, and culture; will safeguard the holy places of all religions; and will loyally uphold the principles of the United Nations Charter. . . .

We appeal to the United Nations to assist the Jewish people in the building of its State and to admit Israel into the family of nations. In the midst of wanton aggression, we yet call upon the Arab inhabitants of the State of Israel to preserve the ways of peace and play their part in the development of the State, on the basis of full and

249

equal citizenship and due representation in all its bodies and institutions — provisional and permanent.

We extend our hand in peace and neighborliness to all the neighboring states and their peoples, and invite them to cooperate with the independent Jewish nation for the common good of all. The State of Israel is prepared to make its contribution to the progress of the Middle East as a whole.

Our call goes out to the Jewish people all over the world to rally to our side in the task of immigration and development and to stand by us in the great struggle for the fulfillment of the dream of generations for the redemption of Israel.

With trust in Almighty God, we set our hand to this Declaration, at this Session of the Provisional State Council, on the soil of the Homeland, in the city of Tel Aviv, on . . . the fourteenth day of May, 1948.

The Leadership of Nasser

The Arab peoples have been united in their hatred of imperialism and in their antagonism toward the state of Israel. Otherwise they have been torn by suspicion among their leaders, by the ancient antagonisms of different Moslem sects, by the territorial ambitions of some of the more powerful states, and by the deep gulf that separates the luxurious life of the small minority from the wretched existence of the masses.

A revolution in Egypt led by a group of army officers overthrew the regime of King Farouk in 1952. Out of this revolution emerged the figure of Gamal Abdel Nasser as absolute ruler of Egypt. President Nasser's ambitions to unite the Arabs under his leadership have made him an object of fear as well as adoration in the Arab world.

Nasser has made several attempts to broaden the base of his regime. So far he remains a dictator, and he has dismissed several carefully selected assemblies because of "reactionary infiltration." Nasser has just begun to attack the social and economic problems of his poverty-stricken land.

In the following selection Nasser discusses his revolutionary past and his dreams for the future.

But what is it we want to do? And how is it to be done?

The truth is I have often known the answers to the first question, and I am sure I was not the only one, for it was the hope and dream of our entire generation. As for the second question — the way to achieve what we want — I admit that this has undergone more change than anything else in my thinking. Also, in my opinion, it is the subject on which we are now most divided.

There can be no doubt that all of us dream of an Egypt free and strong. That is something about which there is not dispute between one Egyptian and another. But as for the way to achieve freedom and strength, that is our Gordian knot [great problem].

I came up against this problem before July 23, 1952,* and it has continued to dominate my thoughts ever since. . . . As my thinking progressed, I began to realize the great necessity for a "positive action."

But *what* action? To write the words "positive action" on a piece of paper is a simple matter. But in real life, and under conditions besetting our generation, and in face of the ordeals which, like vultures, have dug their talons into the life of our country, this is not enough.

For a brief period, positive action in my estimation meant my own enthusiasm and zeal. But this idea changed, and I began to see that it was not enough for me to merely be enthusiastic; I had also to inspire others to enthusiasm.

In those earlier days [under British rule], I led demonstrations in the Nahda Secondary School and I shouted from my heart for complete independence, and many others behind me shouted, too. But our shouts only raised dust which was blown by the wind and produced only weak echoes which shook no mountains and shattered no rocks.

Then I began to think that this positive action would be to demand that the leaders of Egypt unite to agree upon a single policy; so we went around in groups, shouting and excited, to visit their houses, demanding in the name of Egyptian youth that they agree on a single policy. But their agreement, when it came, dealt a severe blow to my expectations. . . .

The Second World War and the short period before it fired the

* The date of the revolution.

Source: Gamal Abdel Nasser, *Egypt's Liberation: The Philosophy of the Revolution,* Washington, D.C.: Public Affairs Press, 1955, pp. 49–52, 105–14. Reprinted by permission of the publishers.

spirit of our youth and moved our whole generation towards violence. I confess — and I trust the public prosecutor will not take me to task — that to my excited imagination at that time political assassinations appeared to be the positive action we had to adopt if we were to rescue the future of our country. I considered the assassination of many individuals, having decided that they were the main obstacles which lay between our beloved country and its destined greatness. I began to study their crimes and to take it upon myself to judge the harmfulness of their actions.

I even considered the assassination of the ex-king and some of his entourage who had such utter disregard for the things we held sacred. And I was not alone in thinking thus. When I had occasion to be with others, we went beyond mere thinking to planning. So many were the projects I made in those days and so many were the sleepless nights in preparing this long-awaited positive action!

Our life during that period was like a thrilling detective story. We had dark secrets and passwords. We lurked in the shadows; we had caches of pistols and hand grenades, and firing bullets was our cherished hope. We made many attempts in this direction, and I can still remember our emotions and feelings as we dashed along that melodramatic path to its end.

When I try to analyze the elements of our strength, there are three main sources which should first be taken into account.

The first of these sources is that we are a community of neighboring peoples linked by all the material and moral ties possible, and that we have characteristics and abilities and a civilization which have given rise to three holy religions — factors which cannot be ignored in the effort to build a secure and peaceful world. So much for the first source.

As for the second source of strength, it is our land itself and its position on the map — that important, strategic position which embraces the crossroads of the world, and thoroughfare of its traders, and the passageway of its armies.

There remains the third source: oil — a sinew of material civilization without which all its machines would cease to function. The great factories, producing every kind of goods; all the instruments of land, sea, and air communication; all the weapons of war, from the mechanical bird above the clouds to the submarine beneath the waves — without oil, all would turn back to naked metal, covered with rust, incapable of motion or use. . . .

If we consider next . . . the continent of Africa — I may say without exaggeration that we cannot under any circumstances, however much we might desire it, remain aloof from the terrible and sanguinary [bloody] conflict going on there today between five million whites and two hundred million Africans. We cannot do so for an important and obvious reason: we are *in* Africa. The peoples of Africa will continue to look to us, who guard their northern gate and who constitute their link with the outside world. We will never in any circumstances be able to relinquish our responsibility to support with all our might the spread of enlightenment and civilization to the remotest depths of the jungle.

There remains another important reason. It is that the Nile is the life artery of our country, bringing water from the heart of the continent. . . .

The Dark Continent is now the scene of a strange and excited turbulence; the white man, representing various European nations, is again trying to redivide the map of Africa. We shall not, in any circumstance, be able to stand idly by in the face of what is going on in the false belief that it will not affect or concern us.

I will continue to dream of the day when I will find in Cairo a great African institute dedicated to unveiling to our view the dark reaches of the continent, to creating in our minds an enlightened African consciousness, and to sharing with others from all over the world the work of advancing the welfare of the peoples of this continent.

There remains . . . the domain of our brothers in faith who, wherever under the sun they may be, turn as we do in the direction of Mecca and whose devout lips speak the same prayers.

When I went with the Egyptian delegation to the Kingdom of Saudi Arabia to offer condolences on the death of its great sovereign, my belief in the possibility of extending the effectiveness of the pilgrimage [to Mecca], building upon the strength of the Islamic tie that binds all Moslems, grew very strong. I stood before the Kaaba,* and in my mind's eye I saw all the regions of the world which Islam has reached. Then I found myself saying that our view of the pilgrimage must change. It should not be regarded as only a ticket of admission into paradise after a long life, or as a means of buying forgiveness after a merry one. It should become an institution of great political power

* **Kaaba:** the major Moslem shrine in Mecca.

and significance. Journalists of the world should hasten to cover the pilgrimage, not because it is a traditional ritual affording interesting reports to the reading public, but because of its function as a periodic political conference in which the envoys of the Islamic states, their leaders of thought, their men learned in every branch of knowledge, their writers, their captains of industry, their merchants, and their youth can meet in order to lay down in this Islamic world parliament the broad lines of their national policies and their pledges of mutual cooperation from one year to another. . . .

When I consider the 80 million Moslems in Indonesia, and the 50 million in China, and the millions in Malaya, Siam, and Burma, and the nearly 100 million in Pakistan, and the more than 100 million in the Middle East, and the 40 million in the Soviet Union, together with the other millions in farflung parts of the world — when I consider these hundreds of millions united by a single creed, I emerge with a sense of the tremendous possibilities which we might realize through the cooperation of all these Moslems, a cooperation going not beyond the bounds of their natural loyalty to their own countries, but nonetheless enabling them and their brothers in faith to wield power wisely and without limit.

The Prospects of Democracy in Africa

European domination and exploitation of Africa, as well as the introduction of European ideas of liberty and self-government, aroused Africans to seek independence from their imperial rulers. At the end of World War II, when sympathy with peoples living under foreign rule was especially strong and Africans became more determined in their demands, the liberation of Africa was at hand. Beginning with Ghana in 1957, independence has been won by one African state after another, until only a few of the traditional colonies remain.

For the most part, the transfer of power from the rulers to the Africans has been peaceful. England and France have remained on excellent terms with most of their former colonies.

In some areas, however, especially the Belgian Congo, the road to nationhood has been full of obstacles. But even in those areas where there have been goodwill and sound preparation for self-government, the new nations still face staggering political and economic problems.

In the following selection Chief Obafemi Awolowo, former Premier of the Western Region of Nigeria and the leader of the major opposition party in the federal parliament of Nigeria, discusses the problems and prospects of a new African nation. Nigeria won full independence in October 1960 and chose to remain a member of the Commonwealth of Nations.

We believe in the democratic way of life: equality under the law, respect for the fundamental rights of individual citizens, and the existence of independent and impartial tribunals where these rights could be enforced. We believe that the generality of the people should enjoy this life and do so in reasonable abundance. The most detestable feature of British administration was that the governed had no say in the appointment of those who governed them. A Nigerian administration by Nigerians must be erected on the general consent and the united goodwill of the majority of the people. In my view there can be no satisfactory alternative to this. At the same time I fully recognize that the healthy growth of a democratic way of life requires the existence of an enlightened community led by a group of people who are imbued with the all-consuming urge to defend, uphold, and protect the human dignity and the legal equality of their fellowmen. But to us it was not going to be an easy task. Right there with us in the region outside Lagos,* democratic practices were unknown. At the local government level, many . . . chiefs were autocrats. . . . Native courts, where justice was expected to be administered in accordance with customary usages, were dens of corruption and the instruments of tyranny and oppression. . . . As things stood we knew on which side we should be — the popular side, the people's side. . . .

With regard to the other freedoms — freedom from ignorance,

* **Lagos:** capital of Nigeria.

Source: Obafemi Awolowo, Awo: The Autobiography of Chief Obafemi Awolowo, London: Cambridge University Press, 1960, pp. 255–56, 266–68, 302–05, 309–10. Reprinted by permission of Cambridge University Press, New York.

freedom from disease, and freedom from want — we knew that we would encounter towering problems . . . when our objectives came to be related to the means — that is money and manpower — for attaining them. . . .

We had promised our people that we would introduce before the end of our five-year term: (1) free universal primary education for all children of school-going age; (2) free medical treatment for all children up to the age of eighteen; (3) one hospital for each of the twenty-four administrative divisions in the region which did not yet possess one; (4) improvement in agricultural technique and higher returns for farmers; (5) better wages for the working class; (6) improvement of existing roads and bridges and the construction of new ones; (7) water supply to urban and rural areas. . . . We did recognize that there were also financial hurdles of a mountainous height to be overcome. But we were determined to blast our way through them all. . . .

In our underdeveloped society I placed the utmost premium on (1) education, (2) health, (3) economic development, and (4) democratization of local government. . . .

I believe that every citizen, however humble and lowly his station in life, has a right to demand from his government the creation of those conditions which will enable him progressively to enjoy, according to civilized standards, the basic necessities of life as well as reasonable comfort and a measure of luxury. In other words, every citizen, regardless of his birth or religion, should be free and reasonably contented. . . .

All men and women should be treated as equal, both as political and economic beings. For this reason all laws, measures, and programs introduced by government must be framed so as to give equal treatment and opportunity to all. . . .

The provision of education and health in a developing country such as Nigeria is as much an instrument of economic development as the provision of roads, water supply, electricity, and the like. To educate the children and enlighten the illiterate adults is to lay a solid foundation not only for future social and economic progress but also for political stability. A truly educated citizenry is, in my view, one of the most powerful deterrents to dictatorship, oligarchy, and feudal autocracy. . . .

There is a newfangled theory now being propounded with erudition and gusto in the countries of the so-called Western democracies. The proponents of this theory hold the view that it is inappropriate and hardly fair to expect a newly emergent African nation to practice democracy as it is known and practiced in the countries of Western Europe and the United States of America. Every mortal blow that is struck by an independent African nation at the vitals of democracy is [excused] by these theorists as the African's peculiar method of adapting democratic usages to his barbaric and primitive environment. The denial of fundamental human rights, the destruction of the rule of law, and the suppression of opposition have been brilliantly . . . rationalized. The outrageous declaration by an African leader that a one-party system is in accord with the democratic way of life has been ably defended by these spokesmen of the Western democracies.

Two things strike me forcibly in this strange and apologetic attitude of the Western democracies toward the debasement of the great ideal of democracy. The first is this. The nationals of these imperial powers, for a number of reasons which are well known, have always had a feeling of superiority toward the peoples of their former colonial territories. . . . It would appear that in their heart óf hearts the white peoples, especially those of the Western world, still regard an African society as a group of inferior races, notwithstanding that they are politically independent. In this connection the British people are the worst offenders. They are never tired of expatiating [speaking at length], to the point of nausea, on the length of time — the number of centuries — it took them to evolve from feudalism to democracy. This is an indisputable historical fact, and British contributions to human civilization are acknowledged. . . . The British must stop imagining and propagating the erroneous view that their achievements in the art of democracy are beyond the reach of others or that the slow and painful course of their evolution must in other cases be strictly followed. It must always be remembered that we are now living in an age in which all that is good and bad on our planet is indivisible. Under existing conditions, latecomers have the singular advantage of benefiting from the experiences and accomplishments of older nations.

The second is a deliberate, subconscious, or unwitting confusion between the ideal on the one hand, and the methods by which the ideal is realized in practice on the other. The ideal of democracy is not liable to modification or distortion, even though mankind has invented different methods for its realization. In a democracy the government must rule with the consent of the governed. The governed are inalienably entitled at periodic intervals to give this consent to the same or a different set of people who form the government. The expression of such consent must be free and unfettered, and must on no account be stultified or rigged. Furthermore, the consent must never be obtained by duress, threat, or intimidation; by undue influence or fraud. These are the principles which underlie the ideal of democracy. Wherever these principles (or any of them) are tampered with or abrogated, the resulting situation is anything but democracy. We all know that while these principles are solemnly observed in India, Britain, and the United States of America for instance, the methods of their application differ as between these countries. So the methods could differ in any African nation. But it is an affront to the African race to suggest that they are incapable of applying these principles.

Democracy and a one-party system of government are, in my opinion, mutually exclusive. Under a one-party system the party in power arrogates to itself the right to be the only ruling party for all time. All other parties, therefore, which differ from or are in opposition to it are either suppressed or absorbed. At subsequent elections, if there are any, the consent of the people cannot be said to be genuinely sought and freely given, because there is only one choice open to the electorate. . . .

In acting as the apologists for those who destroy and discredit democracy, the spokesmen of the Western democracies do grievous harm to that noble ideal which they profoundly cherish and which they are prepared to defend with their lives (as they have done in the past) if its practice in their homelands is at any time threatened . . . .

Under no circumstances should we compromise the racial dignity of the African peoples in particular and of the colored peoples in general; nor must we do or say anything at any time which would make us seem the docile satellite of the British or any government. We are a sister country to Britain, and it is as such that we should behave and expect to be treated.

There are two distinct ideological camps in the world today: the Western democracies and the Communist bloc. For reasons which I will presently give, my preference is unhesitatingly and unequivocally for the Western democracies. No nation in the world is absolutely good or absolutely evil. There is still a color bar in the Western democracies. Negroes in America are still being discriminated against. . . . For her part Britain is still guilty, as before, though in a decreasing order of magnitude, of injustice to the black peoples in East and Central Africa.

But such evils as are committed in the countries of the Western democracies toward the weaker peoples of the world are not only fast diminishing, but are being constantly subjected to strong and sharp criticisms in those countries by their nationals, without any risk to their lives or personal freedom. If you did likewise behind the Iron Curtain you would not live to fight another day.

The world in which we live is still very far from perfection. We have got to take it as we find it and, like conscientious and honest people, strive to contribute toward its peace, progress, and happiness. From time to time things will happen which in his judgment one individual considers to be wrong. Whether the individual is right or wrong in his judgment, he has an inherent and inalienable entitlement to entertain such opinion and to express it. The question is where, as between the Western bloc and the Eastern bloc, can a man freely exercise his natural right to hold and express any opinion, subject to such restrictions as may be laid down by laws enacted by the freely elected parliament of the land? The answer is obvious: it is in the Western bloc.

Ferment in Latin America

Class struggle, revolution, and military dictatorship have filled the pages of history of many of the Latin American republics. A small minority of the population controls the governments and the armies, owns a large portion of the land, fills the important professions, and lives in elegant splendor. The vast majority, powerless and illiterate, lives in poverty and misery. Differences in wealth and power have been accentuated by differences in race, since the masses are often Indian or Negro or of mixed origin.

Such conditions, when accompanied by a lack of responsibility on the part of the rulers and a rapidly increasing population, have provided a good breeding ground for both fascist-type dictators and Communism. Since World War II a number of dictatorships have fallen, but they have not usually been replaced by democracies. Communism has acquired control in Cuba and has gained many adherents in other republics. A number of the republics have struggled to raise the standard of living of their *people, and the United States has undertaken to aid them in this endeavor. The problems of Latin America, however, are still a long way from any solution.*

Throughout most of the nineteenth century, following independence, there were three elements which exercised profound influence in the daily life and thought of all Latin American peoples, whether they were literate or illiterate, white, red, black, or brown, and whatever their religion might be.

The first element was the Roman Catholic Church, possibly more accurately referred to here as the Latin American Catholic Church, which, from earliest colonial days, shared with the crown and other political forces responsibility for government and education. The secular clergy — composed of priests, bishops, archbishops, and so on — maintained the tenets of the Catholic religion among the people of the settled areas. The regular clergy, composed of the various orders — Jesuits, Franciscans, Dominicans, and so on — engaged in missionary activities and the conversion of large numbers of natives. . . .

A second element in this picture of nineteenth-century Latin American political society was the aristocracy. These old families, relatively few in number, owned most of the land, except that owned by the Church, and they controlled the government, frequently fighting among themselves for political power and dominance. Many were absentee landlords who banked their incomes abroad. They exploited the mass of agricultural workers, some of whom were held in virtual slavery or peonage, and they kept wages at the lowest possible level.

A third element in Latin American political affairs was the military. The officer class was composed chiefly of older sons of the aristocracy who entered the military service for the social prestige it gave them. With control of military forces it was not difficult for the aristocracy to control the government. And because some of the younger sons frequently went into the clergy, the aristocracy became allied with this group, forming a three-way combination. . . .

At the bottom of the social scale in the nineteenth century, but not an active element and without political influence, were the majority

Source: A. Curtis Wilgus, "The Chemistry of Political Change in Latin America," in *The Annals of the American Academy of Political and Social Science*, Vol. 342, July 1962, pp. 44–50. Reprinted by permission of the American Academy of Political and Social Science.

of men, women, and children of the Latin American countries. Some of these people were pure-blooded Indians or Negroes, some were mixed Indians and Negroes, some were mixed whites and Negroes, and some mixed whites and Indians. . . . These elements could and did cause political ferment in the nineteenth century, and because none of the countries had really effective and workable constitutions, there were frequent explosions in the body politic.

Each of these elements persisted into the twentieth century, and each group conceived and interpreted democracy in its own way. The Church attempted and failed to exercise a leveling influence on society. The aristocracy maintained a grip on political thinking and developed political philosophies, sometimes democratic and sometimes demagogic, which resulted in varying degrees of bureaucracy and oligarchy. The military was used by the government generally to maintain order and in many instances to vote or to influence the vote in national, but fraudulent, elections. As a matter of fact, for the last century the army in each country has formed a real political pressure group which may swing elections one way or another by ballots or by bullets.

Since the opening of the twentieth century, a middle class has gradually developed in all of the countries. In one sense this is a white-collar class, somewhat similar to our middle class. These people are shopkeepers, businessmen, professional men and women, and persons who have achieved financial positions which enable them to rise culturally and socially above the masses. This new element is one of growing importance and to a considerable extent is guiding the reactions that are developing out of the political, social, and economic experiments in the various countries.

A most important element in the chemistry of political change in Latin America is the Communist or the Leftist group, whether national or international. In different countries, members of this faction cause different reactions, for the moment largely political and economic. But this element is an active agent in the process of political fermentation, and it is becoming more and more recognized as a factor which may produce a radical change in the composition of . . . Latin American political life.

Still another element in the twentieth-century political structure in the Latin American countries is the rising labor group which has become more and more conscious and self-conscious of its growing importance. . . .

261

Two contrasting elements have been disturbing influences for several generations in Latin America: the "haves" and the "have nots." The contrast between wealth and poverty has attracted increased political attention and has resulted in growing legislation, especially since the First World War. In many regions of Latin America the wealthy have been getting richer and the poor poorer — here the so-called "population explosion" is a possible factor — but the people living in poverty have become increasingly aware of the advantages of receiving a living wage. Realizing at last what they have missed because of low income, the poor have found leaders who in some instances have reached economic and political [high positions] in various countries. . . .

Beginning with the student movement in Cordoba, Argentina, in 1918, another element began to play a very important part in Latin American political ferment. This is the Latin American university student, acting individually and collectively. Each country has its own national educational institutions which are government supported. At the same time there are a number of Catholic church-affiliated schools of higher learning. Generally speaking, students are the same in both types of institutions, and like students everywhere they have become interested in political problems of every description, even though they may not be able to vote. With this interest students have developed opinions, and with opinions there has come agitation, and with agitation has come a political ferment that has had . . . repercussions in all phases of national life. Frequently, the government has made reprisals against the students by closing the universities, but this does not dampen the students' ardor. Instead, it frees them from the responsibility of classes and turns them out into the street where they can engage in more effective agitation. In recent years student complaints and demands have resulted in improved educational instruction in various universities and even in schools at lower levels. More technical and vocational schools are being established, and new normal [teacher-training] schools are springing up in all countries. . . .

Political factions rather than political parties exist in Latin America. In most cases, they are organized about a single individual who may not be too explicit about his public policies for fear of losing the votes of his followers who might disagree with him, but all emphasize God, Country, and Home. . . .

In Latin American countries political campaigns are always interesting and frequently exciting and dangerous. When a campaign for the presidency begins, there may be as many as two dozen aspiring candidates. These men come from all walks of life: the military, sometimes the clergy, the aristocracy, labor groups, educators, lawyers, engineers, veterinarians, doctors, dentists, artists, novelists, essayists, fiction writers, poets, and people of varying degrees of wealth and color.

The outgoing government inevitably supports one of the candidates. This may also mean that the military will support the same candidate. . . .

Once in the presidency, the Latin American finds his executive authority constitutionally greater than that of the President of the United States. Constitutional loopholes and political pressures on the president encourage and enable him to exercise his individuality in taking what he personally considers proper action for the good of his country. . . .

Dictators grow logically out of the presidency. All Latin American countries have had dictators. . . . They convince themselves that they have the good of their country at heart and that whatever they do is both logical and right. All too often a dictator must use force to remain in power; this in turn invites the use of force against him. The result is a revolution which may or may not achieve the overthrow of the dictator. In some Latin American countries the assassination of dictators has been a laudable, frequent, and fashionable avocation. Hence many countries have had many presidents, and, at times, some countries have had two or three simultaneously.

Some dictators have been popular, and a few have made it possible for their countries to make fundamental and rapid national progress. Many dictators raise monuments to themselves by the construction of public works and by putting up buildings with their names on them. If they are not afraid of assassination, they spend considerable time traveling throughout their country, ingratiating themselves with their people. They make appealing political promises in public speeches, kiss . . . babies, open schools and museums, and shake hands with everyone within reach. But the life of a dictator is usually short and few die quietly in their beds, for the practice of dictatorship carries an occupational hazard.

Revolutions in Latin America are inevitable. Several countries have achieved political stability to such an extent that some observers predict they will never again have a revolution. Such an opinion is absurd. Revolutions afford an effective means of wiping clean the political slate and of getting rid of an impossible [obstacle] in order to start all over again. . . . Some of them might be considered antibiotics in the body politic. The medicine does not kill the patient, although the remedy with its side effects may sometimes prove violent, and a long period of political sickness and convalescence may result.

Latin Americans are realistic, and they view their politics in a practical way. They are the first to realize that revolutions are only a means to an end — and not necessarily a bitter end either. The Latin Americans in their political laboratories have prepared a variety of political mixtures as a result of agitation and interaction of many elements. The chemistry of political change in Latin America is certainly clear to those who are prepared to understand it.

Pope John XXIII's Plea for Peace on Earth

Pope John XXIII was elevated to the papacy when he was nearly seventy-seven years old, and at the time of his death in June 1963 he had reigned for less than five years. He was already renowned as a champion of peace when he issued his eighth encyclical, Pacem in Terris (Peace on Earth), in April of 1963. On many occasions he had appealed to rulers of nations to shun the use of force and to seek peaceful means to settle international disputes. In Pacem in Terris he ranges over the whole field of human relations — relations between men, between individuals and public authorities, and between nations. Addressing himself to all men of goodwill, he makes a plea for the establishment of a strong United Nations which would enforce peace and maintain human rights everywhere.

Peace on earth, which men of every era have most eagerly yearned for, can be firmly established only if the order laid down by God be dutifully observed. . . .

I. Order Between Men

Any human society, if it is to be well ordered and productive, must lay down as a foundation this principle: namely, that every human being is a person; that is, his nature is endowed with intelligence and free will. By virtue of this, he has rights and duties of his own . . . which are therefore universal, inviolable, and inalienable. . . .

We see that every man has the right to life . . . and to the means which are necessary and suitable for the proper development of life. These are primarily food, clothing, shelter, rest, medical care, and finally, the necessary social services. Therefore a human being also has the right to security in cases of sickness, inability to work, widowhood, old age, unemployment, or in any other case in which he is deprived of the means of subsistence through no fault of his own. . . .

Every human being has the right to respect for his person, to his good reputation, the right to freedom in searching for truth, and in expressing and communicating his opinions. . . .

Every human being has the right to honor God according to the dictates of an upright conscience. . . .

Human beings have the natural right to free initiative in the economic field, and the right to work. . . .

The natural rights with which we have been dealing are, however, inseparably connected . . . with just as many respective duties. . . .

It is also clear that in human society, to one man's right there corresponds a duty in all other persons: the duty, namely, of acknowledging and respecting the right in question. . . . Those, therefore, who claim their own rights, yet altogether forget or neglect to carry out their respective duties, are people who build with one hand and destroy with the other. . . .

II. Relations Between Individuals and the Public Authorities

It is agreed that in our time the common good is chiefly guaranteed when personal rights and duties are maintained. The chief concern of civil authorities must therefore be to insure that these rights are acknowledged, respected, . . . defended, and promoted. . . . To safeguard the inviolable rights of the human person and to facilitate the fulfillment of his duties should be the essential office of every public authority. . . .

Source: *The New York Times*, April 11, 1963. © 1963 by *The New York Times*. Reprinted by permission of the publishers.

It should be possible for all the citizens to share as far as they are able in their country's cultural advantages. . . .

III. Relations Between States

All states are by nature equal in dignity. Each of them accordingly is vested with the right to existence, to self-development, to the means fitting to its attainment, and to be the one primarily responsible for this self-development. . . .

Political communities may have reached different levels of culture, civilization, or economic development. Neither is that a sufficient reason for some to take unjust advantage of their superiority over others. . . .

It is not true that some human beings are by nature superior and others inferior. All men are equal in their natural dignity. Consequently, there are no political communities which are superior by nature and none which are inferior by nature. All political communities are of equal natural dignity. . . .

Justice, . . . right reason, and humanity demand that the arms race should cease; that the stockpiles which exist in various countries should be reduced equally and simultaneously; . . . that nuclear weapons should be banned; and that a general agreement should eventually be reached about progressive disarmament and an effective method of control. . . .

Is there anyone who does not ardently yearn to see war banished, to see peace preserved and daily more firmly established? . . .

IV. Relationship of Men and of Political Communities with the World Community

At the present day no political community is able to pursue its own interests and develop itself in isolation, because the degree of its prosperity and development is a reflection and a component part of the degree of prosperity and development of all the other political communities. . . .

Today the universal common good poses problems of worldwide dimensions which cannot be adequately tackled or solved except by the efforts of public authorities . . . which are in a position to operate in an effective manner on a worldwide basis. The moral order itself, therefore, demands that such a form of public authority be established. . . .

It is our earnest wish that the United Nations Organization — in its structure and in its means — may become ever more equal to the magnitude and nobility of its tasks, and that the day may come when every human being will find therein an effective safeguard for the rights which derive directly from his dignity as a person and which are therefore universal, inviolable, and inalienable rights.

A Partial Ban on Nuclear Testing

The first concrete treaty on nuclear testing was initialed in Moscow on July 25, 1963, by representatives of Great Britain, the United States, and the U.S.S.R. After eighteen years and hundreds of discussions, East and West agreed to refrain from further nuclear testing in the atmosphere, under water, and in space. Such tests can now be detected without on-site inspection. Underground testing, which would require on-site inspection, is not limited by the treaty. The Soviet Union's conflict with Communist China, the cost of the arms race, the continued pollution of the atmosphere, and the discovery of detection devices have all been important factors in bringing about this accord.

In the West the agreement was greeted with expressions of both joy and caution. France, which has its own nuclear force, announced that it would not add its signature. And in the East, Communist China continued to work on developing its own atomic weapons.

The late President John F. Kennedy, addressing the American public on July 26, 1963, voiced his country's divided sentiment: "This treaty is not the millennium. It will not resolve all conflicts, or cause the Communists to forgo their ambitions, or eliminate the dangers of war. . . . But it is an important first step — a step toward peace, a step toward reason, a step away from war."

The Communiqué of the Three Powers, July 25, 1963

The special representatives of the President of the United States of America and of the Prime Minister of the United Kingdom . . . visited Moscow together with their advisers on July 14. [They] were received by the Chairman of the Council of Ministers of the Union of Soviet Socialist Republics, N. S. Khrushchev, who presided on July 15 at the first of a series of meetings to discuss questions relating to the discontinuance of nuclear tests and other questions of mutual interest. The discussions were continued from July 16 to July 25. . . .

The discussions took place in a businesslike, cordial atmosphere. Agreement was reached on the text of a treaty banning nuclear weapons tests in the atmosphere, in outer space, and underwater. . . .

The heads of the three delegations agreed that the test ban treaty constituted an important first step toward the reduction of international tension and the strengthening of peace, and they look forward to further progress in this direction.

The heads of the three delegations discussed the Soviet proposal relating to a pact of nonaggression between the participants in the North Atlantic Treaty Organization and the participants in the Warsaw Treaty. The three governments have agreed fully to inform their respective allies in the two organizations concerning these talks and to consult with them about continuing discussions on this question with the purpose of achieving agreement satisfactory to all participants. A brief exchange of views also took place with regard to other measures directed at a relaxation of tension.

The Treaty

The governments of the United States of America, the United Kingdom of Great Britain and Northern Ireland, and the Union of Soviet Socialist Republics, hereinafter referred to as the "original parties,"

Proclaiming as their principal aim the speediest possible achievement of an agreement on general and complete disarmament under strict international control in accordance with the objectives of the

Source: *The New York Times,* July 26, 1963. © 1963 by *The New York Times.* Reprinted by permission of the publishers.

United Nations, which would put an end to the armaments race and eliminate the incentive to the production and testing of all kinds of weapons, including nuclear weapons,

Seeking to achieve the discontinuance of all test explosions of nuclear weapons for all time, determined to continue negotiations to this end, and desiring to put an end to the contamination of man's environment by radioactive substances,

Have agreed as follows:

Article I

1. Each of the parties to this Treaty undertakes to prohibit, to prevent, and not to carry out any nuclear weapon test explosion or any other nuclear explosion at any place under its jurisdiction or control:

    a. In the atmosphere, beyond its limits, including outer space, or underwater, including territorial waters or high seas; or

    b. In any other environment if such explosion causes radioactive debris to be present outside the territorial limits of the state under whose jurisdiction or control such explosion is conducted. It is understood in this connection that the provisions of this subparagraph are without prejudice to the conclusion of a treaty resulting in the permanent banning of all nuclear test explosions, including all such explosions underground, the conclusions of which, as the parties have stated in the preamble to this Treaty, they seek to achieve.

2. Each of the parties to this Treaty undertakes furthermore to refrain from causing, encouraging, or in any way participating in the carrying out of any nuclear weapon test explosion or any other nuclear explosion anywhere which would take place in any of the environments described, or have the effect referred to in Paragraph 1 of this article. . . .

Article IV

This Treaty shall be of unlimited duration.

Each party shall in exercising its national sovereignty have the right to withdraw from the treaty if it decides that extraordinary events related to the subject matter of this Treaty have jeopardized the supreme interests of its country. It shall give notice of such withdrawal to all other parties to the Treaty three months in advance.

CONTENTS OF VOLUME ONE

THE HUMAN ADVENTURE

CONTENTS

273

PART THREE   The Middle Ages

PART FOUR The Emergence of Modern Europe

PART FIVE Enlightenment, Revolution, and Reaction

PART SIX India, China, and Japan